BUYING & SELLING A HOME IN CALIFORNIA

For Allan

Buying & Selling a Home in California

A Complete Residential Real Estate Guide

DIAN HYMER

CHRONICLE BOOKS · SAN FRANCISCO

Printed in the United States of America.

Library of Congress Cataloging in Publication Data
Hymer, Dian Davis.
    Buying and selling a home in California: a complete residential real estate guide / Dian Hymer.
        p.   cm.
    Includes index.
    ISBN 0-87702-534-1
    1. House buying—California.   2. House selling—California.
    3. Real estate business—California.   4. Real property—California.
    I. Title.
    HD266.C2H95   1989
    333.33′8—dc19   88-26699
                                                                              CIP

Editing: Charles Robbins
Book and cover design: Herman + Company
Composition: Mark Woodworth Typography

10 9 8 7 6 5 4 3 2 1

Chronicle Books
275 Fifth Street
San Francisco, California 94103

The comments, observations, and recommendations in this book are the opinions of the author, and are based on over ten years of experience in the residential real estate field. However, the author is not qualified to render legal, accounting, engineering, or other professional advice. Consult the appropriate expert for legal, tax, or other professional recommendations, and be aware that real estate practices and customs are constantly changing and differ from one area to the next.

CONTENTS

INTRODUCTION

The California residential real estate market has changed drastically over the last ten years. In 1978, mortgage money was cheap, qualifying was easy, the housing market was booming, and home buyers purchased with reckless abandon. At a time when home prices appreciated at about 2 percent a month, no one bothered with general building inspections and few buyers worried about discovering defects after the close of escrow. Deciding on a home loan didn't require much thought: the thirty-year fixed rate loan was the norm. Purchase contracts were uncomplicated.

The heyday of the late seventies was followed by the worst real estate market since World War II. Interest rates skyrocketed to new heights in 1980 and 1981, finally bringing the housing market to a virtual halt in 1982. The gradual recovery of the market began in 1983, accompanied by a massive restructuring of the mortgage financing system as deregulation of the banking industry gave savings and loans more commercial banking powers. Interest rates on home loans dropped and the adjustable rate mortgage made its debut. Shunned initially, adjustable rate mortgages are now commonplace.

Concurrent with changes in the home finance industry, a strong climate of consumerism developed in California, resulting in new laws with a direct impact on residential real estate sales. "Buyer Beware," formerly a basic tenet of the industry, was cast aside in favor of a far more explicit approach to maximizing consumer awareness and protection. Buying or selling a house in California now involves a four-page purchase contract, a disclosure regarding real estate agency relationships, the "Real Estate Transfer Disclosure Statement" having to do with property defects, a seller financing disclosure (if a seller carries financing for a buyer), an adjustable rate financing disclosure (if a buyer obtains an adjustable rate loan from an institutional lender), termite inspection reports, general building inspection reports, and more.

Does this increase in paperwork represent progress? In 1940, the

United States census showed that the median value of all existing dwelling units was only $3,000. In the summer of 1988, the median price of homes sold in California logged in at approximately $167,500, according to the California Association of Realtors. A home is no longer valued merely as a lodging; it's the largest investment most people make in a lifetime and few of us can afford to make a costly mistake.

No wonder California real estate is a hot topic of conversation. Finding, buying, selling, and financing a home in today's market can be a tricky business. How many times have you heard a disgruntled buyer complain about losing a house to another buyer in a multiple offer competition? Or a seller bemoan the fact that a real estate deal fell apart at the last minute? Or a buyer grumble about being turned down for a home loan with no warning?

Buying and Selling a Home in California is designed to provide you with the tools you need to ensure that your real estate purchase or sale is a success story, not a tale of woe. After reading this book you won't worry about qualifying for a loan because you'll know how to prequalify yourself and you'll understand how the loan qualification process works. You'll learn how to decide when is the best time to buy and to sell, how to select the agent who'll best serve your needs, and how the tax laws will affect your move. You'll know how to find your dream home, how to fix up your current home and sell it for top dollar, how to negotiate the purchase contract, and when to order a further inspection.

Whether you're a first-time buyer, a homeowner trading up to a larger home, or a retiree who needs to sell the family home to trade down to a smaller one, you'll find valuable tips on how to structure your purchase or sale. Anyone considering an adjustable rate mortgage will find the list of questions to ask adjustable rate lenders a must. Real estate topics that are rarely discussed are dealt with here, such as termite reports and what to do if you're dissatisfied with your real estate agent. And real estate agents, particularly those new in the business, will find the book useful. Agents become good agents through years of hard work; sharing another agent's years of experience will help to increase your level of professionalism.

The book also provides copies of the actual real estate forms you'll be likely to use in your California real estate transaction: the listing agreement, purchase contract, counteroffer, and the various disclosure forms required by law. Buyers and sellers will reduce their anxiety by reading this book since they will understand in advance how the process works, and they will be able to monitor their real estate transactions to successful completion.

Housing experts are confident that changes in the home finance industry will help to moderate housing cycle fluctuations in the future so we won't have to live through another year like 1982. And even though California home prices are at an all-time high and are expected to go higher, adjustable rate financing offered at 2–3 percent below fixed rate home loans continues to make housing affordable by helping more buyers qualify to buy. So if you've been a would-be player of the great California real estate game, face up to reality: the time to play is now and here are the rules to play by.

Keep in mind that this book is based on the opinions of the author and does not represent the standard of care of any individual realty company. Be sure to read all contracts and forms carefully, front and back. Read the fine print too, even if you think it's a waste of time or the print's too small. If you have any questions during the course of a purchase or sale transaction, call your agent, escrow officer, accountant, attorney, or building inspector for the answer. Ask a lot of questions; the answers will save you plenty.

DECIDING TO MOVE

BALANCING NEEDS AND DESIRES

Deciding to move is exciting, but buying a home doesn't happen overnight. It's a process that takes time, so set a game plan for yourself, before you even start looking.

Take a moment to indulge your fantasies—on paper that is. Buy a notebook and dedicate it to the search for your new home. On the first page, make a "wish list" of the features you desire in a home. Write down everything that comes to mind. For instance, maybe you're a hobby-oriented person who will be happier with a little extra space, even if it's a cubbyhole in a basement, to develop into a workspace or wine cellar.

Next, take a good hard look at the list, dividing it into two sections—the absolutes and the negotiables. The absolutes are your basic needs, such as four bedrooms (or three plus a den), more than one bathroom, a large kitchen, a dining area, or a yard suitable for pets and children. Some home buyers have specialized needs, such as wheelchair access and one-level living to accommodate a disabled member of the family. If you and your spouse are both busy professionals, you may need a space for live-in help.

One variable that's often overlooked is the condition of the new home. If you're extremely busy, are short on cash, and have few mechanical skills, then "move-in condition" should be on your absolutes list. On the other hand, if you can afford to hire professionals to remodel your new home, then "almost perfect condition" can be included on the negotiables list. And if you are short on cash but skilled at house painting, plumbing, and carpentry, you may need to find a home that's not in move-in condition with the intention of working on it yourself in order to buy at all. In this case, "fixer-upper" will be on the absolutes list.

Negotiable items may include a swimming pool, a view, a family room with a fireplace, a gas stove, or a specific style of house

(Mediterranean, English Tudor, or French Provincial). These are the features that distinguish a home that fits your dreams from one that merely suits your needs. They are, however, items you can live without if necessary.

The final step in determining the kind of house you're looking for is to prioritize your absolutes and negotiables. The perfect house does not exist, not at any price. Knowing in advance which of your needs and wants are most important will help you to make a sensible decision.

DETERMINING YOUR PRICE RANGE

Determining what you can afford depends on two basic elements: the amount of mortgage you qualify for and the amount of cash you have available for the down payment and closing costs. A rough indicator of your price range can be found by multiplying your annual gross income by three.

The easiest way to find out the size mortgage you qualify for is to meet with a local loan agent to be lender prequalified. Take information with you regarding your income, current debts, and assets. There is, however, a certain satisfaction to be derived from calculating for yourself approximately what you can afford. A "Home Purchase Affordability Worksheet" is included on page 6 for prospective buyers who are so inclined. Sellers, too, can benefit from familiarizing themselves with the worksheet. By examining the simple equations lenders use to qualify buyers for home loans, you should be able to avoid the problem of having a sale fall apart because the buyers couldn't arrange financing. Understanding the qualification process will enable you to determine at the time the buyers' offer is presented whether they will be able to qualify for the loan they're applying for.

To calculate the amount of the loan you qualify for, divide your gross annual income (not net income) by twelve to arrive at your gross monthly income. If you'll be purchasing a home with another person, be sure to include the amount of a second income. For example, let's say your gross annual income is $50,000, which gives a gross monthly income of approximately $4,167. Multiply this figure by 36 percent (.36) to determine your affordable monthly debt plus housing cost, which in this example is $1,500.12.

Next, subtract any long-term debts such as car payments, student loans, or installment loans that will take longer than six months to pay off. This number is your affordable monthly housing expense. In this case, let's say the buyers have a car payment of $300.12 a month which, when subtracted from $1,500.12, leaves $1,200 to apply toward the affordable monthly housing expense. If you have no long-term debt,

Home Purchase Affordability Worksheet

Gross Annual Income: _____

Divide by 12 to determine

Gross Monthly Income: _____

Multiply by 36 percent (.36) to determine

Affordable Monthly Debt + Housing Cost: _____

Subtract

Long-Term Debts: _____

To determine the

Affordable Monthly Housing Expense (PITI): _____

Multiply by 85 percent (.85) to determine

Affordable Mortgage Payment: _____

(Principal and interest only)

Current Interest Rate: _____

Term of the Loan: _____

See amortization schedule to determine

Affordable Loan Amount: _____

Multiply by 4 percent (.04) to determine

Closing Costs: _____

Total Cash Available: _____

Subtract

Closing Costs: _____

To determine

Down Payment Amount: _____

Add

Affordable Loan Amount: _____

To determine your

Approximate Affordable Purchase Price: _____

simply multiply your gross monthly income by 30 percent to arrive at your affordable monthly housing expense.

The affordable monthly housing expense must cover your monthly principal and interest payments to the lender, as well as property taxes and hazard insurance. These four items are referred to jointly as PITI. Monthly homeowner's association dues, if you are purchasing a condominium or townhouse, and private mortgage insurance (PMI), if it is required by the lender, will be added to the PITI in qualifying you for a loan. PMI is paid by the buyer to protect the lender against the buyer's default on the loan and is often called for when a buyer puts less than 20 percent cash down. PMI is usually calculated as an extra .5 percent interest rate charged on the loan, but this varies with lenders.

The next step is to subtract an amount equal to your monthly property tax and hazard insurance liability (plus homeowner's dues and PMI, if applicable) from your affordable monthly housing expense. The resulting figure will represent your affordable mortgage payment (principal and interest only). Roughly 15 percent of the monthly PITI is usually applied toward taxes and insurance, so you can also multiply your affordable monthly housing expense by 85 percent to arrive at your affordable mortgage payment.

Using our example, $1,200 multiplied by 85 percent (.85) results in an affordable mortgage payment figure of $1,020. The 85 percent figure is approximate and will vary with the interest rate on the loan, the purchase price, and the ratio of the loan amount to the purchase price. Simple formulas are provided below so that you can check the amount deducted for taxes and insurance for accuracy after you have determined an affordable purchase price.

Your gross monthly income is one of two factors limiting the size loan you qualify for. The other is current interest rates, which change over time and also vary from one type of loan to another. The interest rate charged on a loan amortized (paid off in full) over fifteen years is usually lower than the interest rate on a similar loan amortized over thirty years. The initial interest rates on adjustable rate mortgages (ARMs) are lower than the interest rates charged on fixed rate loans.

For information regarding current interest rates in your area, call several local lenders and ask for rate quotes on fifteen- and thirty-year fixed and adjustable rate home loans. This is not the time to make a final decision about what kind of loan you want, but it's wise to start considering it. Looking at the monthly payments required to amortize a loan at different interest rates may help you to decide.

Turn to the amortization schedule at the back of the book. The tables are divided according to interest rates and the term of the loan (fifteen or thirty years). Remember, you have approximately $1,020 of your gross monthly income to apply toward your mortgage payment.

Suppose the interest rate on a fixed rate loan amortized over thirty years is 10.5 percent. Find the thirty-year column for that interest rate on the table. As you read down the list of monthly payments, look for the payment that most closely approximates $1,020. The table ends at $914.74, which is the monthly payment on a $100,000 loan. To find out how much more than $100,000 you can qualify for, subtract $914.74 from $1,020; the remainder is $105.26. Now read up the column. The monthly payment closest to $105.26 is $91.47, which amortizes $10,000. Subtract $91.47 from $105.26; the remainder is $13.79 and read up the column again. $13.79 falls about halfway between the monthly payments on a $1,000 and a $2,000 loan, so let's say you can qualify for an additional $1,500. Add $1,500 to $10,000 and $100,000 for a total affordable loan amount of $111,500.

Compare this to the loan you qualify for if you select a fifteen-year fixed or adjustable (which will be amortized over thirty years). If the interest rate on a fifteen-year fixed loan is 9.75 percent, your affordable loan limit is approximately $96,000. Selecting an adjustable with an initial interest rate of 8 percent will enable you to qualify for a loan amount of $139,000. (For more information about the pros and cons of fixed and adjustable rate home loans, see Chapter Ten.) An interest rate factor chart is included with the amortization schedule at the back of the book for home buyers who want more information on how to compute monthly payments and loan amounts.

To determine what price home you can afford, you need to establish how much cash you have available for a down payment and closing costs. Buyers who are selling one home to buy another will need to know the current market value of the home being sold, as well as an estimate of what the costs of sale will be.

Buyers' closing costs include such expenses as loan origination fees, credit report and appraisal fees, escrow and title insurance fees (depending on where you buy), transfer taxes (again, this varies with location), document preparation and notary fees, proration of taxes, proration of homeowner's association dues, hazard insurance premium, and inspection fees (termite, building, roof, etc.).

An approximate amount for closing costs is determined by multiplying your affordable loan amount by 4 percent. Subtract this amount from your total cash available to arrive at the down payment amount. Then add the down payment to the loan amount; the total is your approximate affordable purchase price.

After you've established what price you can afford, check to make sure that the approximation used to arrive at your affordable mortgage payment is accurate. Remember, you multiplied the affordable monthly housing expense by 85 percent (.85) in order to reduce the PITI figure to principal and interest only. Property taxes in California are limited to 1 percent of the purchase price plus an additional amount to cover bonds for community improvements; a safe number is 1.25 percent, although this will vary from area to area. The cost of hazard insurance, almost always required by the lender, varies with location, deductible amount on the policy, and age of the home. A rough indicator of what an annual policy will cost is found by multiplying the purchase price of the new home by .003 (.3 percent). Add both figures together and divide by twelve to arrive at a monthly figure. Subtract this amount from your affordable monthly housing expense (PITI). The difference should be approximately the same as your affordable monthly payment (principal and interest only).

The amount of cash down payment required to purchase a home varies. Buyers who put less than 20 percent down will find that lenders are somewhat stricter with qualifying criteria. There are alternative sources of financing for marginally qualified buyers. Buyers who put 25 percent cash down needn't worry about rigorous qualifying if they apply for a "quick" qualifier loan and have a good credit history.

What you can qualify for may not be what you feel comfortable paying per month for your housing expense. Most buyers today apply for as much financing as they can afford, since acquisition mortgage interest is tax deductible and other tax shelters have been severely curtailed by recent tax reform. But it's up to you to decide. It doesn't make sense to stretch far beyond your means, particularly if you are living on a fixed income.

WHEN IS THE BEST TIME TO BUY?

Timing is largely dependent on current interest rates. Real estate sales slow during periods of high interest rates, since fewer buyers are able to qualify for financing. And, conversely, sales are usually brisk when interest rates are low.

Don't, however, rule out the possibility of buying when rates are high. These are usually the periods when buyers can find relatively good deals on home prices. Most buyers believe that it's impossible to buy when rates are high so they drop out of the market, leaving less competition for the enterprising few. There are always people who will need to sell no matter what the market is doing. Difficulties in financing during periods of high interest rates can be overcome by assuming a seller's low interest adjustable mortgage, seller financing, or a combination of the two.

Most home buyers feel confident buying when rates are low. Housing is more affordable then, and there is some comfort and sense of security in buying when everyone else is. Home prices tend to rise in a low interest rate real estate market due to high demand. Buyers may find themselves in stiff competition with other buyers for houses that end up selling over the asking price. But it's easy to rationalize paying a few thousand dollars extra when you're sure to make the money back after a few months of price appreciation.

Interest rates are cyclical, and there seems to be no way to determine conclusively at any given time whether rates are rising or falling. But anyone can follow the financial markets by regularly reviewing the business section of a major metropolitan newspaper to track several indicators that have been relatively reliable in the past. Interest rates are influenced by activity in the national and international money markets; recently, the most accurate indicator of home loan rates has been the bond market. When bond rates soar, interest rates on home loans drop, and vice versa. The Federal Reserve Board discount rate is another figure to watch. This is the rate charged to banks when they borrow money. A drop in the discount rate is usually followed by a drop in prime rate, and this is finally reflected in lower mortgage rates. Conversely, a rise in the discount rate signals that mortgage rates will probably move higher. Don't be surprised if home loan rates rise or drop in anticipation of an increase or decrease in the Federal Reserve Board discount rate. The amount of foreign currency invested in government securities affects mortgage interest rates as well. The more foreign investment, the less the government needs to borrow to support itself. A lower demand for money means a lower interest rate on your home loan. On the other hand, when foreign investors go elsewhere the government must borrow more; this creates a higher demand for money and higher interest rates usually follow.

Other indicators to watch are the rates charged on Treasury securities and the money supply figures. Higher Treasury bill (T-bill) rates usually predicate higher interest rates, as can money supply figures if they exceed government expectations.

Regardless of when you choose to buy, don't get yourself into the trap of waiting until the interest rate cycle bottoms out. It's risky to wait if you can qualify to buy and rates are already relatively low. Financial markets can change quickly, and often it's not apparent that interest rates have bottomed out until they're on their way back up again. In addition, low interest rate markets are generally characterized by high levels of home price appreciation, so you might end up paying more if you wait for an extra quarter or half percent drop in interest rates.

TAXES AND OTHER CONSIDERATIONS

Rarely is the quest for tax relief the sole reason for buying a new home, but it's an important consideration. Buying or selling a residence has tax ramifications beyond merely sheltering income, and it's wise to understand ahead of time how you'll be affected financially by your purchase or sale.

The First-Time Buyer

RENT OR BUY?
Prospective first-time buyers often talk themselves out of buying for fear they've already been priced out of the market. Before jumping to conclusions, take a look at the profile of the first-time California home buyer in 1987. Median age: thirty years old. Annual income: just under $40,000. Approximately 54 percent of the buyers came from two-income households. The average purchase price was $122,950 and the approximate home size was 1,250 square feet, according to the California Association of Realtors.

First-time buyers purchased over 38 percent of the homes sold in 1987, a figure down from 40 percent in past years. This decrease is not due to price increases alone, however: it also reflects the fact that the population is aging, a trend which will continue to be manifested by a high proportion of previous homeowners in the market.

Affording the monthly payments is not the primary problem facing most first-time buyers. Statistics show that most renters pay approximately 29 percent of their income toward rent and receive none of the tax benefits of ownership. If you and your spouse are currently paying in the neighborhood of $850 per month on rent and you earn $35,000 to $40,000 per year, you can probably qualify to buy a $120,000 home using adjustable-rate financing. Your monthly principal, interest, property tax, and insurance obligations (PITI) will be approximately $928 per month if you put 20 percent cash down and take out a $96,000 loan at a 9 percent initial interest rate (thirty-year term).

It will cost a mere $78 more per month to own your home, even *before* considering the tax savings. Most of the mortgage payment in the first year (approximately 99 percent on a loan amortized over thirty years) goes to paying interest, which, like property tax, is deductible from your income for tax purposes. In the first year of ownership, you would accumulate a write-off of over $10,000.

The after tax monthly expense of your new home will vary depending on your tax bracket. Using the example above, your monthly mortgage interest and property tax expense for your first year of ownership will be approximately $890 per month. If you are in the 15 percent tax bracket, multiply $890 by .15 and subtract the result, $134, from your entire monthly housing expense (PITI) figure of $928. The balance, $794, is your monthly cost of ownership after taxes. The higher your tax bracket, the larger the tax break and the lower the after tax cost of ownership.

The loan origination fees charged on a purchase mortgage (better known as "points," and customarily 1 percent to 2 percent of the loan amount) are treated as "pre-paid" interest by the IRS and are, therefore, tax deductible. (One point is equivalent to 1 percent of the loan amount.) Two points charged to take out a $96,000 mortgage will cost you $1,920. In most cases this amount can be deducted from your income in the year of purchase, creating a considerable tax savings.

The above comparison of the expenses involved in renting versus buying does not take into account the hidden cost of home maintenance, which is normally not a renter's concern. A first-time buyer is wise to consider purchasing a new, or relatively new, home, condominium, or townhouse for which maintenance expenses are likely to be lower than for an older home.

This example also does not take into account the fact that a portion of the mortgage payment each month goes toward paying off the principal balance remaining on your home loan. This amounts to an enforced savings plan. If you were to continue to pay $850 in rent every month ($10,200 per year), you'd stand little chance of accumulating the equity necessary to allow you to trade up to a more desirable home in the future.

Home price appreciation is an important factor to take into consideration. With rare exceptions, homes in California have appreciated steadily over the past fifty years, and it's anticipated that this trend will continue, at least through the year 2000.

ACCUMULATING THE CASH DOWN PAYMENT

The biggest problem facing 70 percent of first-time buyers is accumulating the cash to cover a down payment and closing costs. This is understandable. With 29 percent of one's income going to rent and 15 – 28 percent going to income taxes, it's easy to see why many people find it difficult to save enough for a down payment even when they have the income to afford mortgage payments.

Resourceful buyers have various options to consider if saving the customary 20 percent cash down payment seems impossible. The most obvious is to borrow the money from a friend or relative. Be aware, though, that borrowing from a friend can put a strain on a valuable personal relationship. Also be aware that most lenders will require verification of the source of the funds needed to close escrow, and they won't permit a buyer to borrow the entire amount of the cash down. A gift letter is often required by the lender when cash is coming from a source other than the buyer's savings. The letter must specify that the buyer is under no obligation to repay the "gift."

Any taxpayer is permitted to give up to $10,000 per year to another person without having to pay a gift tax. If your parents have the financial ability and are so inclined, they can each give you up to $10,000. It's wise to obtain the gift letter and cash from your parents (or other relatives) before making an offer to purchase a piece of property, as it's not uncommon for relatives to change their minds about giving money. Don't find yourself in the awkward position of entering into a binding contract with a seller only to discover you're lacking a significant portion of your cash down payment.

Financing for Buyers Short on Cash

Ninety percent financing is readily available with 10 percent cash down (plus closing costs). In some instances, it's possible to find 95 percent financing requiring only 5 percent cash down. The interest rates will be higher than you'll find on 80 percent loans and qualifying is more difficult, but it may be worth it to you for the privilege of purchasing unassisted by others.

If you have 10 percent cash down and you know someone who is willing to loan you an additional 10 percent (a loan that will be secured by the property, not a gift), you can take advantage of the lower interest rate offered on 80 percent loans. This is referred to as 80, 10 and 10 financing. The bank loans you 80 percent of the purchase price, you make a 10 percent cash down payment, and a third party makes you a 10 percent second loan. Sometimes a seller will be willing to carry the 10 percent second. Real estate agents and mortgage brokers are often in touch with individuals looking to make secure investments through second mortgages.

Veteran's Administration (VA) and Federal Housing Administration (FHA) financing are possibilities for eligible buyers with 5 percent cash down who can't qualify for or afford 95 percent conventional financing. VA and FHA loans have strict limitations on loan amounts: the property must meet certain standards, the qualification process is lengthy, and the seller usually pays costs not required when the buyer obtains conventional financing. VA and FHA financing are, therefore, not attractive options in areas where purchase prices are high or where the market strongly favors the seller.

Equity sharing is another possibility. FHA offers a Shared Equity Mortgage (SEM) program for marginally qualified buyers who are low on cash. Under this program, a buyer purchases the home with an investor or a relative. The cash down payment, mortgage payments, tax benefits, and profits at time of sale are shared between the buyer and the investor. This is a less than ideal arrangement, for although the buyer has the exclusive right to occupy the property, ownership is shared. It's worth investigating, however, if there's no other way to buy.

Equity sharing is not restricted to the SEM program. Some brokers specialize in bringing buyers and investors together for equity sharing ownership. Ask a real estate professional for a recommendation and exercise caution. Consult an attorney with experience in the area to assist you in drafting the necessary contracts and documents. Your agreement should include a provision that gives you the first right to buy out the investor and become the sole owner if you desire.

Another possibility is to purchase with a co-buyer. Under this arrangement, you share not only the financial aspects of ownership but also the living space with your partner. The benefit is that you and your partner can purchase a larger or more expensive home than might otherwise be possible. Again, consult an attorney with experience in drafting home ownership partnership agreements, and be sure you have a partnership arrangement agreed upon in writing before escrow closes.

In slower, "buyer's," markets, several other possibilities are available to buyers short on cash. Builders of new construction developments often offer attractive financing alternatives when they're having difficulty selling a project out; these include 95 percent financing for owner occupants or payment of a portion of the buyer's non-recurring closing costs. Seller financing also becomes more prevalent when the real estate market slows down.

And finally, the lease option is a popular alternative to buyers and sellers in the real estate market when homes are difficult to sell. For a relatively small amount of cash (the option money, which is a negotiable amount), the buyer is able to lease a home for a specified period of time with an option to purchase the property for a specified price.

The option money is applied to the purchase price if the buyer purchases the property, or is forfeited to the seller at the end of the option period if the buyer fails to complete the purchase.

Home ownership offers one of the rare opportunities to purchase a valuable asset with a low cash investment. Buying a home can require as little as 5 percent cash down, which makes real estate one of the higher yielding investments.

But don't count on a quick turnover. It's wise to plan on holding onto a piece of real estate for at least four to five years except in rare instances when prices are rising at a rapid pace. And recognize that real estate is not a liquid investment that can be cashed in whenever you like; there's no guarantee of a quick sale in real estate.

Another word of caution to first-time buyers: don't expect to buy your dream home the first time around. The goal is to become a homeowner. Your first home will be just that: the first, not the ultimate, home you'll own.

The Trade-up Buyer

Repeat or trade-up buyers account for almost half of all home buyers today. The concerns of the trade-up buyer differ from those of the first-time buyer. Accumulating a cash down payment is usually not the major obstacle, since the repeat buyer has benefited from enforced savings through mortgage payments and home price appreciation.

REMODEL OR MOVE?

One dilemma for many homeowners is deciding whether to remodel their existing home or move to another. If you've been happy in your current home and neighborhood and you need more space or a different layout, remodeling is a possibility. Deciding to remodel, like deciding to move, requires careful consideration in order to avoid costly mistakes. The first step is to take a good close look at your wish list of needs and desires. Ask yourself if it's even possible to remodel your present home to suit your needs.

Sometimes, it's not obvious whether remodeling will work, in which case you'll need the aid of an architect or contractor to help you make the decision. You're looking for an architect or contractor who will listen to your needs and who will design a plan that can be built within your price range (not double what you can afford). It's wise to have a consultation done in your home before engaging someone to draw a full set of plans. This will give you an opportunity to determine if the architect's ideas are in line with your own. The cost of a full set of plans is too much if they turn out to be of little use to you. Hire professionals to locate property boundary lines, easements, septic tanks, and wells to make sure your remodeling plans are feasible.

> Bob Webster knew that his home was on a septic sanitary system when he hastily improved his yard with landscaping and a large concrete patio. A year later, Bob and his wife divorced and the house was sold. The new buyers made their offer contingent upon an inspection of the house and the septic system. A thorough search of the grounds revealed that the septic tank was located underneath the new concrete patio, which had to be jack-hammered apart in order for the septic tank to be inspected. Since the buyers' offer was for a house that included a usable patio, Bob had to pay not only the cost of demolishing the original one but also for replacing it with a new one. A septic tank that can't be inspected can't be serviced, so Bob would ultimately have had the same problem even if he hadn't sold his house.

At some point in the decision-making process you need to consider whether you and your family can deal with the difficulties of remodeling. The process is very disruptive, particularly when it involves the kitchen and bathrooms.

Let's say you're still considering a major renovation and you have a set of plans. The next step is to have several licensed contractors bid on the job. While interviewing contractors you should also be determining the current market value of your home and looking into sources of remodel financing. There's been much controversy recently about home equity loans, so shop around and ask for full disclosure of the terms of the loan before making a final decision.

The easiest way to determine the current value of your home is to ask the real estate agent who sold you the home for a current market evaluation. You want to know the value of the home in its present, unremodeled condition. Also tell your agent what your remodeling plans are and ask for an estimate of what your home's value will be after the improvements are completed. If you're adding a bedroom to a three bedroom house, ask for comparable sales information on both three and four bedroom homes in your neighborhood. Your aim is to determine whether you'll be overimproving your home for the neighborhood. The best house on the block is not generally thought to be the best investment.

Home improvements usually add value to a home, but you can't always recover the full cost when you sell. The value of the improvements will also depend on the amenities your home already has and how soon you sell after you remodel. Improvements that usually return 100 percent of an investment are a second bathroom, a third bedroom, or a fireplace (particularly if it is the only fireplace in the house). Other high return improvements are kitchen remodels and skylights (both about 90 percent recoverable), central air conditioning in warm climates (75–100 percent recoverable), a garage (50–100 percent), a deck (70 percent), a patio (35–60 percent). A swimming pool, on the other hand, will return only about 33 percent at the time of sale.

After you receive the contractors' bids, add the estimated cost of the improvements to the current market value of your home. Compare the total to the projected value of your home after the improvements are completed. If the total is considerably less than the projected value, you're probably making a secure investment.

A last, but important, factor needs to be considered before making the decision of whether to remodel or to move: tax consequences. You will, no doubt, need to take out a loan in either case. The points (loan fees, usually 1–2 percent of the loan amount) are treated differently by the IRS on refinance loans than they are on home purchase loans. With a home purchase, you can deduct the total amount of the points from your income in the year of purchase. On a refinance, however, the points must be deducted incrementally over the term of the loan ($\frac{1}{30}$ each year on a thirty-year loan).

The 1986 Tax Reform Act preserved the deductibility of mortgage interest with specific limitations and qualifications that are still undergoing revision. As of this writing, a taxpayer can deduct up to $1 million in mortgage interest on a first and second home as long as this amount does not exceed the amounts paid on acquisition indebtedness and substantial improvements. In addition, there is a $100,000 limit on the interest deduction allowed per year on home equity debt (second trust deeds and lines of credit secured against the home).

If you have a large amount of equity in a home and a large income as well, it may make more sense to trade up than to remodel. For instance, a home that you paid $100,000 for fifteen years ago and that's now worth $400,000 won't qualify for the maximum write-off due to IRS restrictions. If you sell this home, buy another for $500,000, and finance the purchase with an 80 percent loan, your new acquisition indebtedness will be $400,000. The interest on this loan is tax deductible each year and, in addition, you're entitled to a $100,000 per year home equity debt allowance. Consult your tax advisor to determine the precise tax ramifications of moving or remodeling.

BUY OR SELL FIRST?
The biggest concern facing the trade-up buyer is whether to buy or

sell first. The decision usually depends on the real estate market and your financial situation. Finding and purchasing your new home first lets you know precisely where you're going and when before putting your current home on the market. But if you need every dime of equity out of your present home to close escrow on the new one, you may come up short if your current home doesn't sell in time for the anticipated price.

In a slow market, some sellers will agree to accept a purchase contract that is contingent upon the sale of the buyers' home. Sellers who accept a contingent sale offer often require the contract to contain an escape clause (most commonly, a seventy-two-hour escape clause) which allows them to continue offering their home to other buyers. If they receive another attractive offer, the sellers can accept it in a secondary, or "back-up," position. They then notify the buyers who are in first position in writing that they have seventy-two hours to remove the contingency from the contract. If the first buyers remove the contingency within this time frame they stay in contract but their purchase is no longer contingent upon the sale of their current home. If the first buyers are unable to remove the sale contingency the home goes to the second buyers and the first buyers start looking again.

In a fast paced market you're likely to have no trouble selling your home, but you probably won't find a seller willing to accept a contingent sale offer. The good homes sell fast in a seller's market, often with multiple offers. You'll find it impossible to compete with buyers who are able to purchase a new home that is not contingent upon the sale of another home.

Let's say you are a family of five. You need to liquidate the equity on your present home in order to move up, and the thought of selling first and moving to an interim rental is more than you can bear. What do you do in this case?

In a seller's market your house will be in demand, and you'll be in a position to negotiate terms of sale suitable to your needs. Start looking around for a new home first so you're sure that what you want is available, then list your home for sale with a condition that "the seller may need a long close of escrow and/or a rent back."

A normal close of escrow is thirty to sixty days after an offer to purchase is accepted by the sellers. A long close is ninety days or more. A seller rent back provision allows the sellers to rent their home back from the buyers after the close of escrow, usually at a per diem (per day) cost equal to the buyers' principal, interest, taxes, and insurance (PITI). This may be more than you're currently paying monthly to own your home, but after the escrow closes you'll have your equity in cash, which will earn interest until you invest it in another home.

Also, renting your own home back from the new buyers enables you to avoid an interim move, which could be costly. Plus you'll be in a good bargaining position when you find the home you want.

Occasionally a home will be listed for sale, before the seller has found a new home, contingent upon the seller finding a replacement home. This is not the way to sell a home for top dollar. As far as a buyer is concerned, the home is "maybe" for sale. Most buyers will be reluctant to start incurring expenses for such things as home inspections and loan initiation fees with no guarantee that the seller will complete the sale.

Buyers are often willing to allow you to rent back until you find a home as long as you agree to give them notification that you'll be vacating in sufficient time for them to give their landlord a thirty-day notice. The buyers will at least know they have a house, even if they have to wait to move in. With the contingency for a seller to find a replacement home, the buyers have no guarantee that they'll ever be able to move in.

Buyers who agree to accept a contingency for the seller to find a replacement home usually require a price concession on the seller's part. The buyers will also customarily insist on an escape clause that allows them to continue to search for other homes. When they find one they like, they are free to withdraw from the contract and purchase the other home; this puts your house back on the market and you searching for another buyer. If a home appears back on the market several times, it may acquire a stigma that will be difficult to overcome. Buyers often offer less for properties on which several deals have fallen apart.

Another solution to the buy first, sell first dilemma is interim financing, also called "swing" or "bridge" financing. A swing loan is a short-term loan, normally for six months (sometimes with an option to renew for an additional six months), that allows a seller to convert some of the equity in the present home to cash before the house is sold. Interest rates and fees vary, as do qualifying parameters. The amount of cash you can borrow on an interim basis is usually equivalent to 75 or 80 percent of the current market value of the home minus existing debt secured against the property.

The borrower must have the financial ability to qualify to carry the mortgage payments on the old and new home simultaneously. In addition to the expense involved, there is a risk that the old home might not sell within the six-month term of the interim loan.

Rita and Charlie Travis found a fixer-upper with great potential which they purchased with the help of a swing loan. They immediately listed their home for sale, confident that it would sell quickly, and began sprucing up the new house. Four months of double house payments, no offers, and a swing loan due to mature in two months finally convinced them to put their half-completed fixer-upper on the market, hoping that with two houses on the market one would sell. The fixer-upper sold first, leaving Rita and Charlie disappointed but relieved.

THE ROLLOVER RESIDENCE REPLACEMENT RULE

There is one final word on the tax consequences of trading up. The 1986 Tax Reform Act abolished favorable tax treatment for capital gains reported on real estate sales, so the gain is now taxed as ordinary income. If, however, you sell your principal residence and purchase another principal residence within two years, you can defer your gain on the sale. This is known as the rollover residence replacement rule. To qualify to defer capital gain liability, the price of your new home must be equal to, or exceed, the adjusted sales price of your old home. The adjusted sales price is defined by the IRS as the amount realized on the sale of the old house minus fix-up expenses incurred within ninety days before sale.

Trade-up buyers who are building a new home or who buy a less expensive home and reconstruct it are permitted to defer the gain on the previous residence if the acquisition, construction, and reconstruction costs exceed the adjusted sales price of the old home and the work is completed within two years before or after the sale of the old home. Again, be sure to consult your tax advisor before making a move.

The Trade-Down Buyer

The trade-down buyer is typically the buyer who owns and lives in a home designed for raising a family, but whose children no longer live at home. This group currently accounts for less than 20 percent of all home buyers, but it will increase as the population ages. In the last thirty years, the over-sixty-five age group has nearly doubled, from a little over fifteen million people in 1960 to close to thirty million today. This, combined with increased longevity and declining birth-rates, is turning the older adult group into the fastest growing segment of our population (projected to double in size again by the year 2000) The over-fifty-five population has, on the average, two to four times the buying power of the trade-up buyer. Seventy-five percent of this group own their own homes, and 84 percent own them free and clear (the home mortgage has been paid off in full).

Deciding to move is rarely an easy decision for the older adult homeowner. The home may have become a nuisance and sometimes a major expense, but it is usually the source of many fond memories. The major predicament facing this buyer is deciding where to move. If health considerations don't enter into the decision-making process, a different but smaller house is an alternative. Another is to move to an adult retirement community that offers services and security. And finally, if health care is a consideration, there are living facilities that offer full-scale medical services.

Again, the tax consequences of a move are best considered before even starting to look for a new home. The rollover residence replacement rule applies to all taxpayers, so if you purchased a retirement home five years before selling your current home, the IRS will not allow you to roll the gain from the sale of this home into the retirement home.

ONE-TIME BREAK FOR TAXPAYERS OVER FIFTY-FIVE

Since most trade-down buyers purchase less expensive homes, the sale of the current home is likely to result in a taxable gain. Remember, in order to have no taxable gain at the time of sale, the homeowner must purchase a replacement home that is at least equal in price to the adjusted sales price of the current home. Fortunately, the IRS allows taxpayers aged fifty-five and over to take a one-time exclusion of up to $125,000 on the gain from the sale of a principal residence. The exempted amount will not be taxed as gain by the IRS.

To qualify for this exclusion, you or your spouse must be fifty-five or older on the day your current home closes escrow. If you are not fifty-five and your spouse, who would have been fifty-five, is deceased, check with your tax advisor to see if you qualify for the exclusion. Also, there is a residency and ownership requirement that you must have owned and lived in the home you're selling for at least three of the last five years. The $125,000 exclusion is not automatic; you must choose to take it and notify the IRS by submitting a written, signed statement with your tax return. If you take less than the $125,000 maximum exemption allowed, you are not entitled to take the unused portion at a later date. Also, a divorced person whose spouse has used the exemption is not allowed to take further exemptions.

PROPERTY TAX RELIEF FOR TRADE-DOWN BUYERS OVER FIFTY-FIVE

In the past, a deterrent to trading down for many older buyers was the inevitability of property tax reassessment. Let's say, for instance, you own a 2,000-square-foot home on one-third of an acre, worth $200,000. You paid $65,000 for the home in 1975, and your current property taxes are $850 per year. If you sold this home and purchased a 1,700-square-foot, low-maintenance townhouse for $195,000, your new property taxes would be approximately $2,200 per year.

California Assembly Bill 60, which went into effect in 1987, helps to make retirement more affordable for homeowners aged fifty-five and over by giving them the option, on a one-time basis, of transferring their existing property tax burden to a replacement home of equal or lesser value. Rather than paying property taxes based on the fair market value of the replacement residence (as is ordinarily the case), homeowners who qualify pay property tax on the replacement home based on the assessment value of their current home. In the example above, the homeowners could transfer their present $850 property tax to the $195,000 replacement home and avoid the customary property tax reassessment, giving them a savings of $1,350 per year.

Several restrictions apply. One owner must be fifty-five years old or older when the current residence is sold, and the replacement residence must be purchased within two years before or after the current residence is sold. Both residences must be located in the same county, and the purchase price of the replacement home cannot exceed 100 percent of the sale price of the current home if the replacement home is purchased prior to the sale of the current home. This limit increases to 105 percent if the replacement home is purchased within one year after the sale, and to 110 percent if within two years. Proposition 90, passed overwhelmingly by California voters in 1988, authorizes the legislature to extend the benefits of Assembly Bill 60 to seniors who purchase a replacement home located in a different county, but only if that county's board of supervisors elects to participate in the program and accepts transfers from other counties. Because your current property tax assessment will not automatically be transferred to your replacement residence, you must file a form with the county assessor's office in order to take advantage of these benefits.

AFTER THE CHILDREN LEAVE

Many of today's senior citizens do not trade down, preferring to remain in the family home, which they usually own free of debt. One problem they face, however, is that they're living on a fixed retirement income which may not be sufficient to cover living expenses.

One way to tap equity that's tied up in the family home is a home equity line of credit. Once you qualify for a credit line, it is secured as a lien against the home, and you have the ability to write checks up to your approved loan amount limit. You are permitted to pay back the amount borrowed over a number of years. Since the IRS allows you to deduct interest paid on up to $100,000 of home equity debt per year, the credit line is an attractive alternative for seniors who pay taxes. Most home equity credit lines have flexible interest rates, so be sure you fully understand how the loan works before it becomes a lien against your home.

An innovative mortgage geared to the over-sixty-five group, but available only in certain markets, is the reverse annuity mortgage (RAM). This loan is particularly suited to middle- and low-income seniors who have a large amount of equity in their home but are short on cash. The home is used as collateral for the loan, and the lender makes payments (monthly or in one lump sum) to the homeowner. The loan is paid back to the lender when the homeowner sells the home or at the end of the term of the loan, whichever comes first. This mortgage instrument is relatively new and has, therefore, not had the extensive testing in the marketplace that usually results in consumer protection and full disclosure. Be very careful in considering the reverse annuity mortgage.

For more information about reverse mortgages, contact the National Center for Home Equity Conversion (NCHEC) (110 E. Main, Madison, WI 53703) or the American Association of Retired Persons' Home Equity Information Center (1909 Kitchen Street N.W., Washington, D.C. 20049).

Another possibility for the older homeowner who prefers to stay put is the sale-leaseback. With this arrangement, the homeowner sells the home to a relative or investor who leases it back either for a fixed period or for the life of the seller. The seller receives cash proceeds from the sale but continues to occupy the home. The investor may receive tax benefits from owning the property as a rental investment, in addition to equity build-up and price appreciation. Consult an attorney to assist you in drawing up a sale-leaseback agreement and be sure to investigate the estate planning ramifications, particularly if you're entering into this sort of an agreement with a child or heir.

The Temporary Trade-Down Move

Older adults are not the only candidates for a trade-down move. Others include homeowners who desire relief from exorbitant mortgage payments, who are seeking a change in lifestyle, who are considering a career change, or who are divorcing.

If you're trading down in order to permanently reduce housing expense payments, don't forget that you'll have to pay tax on the portion of capital gain that will not be reinvested in a replacement home. Only homeowners over fifty-five qualify for the $125,000 exclusion, and capital gain (which previously received preferential tax treatment) is now taxed as ordinary income. Although it may still be a worthwhile move, you should be aware of the tax consequences and consult with a knowledgeable tax advisor before making the final decision.

Homeowners seeking temporary relief from high mortgage payments or the expenses of home maintenance might be wise to sell the current home and rent awhile. This way you can buy a grace period and still defer capital gains as long as you purchase a replacement home within two years of selling the current home. Keep in mind that you'll need funds for the down payment when you do buy the replacement home. If you're changing careers and your future income is insecure, it's wise to plan on making a 25 percent cash down payment so that you have the option of applying for an "easy" qualifier loan.

The Transferred Homeowner

No move is easy, but the family that is moving a long distance is faced with a particularly traumatic experience. Fortunately, steps can be taken to ease the anxiety. Relocation assistance is sometimes provided by large companies, but even without corporate help, you can assist yourself by asking your new employer to recommend several real estate agents.

Your move will be made easier if you work with a real estate agent who has experience assisting relocating buyers. This means selecting an agent who understands the transferee's special needs and the emotional turmoil the process entails. Ask the agents for names and phone numbers of other buyers they helped to relocate. Find out whether or not these people would choose to work with their agent again.

Another way to find an agent in your new area is to call a local branch of a large national real estate firm and get recommendations from someone in the relocation department. This person can also provide you with a relocation package, which should contain maps of the local area; information on public transportation, hotels, and restaurants; data on schools and test scores; community activities and amenities; a sampling of current home prices; and calendars of current cultural and recreational events.

Once in contact with an agent in the new location, ask to be kept informed of local events. Have your agent send you newspaper clippings about school and neighborhood events as well as information about new listings. Whenever possible, subscribe to the new newspaper or ask your agent to send the Sunday real estate section to you.

Transferees who have the benefit of corporate assistance are the most fortunate. Since executives typically make four moves during their professional careers, relocation companies have developed to help large corporations simplify the moving process. Their services include assistance in finding a home; reimbursement for all or part of the closing, moving, storage, and temporary housing costs; help with financing the new home; equity advance (interim financing); grants for cost of living allowances; counseling; help in finding spousal employment in the new community; and guaranteed home purchase.

The guaranteed home purchase is probably the biggest plum most relocation packages have to offer. In guaranteed purchase programs, the transferring employer contracts with a third party home purchase company to buy the transferee's home if it hasn't sold by a designated time. The home purchase company sets a buyout price that the homeowners have a certain period of time, usually thirty to sixty days, to accept. During this time, if the sellers receive a better offer than the buyout price, they can usually accept that offer, and the home purchase company will handle the transaction to the close of escrow.

Sellers who have the option of a company buyout should insert a clause in the listing agreement allowing them to assign the listing to a third party home purchase company at any time and at their discretion. Most brokers will accept this condition as long as they have a reasonable period of time to attempt to sell the property. The buyout provision enables a seller who runs out of time to turn the listing over to the corporate transfer company and take the buyout offer, in which case no commission is owed to the initial listing broker. Some home purchase companies offer cash incentives to sellers who effectively market their homes through a local real estate agent prior to activating the buyout provision.

The IRS allows taxpayers to deduct the costs of moving, with certain restrictions. Briefly, deductions are allowed if the location of your new job is at least thirty-five miles further away from your current home than was your old job.

WORKING WITH REAL ESTATE AGENTS

Statistics indicate that approximately 80 percent of real estate transactions are conducted with the help of a real estate agent. Fortunately, the image of the real estate agent in California has improved over the years due to concerted efforts on the part of the Department of Real Estate and the California Association of Realtors. It's no longer possible to become licensed to sell real estate in this state by merely passing an exam. To renew a real estate license requires a minimum of forty-five hours of continuing education every four years, including mandatory courses in ethics, and in agency and consumer protection.

AGENTS, BROKERS, REALTORS: DEFINING THE TERMS

A real estate agent is anyone who is licensed by the state to sell real estate. An agent is licensed either as a salesperson or as a broker. Salespeople must work under the supervision of a licensed broker and cannot sell real estate on their own. To obtain a broker's license requires the equivalent of two years' experience as a salesperson, additional college-level course work, and the satisfactory completion of the broker's licensing exam.

Real estate brokers can work independently, and they can serve as the broker of record for other licensed salespeople. A broker may also choose to work for another broker. The words "Broker Associate" on an agent's business card indicate that the agent is a licensed real estate broker working as an associate of another licensed broker.

There is another important designation in the industry: the Realtor. The title "Realtor" next to an agent's name indicates that he or she is not only a licensed salesperson or broker but is also a member of the National Association of Realtors. The significance of this designation for the prospective home buyer or seller is that members of the National Association of Realtors (NAR) subscribe to a strict code of ethics. By agreeing to the NAR code of ethics, real estate licensees pledge that their real estate activities will conform to a high standard of ethical and professional conduct.

Don't assume that every real estate agent is a member of NAR; in fact, only about two out of three real estate agents are Realtors. If you don't see a Realtor trademark on the agent's business card, a call to your local Board of Realtors is all it takes to find out if an agent is a Realtor. Membership in a local Board of Realtors in the state of California automatically entitles an agent to membership to the California Association of Realtors (CAR) and the National Association of Realtors.

How to Shop for an Agent

One of the most important decisions you'll make when buying or selling a home is selecting a real estate agent to represent you. An honest, experienced, hard working, and capable agent can make the difference between a smooth real estate transaction and a horrible experience. It's a good idea to interview several real estate agents before selecting one. There are various ways to find good agents if personal referrals don't generate enough leads. One alternative is to call the manager of a reputable local real estate company and ask for a recommendation of an agent who specializes in the neighborhood of your current home if you're selling, or in the area where you're considering moving if you're buying. Many times prospective buyers or sellers will ask for the top producer. Although the top agent in an office may be perfect for you, be aware that such an agent may also be the busiest and may not have time to adequately serve your needs.

Visiting Sunday open houses is another way to become acquainted with real estate agents. This gives you an opportunity to see an agent in action, as well as to preview the inventory of homes for sale. Drive around your neighborhood and make note of the real estate signs you see most frequently. If you see one agent's name repeatedly, that agent may specialize in your area.

When you walk into a local real estate office and ask to talk to an agent, you'll most likely be turned over the "floor agent," the person on duty to answer calls and inquiries from prospective customers. You don't need an appointment to interview the floor agent, and this visit will give you an opportunity to scrutinize the real estate office.

One innovative buyer called several title companies and asked escrow officers to recommend three good agents, then selected the one agent selected by all three. Why call a title company? Because once a house is bought or sold in California, an agent usually opens escrow at a title company; the escrow officer and real estate agent then work closely with one another throughout the transaction and, as a result, are familiar with one another's professional reputations.

Beware of the out-of-the-area broker. You'll get the best service working with an agent who's an expert in selling real estate in your community. An agent from several counties away who's anxious to help you sell your home probably doesn't have enough local business to stay busy. Also, an out-of-the-area agent is less likely to be informed about local customs and practices. If the agent is a friend, ask to be referred to an agent who specializes in your area.

HOW TO INTERVIEW REAL ESTATE AGENTS

What qualifications should you be looking for in an agent? First, find out if the agent is a Realtor and a member of the local Board of Realtors. Most boards conduct a Multiple Listing Service (MLS). Board members submit their current listings to the Multiple Listing Service, and this information is distributed to all fellow members. The MLS provides an invaluable marketing service for a seller because it increases the amount of exposure a property receives. Buyers working with agents who participate in the MLS have access to many more homes listed for sale than they would if they worked with a non-member agent.

Next, find out if the agent works full-time at real estate and how much experience the agent has. Selecting a part-time real estate agent can be a big mistake in today's complex marketplace. Generally the more experience an agent has, the better, but a well-trained new agent supervised by a broker with experience can be entirely suitable.

Watch out for the agent who tries to entice you into doing business by making negative remarks about competitors. This is a violation of the Realtor code of ethics, as is overstating the value of a property for the purposes of acquiring a listing. (This, by the way, is also against the law.)

Real estate is a people business, so you want someone working for you who's skilled at working with people. The agent you select will be your personal representative in dealings with other real estate agents, loan brokers, title officers, prospective buyers or sellers, insurance agents, and property inspectors. Promptness and personal appearance are factors to take into consideration.

The in-person interview is critical. But before making a final selection, be sure to interview agents over the telephone. Since most of the critical work in a real estate transaction occurs over the telephone, an agent who can't communicate well over the phone is at a disadvantage. Ask the agents you interview for references of previous home buyers or sellers they have worked with. Before making your final agent selection, call two or three of the references. Find out if the buyer or seller was satisfied with the service the agent provided by asking, "Would you buy or sell a home through this agent again?"

California real estate transactions differ from those in other areas in that the agent is integral to the entire process. In many states, agents are merely responsible for bringing buyers and sellers together. Once a house is sold, other professionals, usually attorneys, complete the transaction. Since the service provided by a real estate agent in California will determine the success of your entire endeavor, it is extremely important that you make the correct agent selection. An agent who exhibits professionalism in the interview will be likely to perform a professional job throughout the transaction.

Buyers should expect a prospective agent to discuss their needs and desires as well as their financial capabilities before showing them a single house. Looking at houses that are out of your price range or that don't suit your needs is a waste of time—yours and the agent's. An agent who has endless time probably isn't selling many houses.

A good agent will have made appointments with the sellers to show you their homes and will provide you with a map of your house tour, including address, price, and number of bedrooms and baths. After previewing four or five houses with you, the agent should have a good idea of what you're looking for.

Keep in mind that real estate agents are qualified to give real estate advice, but if you have questions regarding legal or tax matters, you should consult the appropriate professional. Real estate agents also cannot discriminate, so you should not expect them to discuss the racial or ethnic make-up of a neighborhood.

THE COMPARATIVE MARKET ANALYSIS

Sellers should expect each prospective listing agent to provide a comparative market analysis of the home. This is a written estimate of the current market value of the home, based on a comparison with similar homes that have sold in the neighborhood within the last six months. The comparative sales information should include the property address, the sale price, the list price, the date the sale closed escrow, a brief description of the property, and the number of days the home was on the market. The analysis should also include information on similar homes that are presently being offered for sale in the area, as well as a list of the homes that were for sale but never sold.

To complete an accurate comparative market analysis, an agent must first preview your home, paying particular attention to details. Pertinent questions should focus on the age of the roof, the year the exterior was last painted, and any remodeling. Does the agent query you about drainage problems, roof leaks, or structural defects? Not only will the answers to these questions have an effect on the market value of your home, but they will also give you insight into how detail-oriented the agent is.

Your second meeting, to review the comparative market analysis, will allow you to observe the agent's thoroughness and dependability. An agent who takes the time to personalize the presentation is telling you something about the level of service you can expect during the transaction. The presentation should include a written proposal for marketing your home that details precisely how the agent intends to accomplish the sale.

Do not list with an agent who does not offer to complete a comparative market analysis for you. Some agents will guess at a price for your home at your first meeting. One step above this is the agent who shows up for the first appointment accompanied by several other agents from the office. The group waltzes through your home together, then huddles for a moment before producing a collective estimate on the price of your home. Neither of these approaches is professional or acceptable. Insist on an agent who's willing to do the required homework.

Some people feel awkward about interviewing more than one real estate agent. It's understandable that you don't want to waste someone's time and you don't want to be misleading about your intentions. Real estate agents are accustomed to working in competition with other agents, however, and there's no obligation to work with an agent you've interviewed. As a courteous gesture, let the agents you're talking to know that you're interviewing more than one agent. Once you've made a final decision, call the agents you didn't select and let them know how much you appreciate their efforts on your behalf. Pay special attention to the losing agent's responses. An agent who takes the news graciously should be at the top of your list if you run into trouble with your first choice and need to change agents later on.

Real Estate Commissions Are Negotiable

Real estate commissions are negotiable between individual brokers and sellers. It is, however, perfectly legal for a real estate broker to have a set commission, say 6 or 7 percent of the sale price. Most buyers and sellers have no idea what happens to a commission after the escrow has closed. A common misconception is that this amount goes directly to the listing agent. In most cases, this is not so. Ordinarily, the listing broker (the real estate company, not the agent) shares the commission, fifty-fifty, with the selling broker (again, the real estate company, not the individual agent).

Agents have predetermined commission split arrangements with the real estate companies they work for, and this varies from company to company and from agent to agent. It's not uncommon for a company to split a commission fifty-fifty with the agent. The actual listing and buying agents will each receive about 25 percent at the close of escrow.

Determining fair compensation for a listing hinges on many variables. Real estate agents usually work solely on commission, but they have out-of-pocket expenses regardless of whether a listing sells. Expenses include such items as gasoline, car insurance, brochures and other listing expenses, not to mention time. The real estate agent gets paid *only* when a transaction closes escrow.

A listing that sells quickly will result in a nice profit for the listing agent. If the home is hard to sell and numerous deals fall apart before escrow closes, the commission may not even come close to covering the amount of time and money expended by the listing agent. Unfortunately, it's difficult to determine in advance how complicated the sale and escrow will be.

How does this relate to the fact that, by law, commissions are negotiable? Simply put, real estate companies and agents need to make a profit in order to continue doing business. Although it's legal for an individual broker and seller to negotiate a commission, it's also legal for a real estate company to set its own policy regarding commissions. A full service company that provides sellers with an extensive marketing program, including a large commitment to advertising, will probably deviate less from its set commission policy than a minimal service company might.

Supply, demand, and market conditions enter into the picture. A top producing agent with more than enough business who gives clients 110 percent service is less likely to discount the commission than is an agent who's desperate for work. Sellers will have greater success negotiating a reduced commission with a top company or agent in a seller's market, particularly in the upper end price ranges.

An agreement that stipulates a higher commission to the broker if the property sells quickly (say, 6 percent) and a lower rate (5 percent) if the property is not sold within a given time period is actually the reverse of what's sensible. A property that isn't selling will cost the broker more in market expense, not less. Plus, if the market is slow and a lot of homes are sitting around unsold, the homes that are most likely to sell are those offering attractive prices and commissions. The real estate commission owed to the selling broker is included in the Multiple Listing Service information on each house. If agents have a pick of five or so similar houses, it stands to reason that they will show the houses on which the most generous commissions are being offered first. In a slow market, you could negotiate yourself out of a sale by insisting on a cut in the commission. Commission rates are market-sensitive, just as home prices are.

Real estate brokers generally offer discounted commissions for clients who send them a high volume of business, such as builders and relocation companies. It's also fairly common for an agent to agree to a commission reduction, even if this is contrary to company policy, if the commission is not being split with another selling broker or if the agent is representing one client in both a sale and a purchase.

Don't be shy about discussing commissions with prospective agents. If one agent volunteers to represent you for a commission lower than others are offering, let the competition know that someone has agreed to work for you for less. Give yourself the benefit of finding out if another agent will agree to match this fee. Finally, commissions shouldn't be the only factor you consider in choosing an agent. Rapport, dependability, professionalism, comprehensive marketing, and service are the critical ingredients to a successful real estate transaction.

AGENCY DISCLOSURE IS LAW IN CALIFORNIA

A seller's agent can enter into one of two possible agency relationships: the agent can either represent the seller exclusively (single agency) or represent both the seller and the buyer (dual agency). An agent who represents a seller exclusively has a fiduciary responsibility to that person. A fiduciary relationship is one of trust that demands the highest duties known under the law. According to the California Civil Code, a fiduciary owes "utmost care, integrity, honesty and loyalty" in dealings with a principal.

In a dual agency relationship, the agent represents both the buyer and the seller. If the buyer's and seller's agents in a transactions are both associated with the same broker of record, this is also considered dual agency representation. A dual agency relationship is legal in California *only* if it is disclosed in writing and consented to by both buyer and seller.

Because a dual agent owes a fiduciary duty to both the buyer and the seller and since there is a potential conflict of interest with dual agency, California law states that a dual agent shall not disclose to the buyer that the seller will accept less than the list price or disclose to the seller that the buyer will pay more than the offer price, without express written permission. The listing (seller's) agent can never represent the buyer exclusively in a transaction, since the listing agreement creates an agency relationship between the sellers and their agent.

The agent working for a buyer has three possible choices regarding agency representation: the agent can represent the buyer

DISCLOSURE REGARDING
REAL ESTATE AGENCY RELATIONSHIPS
(As required by the Civil Code)
CALIFORNIA ASSOCIATION OF REALTORS© (CAR) STANDARD FORM

When you enter into a discussion with a real estate agent regarding a real estate transaction, you should from the outset understand what type of agency relationship or representation you wish to have with the agent in the transaction.

SELLER'S AGENT

A Seller's agent under a listing agreement with Seller acts as the agent for the Seller only. A Seller's agent or a subagent of that agent has the following affirmative obligations:
To the Seller:
(a)   A Fiduciary duty of utmost care, integrity, honesty, and loyalty in dealings with the Seller.
To the Buyer & the Seller:
(a)   Diligent exercise of reasonable skill and care in performance of the agent's duties.
(b)   A duty of honest and fair dealing and good faith.
(c)   A duty to disclose all facts known to the agent materially affecting the value or desirability of property that are not known to, or within the diligent attention and observation of, the parties.

An agent is not obligated to reveal to either party any confidential information obtained from the other party which does not involve the affirmative duties set forth above.

BUYER'S AGENT

A selling agent can, with a Buyer's consent, agree to act as agent for the Buyer only. In these situations, the agent is not the Seller's agent, even if by agreement the agent may receive compensation for services rendered, either in full or in part from the Seller. An agent acting only for a Buyer has the following affirmative obligations.
To the Buyer:
(a)   A fiduciary duty of utmost care, integrity, honesty, and loyalty in dealings with the Buyer.
To the Buyer & Seller:
(a)   Diligent exercise of reasonable skill and care in performance of the agent's duties.
(b)   A duty of honest and fair dealing and good faith.
(c)   A duty to disclose all facts known to the agent materially affecting the value or desirability of the property that are not known to, or within the diligent attention and observation of, the parties.

An agent is not obligated to reveal to either party any confidential information obtained from the other party which does not involve the affirmative duties set forth above.

AGENT REPRESENTING BOTH SELLER & BUYER

A real estate agent, either acting directly or through one or more associate licensees, can legally be the agent of both the Seller and the Buyer in a transaction, but only with the knowledge and consent of both the Seller and the Buyer.

In a dual agency situation, the agent has the following affirmative obligations to both the Seller and the Buyer:
(a)   A fiduciary duty of utmost care, integrity, honesty and loyalty in the dealings with either Seller or the Buyer.
(b)   Other duties to the Seller and the Buyer as stated above in their respective sections.

In representing both Seller and Buyer, the agent may not, without the express permission of the respective party, disclose to the other party that the Seller will accept a price less than the listing price or that the Buyer will pay a price greater than the price offered.

The above duties of the agent in a real estate transaction do not relieve a Seller or a Buyer from the responsibility to protect their own interests. You should carefully read all agreements to assure that they adequately express your understanding of the transaction. A real estate agent is a person qualified to advise about real estate. If legal or tax advice is desired, consult a competent professional.

Throughout your real property transaction you may receive more than one disclosure form, depending upon the number of agents assisting in the transaction. The law requires each agent with whom you have more than a casual relationship to present you with this disclosure form. You should read its contents each time it is presented to you, considering the relationship between you and the real estate agent in your specific transaction.

This disclosure form includes the provisions of article 2.5 (commencing with Section 2373) of Chapter 2 of Title 9 of Part 4 of Division 3 of the Civil Code set forth on the reverse hereof. Read it carefully.

I/WE ACKNOWLEDGE RECEIPT OF A COPY OF THIS DISCLOSURE.

BUYER/SELLER_____ Date_____ TIME_____ AM/PM

BUYER/SELLER_____ Date_____ TIME_____ AM/PM

AGENT _____ By _____ Date_____
         (Please Print)   (Associate Licensee or Broker-Signature)

A REAL ESTATE BROKER IS QUALIFIED TO ADVISE ON REAL ESTATE. IF YOU DESIRE LEGAL ADVICE, CONSULT YOUR ATTORNEY.

This form is available for use by the entire real estate industry. The use of this form is not intended to identify the user as a REALTOR®. REALTOR® is a registered collective membership mark which may be used only by real estate licensees who are members of the NATIONAL ASSOCIATION OF REALTORS® and who subscribe to its Code of Ethics.

Copyright© 1987, CALIFORNIA ASSOCIATION OF REALTORS·
525 South Virgil Avenue, Los Angeles, California 90020   FORM AD-11

| OFFICE USE ONLY |
| Reviewed by Broker or Designee _____ |
| Date _____ |

EQUAL HOUSING
OPPORTUNITY

SF-Oct-87

CHAPTER 2 OF TITLE 9 OF PART 4 OF DIVISION 3 OF THE CIVIL CODE

Article 2.5. Agency Relationships in Residential Real Property Transactions

2373. As used in this article, the following terms have the following meanings:

(a) "Agent" means a person acting under provisions of this title in a real property transaction, and includes a person who is licensed as a real estate broker under Chapter 3 (commencing with Section 10130) of Part 1 of Division 4 of the Business & Professions Code, and under whose license a listing is executed or an offer to purchase is obtained.

(b) "Associate licensee" means a person who is licensed as a real estate broker or salesperson under Chapter 3 (commencing with Section 10130) of Part 1 of Division 4 of the Business & Professions Code and who is either licensed under a broker or has entered into a written contract with a broker to act as the broker's agent in connection with acts requiring a real estate license and to function under the broker's supervision in the capacity of an associate licensee.

The agent in the real property transaction bears responsibility for his or her associate licensees who perform as agents of the agent. When an associate licensee owes a duty to any principal, or to any buyer or seller who is not a principal, in a real property transaction, that duty is equivalent to the duty owed to that party by the broker for whom the associate licensee functions.

(c) "Buyer" means a transferee in a real property transaction, and includes a person who executes an offer to purchase real property from a seller through an agent, or who seeks the services of an agent in more than a casual, transitory, or preliminary manner, with the object of entering into a real property transaction. "Buyer" includes vendee or lessee.

(d) "Dual agent" means an agent acting, either directly or through an associate licensee, as agent for both the seller and the buyer in a real property transaction.

(e) "Listing agreement" means a contract between an owner of real property and an agent, by which the agent has been authorized to sell the real property or to find or obtain a buyer.

(f) "Listing agent" means a person who has obtained a listing of real property to act as an agent for compensation.

(g) "Listing price" is the amount expressed in dollars specified in the listing for which the seller is willing to sell the real property through the listing agent.

(h) "Offering price" is the amount expressed in dollars specified in an offer to purchase for which the buyer is willing to buy the real property.

(i) "Offer to purchase" means a written contract executed by a buyer acting through a selling agent which becomes the contract for the sale of the real property upon acceptance by the seller.

(j) "Real property" means any estate specified by subdivision (1) or (2) of Section 761 in property which constitutes or is improved with one to four dwelling units, any leasehold in this type of property exceeding one year's duration, and mobilehomes, when offered for sale or sold through an agent pursuant to the authority contained in Section 10131.6 of the Business & Professions Code.

(k) "Real property transaction" means a transaction for the sale of real property in which an agent is employed by one or more of the principals to act in that transaction, and includes a listing or an offer to purchase.

(l) "Sell," "sale," or "sold" refers to a transaction for the transfer of real property from the seller to the buyer, and includes exchanges of real property between the seller and buyer, transactions for the creation of a real property sales contract within the meaning of Section 2985, and transactions for the creation of a leasehold exceeding one year's duration.

(m) "Seller" means the transferor in a real property transaction, and includes an owner who lists real property with an agent, whether or not a transfer results, or who receives an offer to purchase real property of which he or she is the owner from an agent on behalf of another. "Seller" includes both a vendor and a lessor.

(n) "Selling agent" means a listing agent who acts alone, or an agent who acts in cooperation with a listing agent, and who sells or finds and obtains a buyer for the real property, or an agent who locates property for a buyer for the property for which no listing exists and presents an offer to purchase to the seller.

(o) "Subagent" means a person to whom an agent delegates agency powers as provided in Article 5 (commencing with Section 2349) of Chapter I. However, "subagent" does not include an associate licensee who is acting under the supervision of an agent in a real property transaction.

2374. Listing agents and selling agents shall provide the seller and buyer in a real property transaction with a copy of the disclosure form specified in Section 2375 and, except as provided in subdivision (c), shall obtain a signed acknowledgement of receipt from that seller or buyer, except as provided in this section of Section 2374.5, as follows:

(a) The listing agent, if any, shall provide the disclosure form to the seller prior to entering into the listing agreement.

(b) The selling agent shall provide the disclosure form to the seller as soon as practicable prior to presenting the seller with an offer to purchase, unless the selling agent previously provided the seller with a copy of the disclosure form pursuant to subdivision (a).

(c) Where the selling agent does not deal on a face-to-face basis with the seller, the disclosure form prepared by the selling agent may be furnished to the seller (and acknowledgement of receipt obtained for the selling agent from the seller) by the listing agent, or the selling agent may deliver the disclosure form by certified mail addressed to the seller at his or her last known address, in which case no signed acknowledgement of receipt is required.

(d) The selling agent shall provide the disclosure form to the buyer as soon as practicable prior to execution of the buyer's offer to purchase, except that if the offer to purchase is not prepared by the selling agent, the selling agent shall present the disclosure form to the buyer not later than the next business day after the selling agent receives the offer to purchase from the buyer.

2374.5 In any circumstance in which the seller or buyer refuses to sign an acknowledgement of receipt pursuant to Section 2374, the agent, or an associate licensee acting for an agent, shall set forth, sign and date a written declaration of the facts of the refusal.

2375.5 (a) As soon as practicable, the selling agent shall disclose to the buyer and seller whether the selling agent is acting in the real property transaction exclusively as the buyer's agent, exclusively as the seller's agent, or as a dual agent representing both the buyer and the seller and this relationship shall be confirmed in the contract to purchase and sell real property or in a separate writing executed or acknowledged by the seller, the buyer, and the selling agent prior to or coincident with execution of that contract by the buyer and the seller, respectively.

(b) As soon as practicable, the listing agent shall disclose to the seller whether the listing agent is acting in the real property transaction exclusively as the seller's agent, or as a dual agent representing both the buyer and seller and this relationship shall be confirmed in the contract to purchase and sell real property or in a separate writing executed or acknowledged by the seller and the listing agent prior to or coincident with the execution of that contract by the seller.

(c) The confirmation required by subdivisions (a) and (b) shall be in the following form.

_____ is the agent of (check one):
(Name of Listing Agent)

[   ] the seller exclusively; or
[   ] both the buyer and seller.

_____ is the agent of (check one):
(Name of Selling Agent if not the same as the Listing Agent)

[   ] the buyer exclusively; or
[   ] the seller exclusively; or
[   ] both the buyer and seller.

(d) The disclosures and confirmation required by this section shall be in addition to the disclosure required by Section 2374.

2376. No selling agent in a real property transaction may act as an agent for the buyer only, when the selling agent is also acting as the listing agent in the transaction.

2377. The payment of compensation or the obligation to pay compensation to an agent by the seller or buyer is not necessarily determinative of a particular agency relationship between an agent and the seller or buyer. A listing agent and a selling agent may agree to share any compensation or commission paid, or any right to any compensation or commission for which an obligation arises as the result of a real estate transaction, and the terms of any such agreement shall not necessarily be determinative of a particular relationship.

2378. Nothing in this article prevents an agent from selecting, as a condition of the agent's employment, a specific form of agency relationship not specifically prohibited by this article if the requirements of Section 2374 and Section 2375.5 are complied with.

2379. A dual agent shall not disclose to the buyer that the seller is willing to sell the property at a price less than the listing price, without the express written consent of the seller. A dual agent shall not disclose to the seller that the buyer is willing to pay a price greater than the offering price, without the express written consent of the buyer.

This section does not alter in any way the duty or responsibility of a dual agent to any principal with respect to confidential information other than price.

2380. Nothing in this article precludes a listing agent from also being a selling agent, and the combination of these functions in one agent does not, of itself, make that agent a dual agent.

2381. A contract between the principal and agent may be modified or altered to change the agency relationship at any time before the performance of the act which is the object of the agency with the written consent of the parties to the agency relationship.

2382. Nothing in this article shall be construed to either diminish the duty of disclosure owed buyers and sellers by agents and their associate licensees, subagents, and employees or to relieve agents and their associate licensees, subagents, and employees from liability for their conduct in connection with acts governed by this article or for any breach of a fiduciary duty or a duty of disclosure.

exclusively (single agency), represent the seller exclusively (sub-agency), or represent both buyer and seller (dual agency).

According to the California Civil Code, real estate agents must disclose to buyers and sellers all possible agency relationships before they enter into a residential real estate transaction. This involves providing a prospective buyer or seller with a standard disclosure form which describes both the possible agency relationships and the relevant provisions of the civil code. The intent of this law is to clarify the agent's responsibilities and obligations.

Following agency disclosure (which is acknowledged by principals and their agents signing at the bottom of the disclosure form), agents are required to inform the buyer and/or seller, "as soon as practicable," of every party that they are representing in the transaction. This must be followed by confirmation, in writing, of the agency relationships that will exist in the transaction.

Before agency disclosure became law in California, the buyer's agent customarily worked exclusively for the seller, and not for the buyer, through an agency relationship called sub-agency in which one agent works for another agent. A buyer's agent who is a sub-agent to the seller's agent owes a fiduciary responsibility to the seller, not to the buyer. As a sub-agent representing the seller, an agent is working to bring the seller the highest possible price, not to negotiate the lowest possible price for the buyer.

Many states do not yet have an agency disclosure law. If you are buying a home outside California, find out if your agent is acting as a sub-agent of the seller. Also, investigate whether it's possible to hire a buyer's broker, who will owe a fiduciary responsibility to you, not to the seller.

California law is very clear on an agent's obligations to both buyer and seller in a transaction. These responsibilities include diligent performance of an agent's duties; honesty, fairness, and good faith to both parties; and a "duty to disclose all facts known to the agent materially affecting the value or desirability of the property that are not known to, or within the diligent attention and observation of, the parties."

THE PROS AND CONS OF WORKING WITH MORE THAN ONE AGENT
There's no written rule that says a buyer must look for a new home with only one agent. Practically speaking, however, working with one agent exclusively is usually the best arrangement. Since most buyers are in a hurry, working with one agent helps avoid the time consuming duplication of efforts that can occur with several agents. Most homes are listed on the Multiple Listing Service, so if you work with a Realtor who belongs to the local Board of Realtors and who is active

in the business, you're likely to be exposed to the full inventory of listings as they become available.

As a seller, there's really not much choice. Most listing agents will work only on an exclusive basis. This is another aspect of the real estate business that causes confusion, yet it is possible to list with one agent and obtain maximum exposure at the same time. This is done by signing an Exclusive Listing Agreement, with a clause in the agreement that instructs the agent to list your home on the Multiple Listing Service. Again, to accomplish this you must list with an agent who belongs to the local Board of Realtors.

Be courteous to real estate agents, but don't let yourself be intimidated by them. Buyers must feel comfortable with their agents. An agent you meet by chance may turn out to be terrific for you, but if you have reservations or if the listing agent has exposed you to the property and you don't want to be represented by the same person who represents the seller, find another agent. Agents sometimes get into commission disputes in these situations. A truly professional agent respects your decision to select the representative you feel comfortable with and never involves you in agent disputes.

COMMON COMPLAINTS ABOUT REAL ESTATE AGENTS

The most common complaint, which is often completely justified, is that buyers or sellers feel they're being hustled by real estate agents. Real estate is a competitive business, and the good agents are continually looking for new customers. It's also a very personal business, so you must relate well with an agent who represents you in order to have an agreeable transaction. If an agent's approach is too "hard sell" for your liking, find another agent. The most successful agents are masters at the "soft sell" approach to doing business.

Another common complaint is that the agent consistently shows homes that are above the buyer's price range. Good agents will qualify their buyers first and won't show homes out of the predetermined price range.

Buyers who have looked for some time and have found nothing often complain that their agent hasn't been listening to them and is always showing them houses that are not quite right. In most cases either the buyers are not clearly communicating their wants and needs to their agent or what they are looking for is not presently available.

Agents can't be expected to be mind readers. From an agent's standpoint, the hardest buyers to please are the ones who say nothing about what they like and don't like, or the ones who think every home they see is wonderful (which usually means they don't know what they like). If you're clear with your agent about what you're looking for, your agent should be able to describe your dream home after showing you no more than three or four houses.

A final, legitimate complaint made by both buyers and sellers is that their agent does not work hard enough for them. Buyers who discover they're missing out on one good house after another should find another agent who will work actively on their behalf. An even bigger problem is when buyers or sellers discover, after the purchase contract is negotiated, that their agents won't return phone calls and fail to follow through with the critical details of the escrow and closing.

What to Do If You're Dissatisfied with Your Agent

Firing real estate agents before they're hired is easy enough: tell them you already have another agent to represent you. If, after you're into the escrow period, you discover that your agent has left you to fend for yourself, you have several ways to protect yourself.

Let your agent know you're unhappy with the lack of attention to your transaction. Ask to be informed every two days about the escrow's progress. If this doesn't result in improved service, continue to call every few days or so to monitor the transaction yourself.

Never forget that you are the boss and you have the right to expect high quality representation. If, after repeated discussions with your agent, you continue to be dissatisfied, call the agent's manager or broker of record. Be candid about your concerns. If the manager is unable to solve the problem, then request that another agent be assigned to handle your transaction.

CHAPTER 4

LISTING YOUR HOME FOR SALE

WHEN IS THE BEST TIME TO SELL?

Sellers commonly wonder when is the best time to sell. Statistics are available that can help determine the answer, and the Multiple Listing Service is continually compiling information on local real estate market conditions. Ask your agent the length of time it's taking to sell homes similar to yours, the average percentage of listing price obtained, the number of recent sales in your neighborhood, the number of recent sales in your price range, and the most common type of financing used.

In an active real estate market, homes usually sell within sixty to ninety days for close to list price, and buyers usually obtain new financing to complete their purchases. In a slow market, you'll find fewer sales taking a longer period of time, lower sale prices, and more seller financing. Most sellers, approximately 50 percent according to a recent survey, have an urgent need to sell; that is why, in a relatively slow market, competitive pricing is critical.

Weather conditions can also be a consideration. Homes tend to show better and buyers are more eager to buy when the sun is shining. In recent years, however, interest rates, not the weather, have governed real estate market activity. Don't discount selling in the dead of winter if rates are low. The school calendar may affect the timing of sellers who have children, but keep in mind that most home buyers gauge their activities around interest rates, not the school year.

LISTING AGREEMENTS

There are several types of listings. An open listing is a nonexclusive agreement in which the seller agrees to pay a commission only to the broker who sells the property. A seller may enter into an open listing with many different brokers but reserve the right to sell the property personally; in this case no commission is owed to a broker. The drawback of this arrangement is that brokers are not likely to spend much time trying to sell the property, since there's little chance of being paid for the effort.

An Exclusive Agency listing authorizes only one broker to sell the property, but still preserves the seller's right to make a personal sale. Again, the drawback is that the seller is likely to get less than full-time effort, since the broker's marketing endeavors could be wasted.

The most popular listing agreement in the residential home industry is the Exclusive Authorization and Right to Sell listing. Under this agreement, only the listing broker has the right to sell the home and will receive a commission, if the property is sold on the seller's terms and conditions, no matter who finds the buyer. Most exclusive listing contracts also contain provisions for the seller's broker to submit the property to the Multiple Listing Service and for the commission to be split between the listing and broker's buyers. This way, the seller receives not only broker representation but maximum marketing exposure as well. A home may or may not sell during the time period of the listing agreement, but if it does, the listing broker will at least be compensated for the effort. Marketing a home comprehensively costs money, and few good brokers are willing to incur those expenses without at least having a chance of being compensated.

ADVICE ON HOW MUCH TO FIX UP FOR SALE

First impressions have a lasting impact. Imagine yourself as a buyer walking up to a house that has a shoddy facade, fence posts hanging from rusty old nails, exterior house paint blistered and peeling, and crab grass growing everywhere. You immediately wonder what horrors await behind the front door.

No one would recommend that you completely make over your home for a quick and profitable sale. Making the most of what you own, however, is only sensible if, like most people, you need to squeeze every dime possible out of the current home. Cosmetic repairs that cost relatively little but return a lot on the investment plus routine cleaning are what a savvy homeowner should concentrate on.

The entry to Jerry Thomas's house, for instance, consisted of an immense deck and stairway system with such bad dry rot that Jerry had placed pots upside down over holes in the deck to keep guests from tripping and falling. The roof and gutters had deteriorated to the point that water poured from the roof onto the head of anyone standing at the front door during a rain storm. Jerry's Realtor predicted that, with the deck and roof in their current condition, the house would sell for around $200,000 and that the buyer would probably ask Jerry to pay for the repair work. The Realtor convinced Jerry to replace the deck and roof before marketing the home, which sold with multiple offers for $250,000. Jerry more than doubled the return on the money he invested in fixing up the property for sale.

Start by taking a critical look at your home. Try to put yourself in the frame of mind of a picky buyer, and have a notepad handy. Make a list of everything you see that should be repaired, replaced, or removed before you market the home.

Real estate agents often say that curb appeal, the way the property looks from the street, sells the house, so begin by making a study of the exterior. Dead or dying shrubs should be removed and replaced. If the lawn is shot, consider rolling in new sod, but a sickly lawn may just need fertilizing and more water, so try this first. Replace missing fence slats and repair lopsided gates or shutters. Fix a leaky sprinkler system and add color to the yard with flats of flowering annuals to line walkways and planting beds. Colorful container plants at the front entry provide a cheerful welcome.

Pay special attention to the condition of the driveway, particularly if it's in front of the house. Remove grease stains with a chemical solvent, patch holes, and consider resurfacing if the driveway is beyond repair. The impression you want to convey is that the property is well maintained.

The exterior paint should be in good condition. If it looks good, touch up where necessary; otherwise, consider a complete paint job. Keep in mind that if you don't paint a house that needs it, the buyer will have to overcome a negative first impression, which may cost you more than it would to have painted the house in advance.

Exterior paint color preferences change, and it doesn't make sense to repaint your home without first considering a change in color scheme. This is particularly the case if a new color will make your home more salable or bring a higher price. Blue, yellow, green, black, purple, and slate gray have been difficult colors to sell in the past. Currently, pastels and earth tones are popular. A beige, taupe, or grey with a contrasting trim is usually a safe bet, depending on the house style. Ask your agent and several painters for color recommendations. Drive around your neighborhood and note the color combinations that are particularly attractive. If you're still in doubt, contact a color consultant.

The roof, gutters, and down drains should be in good repair. Caulk areas where you've had leaks in the past: chimneys, vent pipes, and skylights are common culprits. Replace loose, cracked, and missing shakes and shingles.

A word of caution about your fix-up projects: Keep a record of the items you're correcting that should be disclosed to the new buyer. For instance, a skylight that has leaked in the past and needs routine caulking should be disclosed. Informing the buyer, in writing, of the general maintenance items that must be taken care of to ensure the continued good condition of the property is likely to relieve you of future liability.

Before calling the roofer to make repairs or to clean your gutters, look for signs of moisture entry from inside your house. Water stains and cracked, blistered, or peeling paint on ceilings or walls are the indicators. Have the roofer repair where indicated and ask for a water test to be sure that the problem is corrected before making cosmetic repairs to the interior.

Other things to look out for in your yard are weeds, debris, fallen leaves, excess ivy, or murky water in the pool. Trim hedges and paths, clean up the yard, haul away yesterday's treasures that have no value to you, and have the pool water treated until it sparkles. Don't overlook the subterranean drainage system around your house. Call a rooting company to unclog plugged drains.

Be sure to emphasize good outdoor living, if this is a selling feature of your home. An empty deck or patio can be dressed up with outdoor furniture and containers of flowering plants. Good looking, inexpensive varieties of patio furniture are available.

Now, for the inside. The areas that buyers will see first are the most important. Keep this in mind if you are short on time or funds. Before opening the front door, test the door bell and entry porch light. Purchase a new welcome mat to replace an old one that's frayed and weathered.

Imagine yourself as a prospective buyer. Open the door and walk inside. Stand in your entry hall and concentrate on the first impression. If the immediate surroundings appear dark, dingy, crowded, garish, or cluttered, change them to create an interior that's light, spacious, airy, and fresh.

Remove furniture from crowded rooms and hallways. Use the extra pieces elsewhere, or tag them for storage or sale. Generally speaking, under-furnished is better than over-furnished, because it creates an illusion of spaciousness. If you're having difficulty rearranging your belongings, ask your agent for help, or seek the advice of an interior decorator who specializes in "fix-up-for-sale."

Dingy walls should first be cleaned, with specific effort directed toward removing crayon or pencil marks and finger prints, particularly around light switch plates. If walls don't brighten with cleaning or if the existing colors are overpowering, repaper or paint as needed.

Stick to neutrals and pastel shades that won't clash with a buyer's decor.

Pay attention to floor coverings. Carpet that looks outdated, tattered, and worn should be replaced, unless you have hardwood flooring underneath the carpet. If the floors are in good shape, you can leave them bare and save the cost of recarpeting; if they are a bit rough, get several bids to determine the cost of refinishing. Find out from your agent whether hardwood floors or wall-to-wall carpets are more popular with buyers before deciding whether to refinish the floor or replace the carpet.

Another reminder about disclosure obligations: Sellers who discover burn marks or stains in wood floors when they are replacing wall-to-wall carpeting should disclose this to prospective buyers. If you patch, paint, or wallpaper walls that are uneven, cracked, or have holes in them, disclose this also to avoid being accused of concealing a defect. Keep a record of these items as you redecorate for sale to aid you in filling out the seller disclosure form (discussed later in this chapter). Also, keep receipts for all of the fix-up work since some expenses are tax deductible.

Kitchens and bathrooms are focal points for most buyers. Be sure that both are spotless and free of clutter. Keep toilet articles out of sight; replace tired-looking shower curtains, bath mats, and towels. Antiquated light fixtures can be updated relatively inexpensively. Always keep in mind: the more light the better. If you've had a termite report that calls for replacing the kitchen or bathroom floor, consider having the work done before you market your home.

Little improvements can make a big difference. Designer light switch plates throughout the house cost very little and can be added with a screwdriver. Old cabinets look new when battered knobs and pulls are replaced.

Be sure to fix leaky faucets, a toilet that runs continually, and clogged drains. Add to your fix-up list torn screens, squeaky or sticky doors and windows, broken windows, or a sliding door that pops off its track. Tighten hardware, particularly loose door knobs, and replace burned out light bulbs and missing tiles.

Clean out and organize closets, as storage space is another top priority for most home buyers. Throw away anything you don't need; it makes no sense to move with unwanted items, anyway. Consider investing in closet organizers if your closets are small. And don't forget to clean and reorganize the garage, attic, and basement to emphasize their storage potential.

Make the most out of every square inch of your house. Turn the junk room into a room with a purpose. A room that's too small to be used as a bedroom might be ideal as an office, hobby center, nursery, study, or computer corner.

Don't overlook the views from your windows. Overgrown trees and hedges should be trimmed. Add a sheer window covering or a blind to a window that has an unpleasant outlook.

Pet and smoker odors are offensive to most buyers. Clean thoroughly and air out the house. Pet stores have products that eliminate most pet odors from carpets. The scentless variety is preferable.

The look you're aiming for is squeaky clean. Floors should be scrubbed and waxed. If you're not replacing carpets, have them professionally cleaned (or rent professional equipment and do it yourself), and, while you're at it, clean upholstered furniture. Finally, wash all windows, inside and out.

By now you're probably exhausted from just thinking about all that needs to be done to get a home ready to sell. Working people will be particularly overwhelmed. Finalize the list and get bids for having the work done in advance. Take a few days off, if you can, to supervise or assist with the fix-up. Hiring a professional cleaning company to come in after all the projects are completed will save you time, and it's worth the expense if you're busy. At the end of it all, your home will look great. Don't be surprised if you find yourself wondering why you didn't take care of all these chores earlier. If you feel this way, you're not alone. Most people's homes never look as good as they do when they go on the market.

The Exclusive Authorization and Right to Sell

The listing agreement is an employment contract between you and your broker. The California Association of Realtors (CAR) has developed standard forms that are available for use by the entire real estate industry. A copy of the CAR "Exclusive Authorization and Right to Sell" listing is included and will be reviewed in this section. Individual real estate companies may have their own forms that differ somewhat from the CAR forms; however, there is consistency regarding the basic elements included in most exclusive right to sell listing agreements.

The listing agreement begins with a grant clause giving a real estate broker the exclusive right to sell a property for a specified period of time. The length of the listing period is negotiable, but it's usually 90 to 180 days. In an active real estate market, a well-priced home should sell within ninety days. In a slower market, a home may take in excess of six months to sell. The length of a listing can be extended by mutual consent of the seller and the broker. Sellers listing with an agent they haven't worked with before ought to list for ninety days and extend later if necessary. If you're not pleased with the agent's performance, you'll be free to find a replacement at that time.

EXCLUSIVE AUTHORIZATION AND RIGHT TO SELL
MULTIPLE LISTING AUTHORIZATION
THIS IS INTENDED TO BE A LEGALLY BINDING AGREEMENT — READ IT CAREFULLY.
CALIFORNIA ASSOCIATION OF REALTORS® (CAR) STANDARD FORM

1. **EXCLUSIVE RIGHT TO SELL:** I hereby employ and grant_____
hereinafter called "Broker," the exclusive and irrevocable right commencing on _____ , 19____ , and expiring at
midnight on _____ , 19____ , to sell or exchange the real property situated in the city of_____ ,
County of _____ , California described in the attached information sheet and as follows:_____
_____ .

2. **TERMS OF SALE:** The purchase price shall be _____
_____ ($_____), to be paid as follows_____
_____

The following items of personal property are included in the above stated price: _____
_____

3. **MULTIPLE LISTING SERVICE (MLS):** Broker is a Participant of_____
BOARD OF REALTORS® Multiple Listing Service (MLS) and this listing information will be provided to the MLS to be published and
disseminated to its Participants. The Broker is authorized to appoint subagents and to report the sale, its price, terms and financing for the
publication, dissemination, information and use by authorized Board members, MLS Participants and Subscribers.

4. **TITLE INSURANCE:** Evidence of title shall be a California Land Title Association standard coverage policy of title insurance in the
amount of the selling price.

**Notice: The amount or rate of real estate commissions is not fixed by law. They are set by each Broker individually
and may be negotiable between the Seller and Broker.**

5. **COMPENSATION TO BROKER:** I hereby agree to compensate Broker, irrespective of agency relationship(s), as follows:
(a) _____ percent of the selling price, or $_____ , if the property is sold during the term hereof, or any extension
thereof, by Broker on the terms herein set forth or any other price and terms I may accept, or through any other person, or by me,
or____ percent of the price shown in 2, or $ _____ , if said property is withdrawn from sale, transferred,
conveyed, leased, or rented without the consent of Broker, or made unmarketable by my voluntary act during the term hereof or any
other extension thereof.
(b) the compensation provided for in subparagraph (a) above if property is sold, conveyed or otherwise transferred within _____
calendar days after the termination of this authority or any extension thereof to anyone with whom Broker has had negotiations prior
to final termination, provided I have received notice in writing, including the names of the prospective purchasers, before or upon
termination of this agreement or any extension hereof. However, I shall not be obligated to pay the compensation provided for in
subparagraph (a) if a valid listing agreement is entered into during the term of said protection period with another licensed real estate
broker and a sale, lease or exchange of the property is made during the term of said valid listing agreement.
(c) I authorize Broker to cooperate with other brokers, to appoint subagents, and to divide with other brokers such compensation in any
manner acceptable to brokers.
(d) In the event of an exchange, permission is hereby given Broker to represent all parties and collect compensation or commissions
from them, provided there is full disclosure to all principals of such agency. Broker is authorized to divide with other brokers such
compensation or commissions in any manner acceptable to brokers.
(e) If requested by Broker, Seller shall execute and deliver an escrow instruction irrevocably assigning Broker's compensation in an
amount equal to the compensation provided in subparagraph (a) (above) from the Seller's proceeds.

6. **DEPOSIT:** Broker is authorized to accept and hold on Sellers behalf a deposit on the account of the purchase price.

PROTECTION PLAN: Seller is informed that home protection plan_____ ide additional protection
____ d Buyer. Cost and coverage ____

Setting the list price is one of the most important aspects of the
listing agreement. Arriving at an accurate price is easier to accomplish in some neighborhoods than in others. Homes located in planned
developments, where there are several standard models, are usually
easier to price than homes in areas where there is tremendous varia-
bility in house types. Another factor to keep in mind is that the real
estate market is continually changing, and market fluctuations have
an effect on property values.

The comparative market analysis, discussed in Chapter Three,
provides the background data on which to base your list price decision. Study the comparable sales material presented to you by the
different agents you interviewed initially. If all agents agreed on a price
range for your home, go with the consensus.

7. **HOME ~~~~** ~~~~ are available. Such plans may provide ~~~~
and benefit to a Seller and ~~~~ ~~~~ may vary.

*8. **KEYBOX:** I authorize Broker to install a KEYBOX: (Initial) YES (____/____) NO (____/____)
Refer to reverse side for important keybox information.

9. **SIGN:** Authorization to install a FOR SALE/SOLD sign on the property: (Initial) YES (____/____) NO (____/____)

10. **PEST CONTROL:** Seller shall furnish a current Structural Pest Control Report of the
main building and all structures of the property, except _____   (Initial) YES (____/____) NO (____/____)

*11. **DISCLOSURE:** Seller's disclosure obligations are set forth on the reverse side. Seller shall provide a Real
Estate Transfer Disclosure Statement concerning the condition of the property. I agree to save and hold
Broker harmless from all claims, disputes, litigation, and/or judgments arising from any incorrect
information supplied by me, or from any material fact known by me which I fail to disclose.   (Initial) (____/____)

*12. **TAX WITHHOLDING:** Seller agrees to perform any act reasonably necessary to carry out the provisions of FIRPTA (IRC 1445) and
regulations promulgated thereunder. Refer to the reverse side for withholding provisions and exemptions.

13. **EQUAL HOUSING OPPORTUNITY:** This property is offered in compliance with local, state, and federal anti-discrimination laws.

14. **ATTORNEY'S FEES:** In any action or proceeding arising out of this agreement, the prevailing party shall be entitled to reasonable
attorney's fees and costs.

15. **ADDITIONAL TERMS:** _____

16. **ENTIRE AGREEMENT:** I, the Seller, warrant that I am the owner of the property or have the authority to execute this agreement. The Seller
and Broker further intend that this agreement constitutes the complete and exclusive statement of its terms and that no extrinsic evidence
whatsoever may be introduced in any judicial or arbitration proceeding, if any, involving this agreement.

**I acknowledge that I have read and understand this agreement, including the important information on the reverse side, and
have received a copy.**

Date _____ , 19 _____ , California

Seller _____ Address _____

Seller _____ City _____ State _____ Phone _____
In consideration of the above, Broker agrees to use diligence in procuring a purchaser.

Real Estate Broker _____ By _____

Address _____ City _____ Date _____

OFFICE USE ONLY
Reviewed by Broker or Designee _____
Date _____

EQUAL HOUSING OPPORTUNITY
SF-Oct-87

How you position yourself in the market, in relation to your competition, is very important. Some sellers find it helpful to visit Sunday open houses in their area. If the open house agent tells you that offers are being written and the home is new on the market, the home is probably priced right. A home that has been on the market for months with no offers is probably overpriced, particularly if similar homes in the area have sold quickly.

A good rule of thumb is to list a home within 5 percent of the expected selling price. This leaves some room to negotiate with a buyer. Overpricing a home discourages buyers and real estate agents, resulting in a home that sits on the market. Buyers and agents often wonder if something's wrong with such a house. Often the only thing wrong is the price, but stigmas are difficult to overcome. Also, keep in mind that 95 percent of home buyers cite price as the major factor in deciding whether to buy a given house. Price it right and it's sold.

The listing agreement contains a provision, under the Terms of

8. **KEYBOX:** A keybox designed as a repository of a key to the above premises, will permit access to the interior of the premises by Participants of the Multiple Listing Service (MLS), their authorized licensees and prospective buyers. If property is not seller occupied, seller shall be responsible for obtaining occupants' written permission for use of the keybox. Neither listing nor selling broker, MLS or Board of REALTORS® is an insurer against theft, loss, vandalism or damage attributed to the use of keybox. SELLER is advised to verify the existence of, or obtain appropriate insurance through their own insurance broker.

11. **DISCLOSURE:** Sellers of real property should be aware of their disclosure obligations under the California Court Cases, Statutes and Real Estate Law commentaries excerpted or paraphrased below:

12. **TAX WITHHOLDING:** Under the Foreign Investment In Real Property Tax Act (FIRPTA), IRC 1445, *every* Buyer of U.S. real property *must*, unless an exemption applies, deduct and withhold from Seller's proceeds ten percent (10%) of the gross sales price. The primary exemptions are: No withholding is required if (a) Seller provides Buyer with an affidavit under penalty of perjury, that Seller is not a foreign person," or (b) provides Buyer with a "qualifying statement" issued by the Internal Revenue Service, or (c) if Buyer purchases real property for use as a residence and the purchase price is $300,000.00 or less and if Buyer or a member of Buyer's family has definite plans to reside at the property for at least 50% of the number of days it is in use during each of the first two twelve-months periods after transfer. Seller agrees to execute and deliver as required any instrument, affidavit or statement to carry out the provisions of FIRPTA.

SELLER DISCLOSURE OBLIGATIONS
UNDER CIVIL CODE SECTION 1102, ET SEQ.

Effective January 1, 1987, a transferor (seller) of real property including a residential stock cooperative containing 1 to 4 residential units (unless exempted under § 1102.1) must supply a transferee (buyer) with a completed Real Estate Transfer Disclosure Statement in the form prescribed in Civil Code §1102.6.

EXEMPTED TRANSFERS: Summary of exempted transfers (Civil Code Section 1102.1) where Real Estate Transfer Disclosure Statement is **not** required:

a. Transfers requiring "a public report pursuant to §11018.1 of the Business & Professions Code" and transfers pursuant to §11010.4 of Business & Professions Code where no public report is required;
b. "Transfers pursuant to court order" (such as probate sales, sales by a bankruptcy trustee, etc.);
c. Transfers by foreclosure (including a deed in lieu of foreclosure and a transfer by a beneficiary who has acquired the property by foreclosure or deed in lieu of foreclosure);
d. "Transfers by a fiduciary in the course of the administration of a decedent's estate, guardianship, conservatorship, or trust."
e. "Transfers from one co-owner to one or more other co-owners."
f. "Transfer made to a spouse" or to a direct blood relative;
g. "Transfers between spouses" in connection with a dissolution of marriage or similar proceeding;
h. Transfers by the State Controller pursuant to the Unclaimed Property Law;
i. Transfers as a result of failure to pay property taxes;
j. "Transfers or exchanges to or from any government entity."

TIMING OF DISCLOSURE AND RIGHT TO CANCEL (CIVIL CODE SECTION 1102.2):

a. In the case of a sale, the disclosures to the buyer shall be made "as soon as practicable before transfer of title."
b. "In the case of transfer by a Real Property Sales Contract, (Installment Land Sales Contract) . . . or, by a lease together with an option to purchase, or ground lease coupled with improvements, as soon as practical before . . . the making or acceptance of an offer."

"If any disclosure, or any material amendment of any disclosure, required to be made by this article, is delivered after the execution of an offer to purchase, the transferee shall have three days after delivery in person or five days after delivery by deposit in the mail, to terminate his or her offer by delivery of a written notice of termination to the transferor of the transferor's agent."

...ITED DISCLOSURES (CIVIL CODE SECTION 1102.4):

Sale section, for specifying how the purchase price is to be paid. "All cash to seller" is the most common preference, particularly in a low interest rate market, or if the seller needs all of the equity in cash in order to buy a new home. In a slow, high interest rate market, or if a seller is trading down and doesn't need all the equity at the time of sale, the listing might indicate "seller is willing to carry financing for a qualified buyer."

Sellers who have an existing assumable home loan should make a copy of the note available to the listing agent for prospective buyers to review. If the note has disappeared, ask your lender for a copy, along with an explanation of the terms under which the loan is assumable. Sometimes an agent can obtain this information for a seller. While you're at it, find out if your note contains a prepayment penalty, since

SUBST~~IT~~

a. Neither the transferor nor ~~any listing or selling~~ agent shall be liable for any error, inaccuracy, or omission of any information delivered pursuant to this article if the error, inaccuracy, or omission was not within the personal knowledge of the transferor or that listing or selling agent, was based on information timely provided by public agencies or by other persons providing information as specified in subdivision (c) that is required to be disclosed pursuant to this article, and ordinary care was exercised in obtaining and transmitting it.

b. The delivery of any information required to be disclosed by this article to a prospective transferee by public agency or other person providing information required to be disclosed pursuant to this article shall be deemed to comply with the requirements of this article and shall relieve the transferor or any listing or selling agent of any further duty under this article with respect to that item of information.

c. The delivery of a report or opinion prepared by a licensed engineer, land surveyor, geologist, structural pest control operator, contractor, or other expert, dealing with matters within the scope of the professional's license or expertise, shall be sufficient compliance for application of the exemption provided by subdivision (a) if information is provided to the prospective transferee pursuant to a request therefor, whether written or oral. In responding to such a request, an expert may indicate, in writing, an understanding that the information provided will be used in fulfilling the requirements of Section 1102.6 and, if so, shall indicate the required disclosures, or parts thereof, to which the information being furnished is applicable. Where such a statement is furnished, the expert shall not be responsible for any items of information, or parts thereof, other than those expressly set forth in the statement.

OTHER DISCLOSURE REQUIREMENTS

I "…Where the seller knows of facts materially affecting the value or desirability of the property which are known or accessible only to him and also knows that such facts are not known to, or within the reach of the diligent attention and observation of the buyer, the seller is under a duty to disclose them to the buyer." Lingsch v. Savage, 213 Cal. App. 2d 729

II "Concealment may constitute actionable fraud where seller knows of facts which materially affect desirability of property and seller knows such facts are unknown to buyer." Koch v. Williams 193 Cal. App. 2d 537,541.

III "Deceit may arise from mere nondisclosure." Massei v. Lettunich, 248 Cal. App. 2d 68,72.

IV Failure of the seller to fulfill such duty of disclosure constitutes actual fraud. [Civil Code Section 1572(3)]

V **California Civil Code: §1709. Deceit—Damages** One who willfully deceives another with intent to induce another to alter his position to his injury or risk is liable for any damages which he thereby suffers. §1710. **Elements of Actionable Fraud** A deceit, within the meaning of the last section, is either: (1) The suggestion, as a fact, of that which is not true, by one who does not believe it to be true; (2) The assertion, as a fact, of that which is not true, by one who has no reasonable ground for believing it to be true; (3) The suppression of a fact, by one who is bound to disclose it, or who give information of other facts which are likely to mislead for want of communication of that fact; or (4) A promise, made without any intention of performing it.

VI "The maker of a fraudulent misrepresentation (seller) is subject to liability … to another (buyer) who acts in justifiable reliance upon it if the misrepresentation, although not made directly to the other (buyer), and that it will influence his conduct…" [parenthetical material added]. Restatement (2d) of Torts §533.

VII "The Seller may have an affirmative duty to disclose certain significant facts regarding the condition of his property. It is not enough for the seller to say nothing because he is not asked." California Real Estate Sales Transactions. §12.2, p. 463 (Cal. C.E.B. 1967).

VIII "A buyer who has been defrauded by the seller has the choice of either: (A) Using the seller's fraud as a basis for an action for affirmative relief in the form of an action for damages or for rescission of the contract."

IX Exculpatory Clauses: "It is better for the seller to disclose the specific condition than to attempt to exculpate himself against its nondisclosure. In general, the exculpatory (e.g., "as is") clause provides little, if any, protection." California Real Estate Sales Transactions p. 483 (Cal. C.E.B. 1967).

[The Above is a general statement of the seller disclosure obligations. Other disclosures may be required].

if it does, this could drain thousands of dollars from your proceeds at closing. Be sure to verify in advance whether your net from the sale will be affected by a prepayment penalty.

A seller will usually specify in the listing agreement the items of personal property included in the purchase price. Appliances that are not built in (washer, dryer, refrigerator, portable dishwasher, portable microwave, freestanding stove) are all negotiable. Sellers who are undecided at the time of listing about which appliances will stay with the house can either leave this section blank or state that the appliances are negotiable. Built-in appliances, window coverings, tacked down carpets, and fixtures permanently attached to the property are assumed to be included. So if you want to take your bedroom drapes because they match the bedspread, or a dining room chandelier that has sentimental value, you should specifically exclude these items from the sale.

The Multiple Listing Authorization clause authorizes the broker to submit the listing information on the property to the Board of Realtors' Multiple Listing Service (MLS). To obtain access to the MLS an agent must be a member of the local Board of Realtors, so list with a Realtor to guarantee an effective, professional marketing effort. A home located in an area within the marketing sphere of two boards should be included on both Multiple Listing Services on the basis of reciprocal arrangements that neighboring boards have with one another.

Many sellers shy away from multiple listing of their home because they think it's synonymous with permitting any and all to have access to the property. Actually, multiple listing gives the seller maximum exposure, and the listing agent can set up any showing arrangement that's agreeable to the sellers. It's advisable to make a home as accessible for showing as possible. However, if you're selling a multi-million-dollar property and you want prospective buyers to be financially prequalified before the property is shown, include this as a provision of the listing agreement.

Some agents will try to convince sellers to sell their homes in-house, without multiple listing exposure. An in-house sale is one in which the listing (seller's) and selling (buyer's) agents both work for the same real estate firm. The only one to come out ahead with this arrangement is the real estate broker, who keeps marketing expenses down by effecting a quick sale and by not having to split the commission with an outside broker. The way to sell for top dollar is to expose a property as extensively as possible to all prospective buyers. Don't sell yourself short by accepting an in-house offer before your home has been adequately marketed. Exposure in a seller's market can result in multiple offers, sometimes for over the list price.

The Compensation to Broker portion of the listing agreement will be filled in according to the commission you and your broker agree upon.

Home protection plans are available, which may provide additional benefits to the seller and buyer after the close of escrow. A home protection plan is an insurance policy covering the major systems of the house: plumbing, electrical, furnace, hot water heater, and some appliances. The policy usually goes into effect at close of escrow and runs for one year. When a malfunction occurs in one of the insured systems, the buyer calls the protection plan company and pays a service charge; the protection plan company pays the cost of the repair work or replacement.

Sellers can offer to pay for a home protection plan when they list their home, or this may become a negotiable item in the purchase contract. If a policy is purchased before or at the close of escrow, the warranty company usually does not require that an independent in-spection be made of the property and payment is usually made at the close of escrow. Policies are available for the marketing and escrow periods at a per diem cost that is usually less than a dollar per day. Read the policies carefully; limitations on coverage do apply.

A seller must decide at the time of listing whether to have a keybox (also called lockbox) installed on the property. A keybox is a metal box containing the house key, which is hung on, or close to, the front door. The keybox is opened by special keys issued only to agents who are members of the Multiple Listing Service. These keys cannot be duplicated.

Having a keybox on your home makes the property easily acces-sible to Realtors and their buyers. It is not, however, mandatory. If you do not use the keybox, you should make a key available to agents through your listing agent. Be sure to get written authorization to have a keybox placed on the home if it is occupied by someone other than yourself (a tenant, for instance).

The "for sale" sign is one of the best forms of advertising. If you shudder at the thought of a sign in your front yard, consider that most buyers drive around the neighborhoods where they want to live, and many call a real estate office or agent asking about houses where they have seen signs. They're usually inquiring about the price and size of the home. Contrast this with buyers who call inquiring about ads: they have no idea what the house looks like or where it's located.

Many sellers initially object to posting a sign because they don't want their neighbors to know their home is for sale. This is usually an emotional reaction to the thought of moving away from old friends. But in fact, sellers should want their neighbors to know their home is for sale. Often neighbors have friends who have asked to be kept informed of any new listing that comes on the market.

When you authorize a sign, you are also granting permission for a "sold" sign to be put up once your home is sold. Ask your agent when this sign will be displayed: when an offer is accepted? When all con-tingencies are removed from the contract? Or just prior to the close of escrow?

A "pending sale" sign is preferred by some agents because it lets the public know the seller has accepted an offer but that there may still be contingencies to be removed from the contract. A "pending sale" sign might encourage interested prospects to continue calling, so your agent can keep a list of interested people should the trans-action fall apart. Don't forget to ask your agent to have a "do not disturb occupant" sign attached to the "for sale" sign.

A Structural Pest Control ("termite") Report is obtained during the course of most home sales in California. Custom varies from one area to the next as to whether the buyer or seller pays the cost of the termite inspection report, which is approximately $125. Since it's usually the seller who pays the cost of the corrective work (and this could amount to thousands of dollars), it makes sense for the seller to order a termite report at the time the home is listed for sale. This way the seller will know the extent of the termite liability before weighing an offer to purchase the home. Sellers who elect to provide a presale termite report will want to limit that report to the main building, excluding old tool sheds or a detached garage.

Seller disclosure is a critical part of selling a home today. Effective January 1, 1987, a seller of residential property in California must provide a buyer with a completed Real Estate Transfer Disclosure Statement. (For more information about the Real Estate Transfer Disclosure Statement, read the remainder of this chapter and see Chapter Nine.)

The tax withholding clause of the listing agreement secures the seller's agreement to comply with the provisions of the Foreign Investment in Real Property Tax Act (FIRPTA). Briefly, FIRPTA requires every buyer of real property in the United States to withhold from the seller's proceeds 10 percent of the gross sales price if the seller is of foreign nationality. There are several exemptions, one of which is property with a sale price of less than $300,000 being purchased as a primary residence.

An arbitration clause will appear in some listing agreements that offer binding arbitration as an option to Realtors and principals as a method of resolving disputes. The Additional Terms section of the listing agreement is provided for any other pertinent conditions that apply to the listing. A seller who has a number of additional conditions should enter "See Addendum to Listing Agreement Attached" in the space provided. Title the supplement "Addendum to the Listing Agreement" and have it signed by both you and your agent.

Additional terms can include a long close of escrow or a provision for the sellers to rent back their home after the close of escrow. The seller might require a close of escrow after a specific date, or the sale could be contingent upon the simultaneous close of escrow with the buyer's new home. Specific items of personal property could be included or excluded from the sale, or the seller might retain the right to assign the listing to a relocation company.

Sellers marketing tenant-occupied properties need to make it clear to prospective buyers that the property is currently occupied by renters who have certain legal rights. These rights depend upon rental arrangements and local rent control ordinances.

Occasionally, a friend or acquaintance of a prospective seller will express an interest in buying the home. It is possible to exclude such a person from the listing agreement. If an "exclusion" from a listing agreement contracts with the seller to purchase the home, a commission is not owed to the listing agent.

An exclusion is worth considering as long as you keep several facts in mind. Most people who claim they want to buy your home, if you ever sell, never do. In addition, attempting to market a home with an exclusion in the listing agreement is difficult, as an exclusion puts every other buyer at a disadvantage. Qualified buyers are sometimes reluctant to spend the time and energy required to make an offer on a property that they know someone else has the opportunity to purchase for less. Many busy agents refuse to work on properties with exclusions.

The best way to deal with someone who wants to be excluded from your listing agreement is to put a finite time on the length of the exclusion, say one or two weeks at most. This will force the prospective buyer to make a decision, and a serious buyer will. It's advisable, in this situation, to hold off submitting the listing to the Multiple Listing Service until the person excluded has either purchased your home or is no longer excluded from the listing agreement. This way you don't muddy your marketing efforts by having to disclose an exclusion to prospective buyers. Keep in mind that your home is most salable when it first hits the market, so don't let anyone sabotage your initial market impact only to let you down later.

THE REAL ESTATE TRANSFER DISCLOSURE STATEMENT

California Civil Code Section 1102 requires sellers of residential property (one to four units) to provide a buyer with a Real Estate Transfer Disclosure Statement. A seller must comply with this requirement, whether or not there is a real estate agent involved in the transaction. Some residential property transfers are exempted from the requirement, such as probate, trustee, guardianship, foreclosure, and bankruptcy sales. A complete list of exempt transfers, along with explanatory material including an explicit citation of disclosure requirements, can be found on the reverse side of the first page of the disclosure form.

Much has been said about the care a buyer should take in making a home purchase. Equal care should be taken in selling a home. Ask your agent to supply you with a form before your listing appointment. Fill out as much of the form as you can on your own; check any items you question and complete them later when you better understand what is being asked.

A seller has a duty to disclose "facts materially affecting the value or desirability of the property which are known or accessible only to

him" and which "facts are not known to, or within the reach of the diligent attention and observation of the buyer. . . ." Failure to disclose can constitute fraud. Furthermore, it's not sufficient to fail to disclose something simply because you are not specifically asked to. For instance, if you are selling a condominium and your condominium association is currently involved in litigation against the builder, you must disclose this to a buyer, whether or not the buyer asks you about it. Precisely what is considered a material fact will differ from one situation to the next.

The disclosure form isn't complicated, but in most cases it should be supplemented with additional information from the seller. Section I (see sample form) asks the seller to itemize "substituted disclosures," and several spaces are allotted for this purpose. A substitute disclosure

☐ Central Hea~~ting~~   ~~ning~~   ☐ Evaporator Cooler(s)
☐ Wall/Window Air Conditioning   ~~☐~~ Sprinklers   ☐ Public Sewer System
☐ Septic Tank   ☐ Sump Pump   ☐ Water Softener
☐ Patio/Decking   ☐ Built-in Barbeque   ☐ Gazebo
☐ Sauna   ☐ Pool   ☐ Spa ☐ Hot Tub
☐ Security Gate(s)   ☐ Garage Door Opener(s)   ☐ Number of Remote Controls _____
Garage: ☐ Attached   ☐ Not Attached   ☐ Carport
Pool/Spa Heater: ☐ Gas   ☐ Solar   ☐ Electric
Water Heater: ☐ Gas   ☐ Solar   ☐ Electric
Water Supply: ☐ City   ☐ Well   ☐ Private Utility   ☐ Other _____
Gas Supply: ☐ Utility   ☐ Bottled
Exhaust Fan(s) in _____ 220 Volt Wiring in_____
Fireplace(s) in _____ ☐ Gas Starter
☐ Roof(s): Type: _____ Age: _____ (approx.)
☐ Other:_____
Are there, to the best of your (Seller's) knowledge, any of the above that are not in operating condition? ☐ Yes ☐ No If yes, then describe.
(Attach additional sheets if necessary.): _____
_____
_____

B. Are you (Seller) aware of any significant defects/malfunctions in any of the following? ☐ Yes ☐ No If yes, check
appropriate space(s) below.
☐ Interior Walls ☐ Ceilings ☐ Floors ☐ Exterior Walls ☐ Insulation ☐ Roof(s) ☐ Windows ☐ Doors ☐ Foundation ☐ Slab(s)
☐ Driveways ☐ Sidewalks ☐ Walls/Fences ☐ Electrical Systems ☐ Plumbing/Sewers/Septics ☐ Other Structural Components
(Describe: _____
_____)

If any of the above is checked, explain. (Attach additional sheets if necessary.): _____
_____
_____

Buyer and Seller acknowledge receipt of a copy of this page, which constitutes Page 1 of 2 Pages.
Buyer's Initials (_____) (_____)   Seller's Initials (_____) (_____)

┌─ OFFICE USE ONLY ─┐
Reviewed by Broker or Designee _____
Date _____

EQUAL HOUSING
OPPORTUNITY
SF-Aug-87

REAL ESTATE TRANSFER DISCLOSURE STATEMENT (TDS-14 PAGE 1 OF 2)

is any documentation you have, or will obtain, that is intended to satisfy the disclosure obligations, such as termite, roof, drainage, soils, septic tank, well, structural, and general house inspection reports. Current, as well as past, reports should be listed, and relevant copies of each report or estimate for repair work should be attached to the disclosure statement.

Section II of the disclosure form has three parts. Part A asks if the seller occupies the property and what appliances and specific items are part of the property. It also asks if any of the items included with the property are not in operating condition. Part B asks if the seller is aware of any significant defects, and Part C is a list of fifteen questions about the property. Explain each defect completely, attaching additional sheets of paper to the form if necessary. Don't forget to include any fix-up-for-sale work that conceals defects requiring disclosure (new carpet over stains on a wood floor; wallpaper hiding cracks or voids in walls).

DISCLOSURE

Sellers of real property should be aware of their disclosure obligations under the California Court Cases, Statutes and Real Estate Law commentaries excerpted or paraphrased below:

**SELLER DISCLOSURE OBLIGATIONS
UNDER CIVIL CODE SECTION 1102, ET SEQ.**

Effective January 1, 1987, a transferor (seller) of real property including a residential stock cooperative containing 1 to 4 residential units (unless exempted under §1102.1) must supply a transferee (buyer) with a completed Real Estate Transfer Disclosure Statement in the form prescribed in Civil Code §1102.6.

EXEMPTED TRANSFERS: Summary of exempted transfers (Civil Code Section 1102.1) where Real Estate Transfer Disclosure Statement is **not** required:

a. Transfers requiring "a public report pursuant to §11018.1 of the Business & Professions Code" and transfers pursuant to §11010.4 of Business & Professions Code where no public report is required;
b. "Transfers pursuant to court order" (such as probate sales, sales by a bankruptcy trustee, etc.);
c. Transfers by foreclosure (including a deed in lieu of foreclosure and a transfer by a beneficiary who has acquired the property by foreclosure or deed in lieu of foreclosure);
d. "Transfers by a fiduciary in the course of the administration of a decendent's estate, guardianship, conservatorship, or trust."
e. "Transfers from one co-owner to one or more other co-owners."
f. "Transfer made to a spouse" or to a direct blood relative;
g. "Transfers between spouses" in connection with a dissolution of marriage or similar proceeding;
h. Transfers by the State Controller pursuant to the Unclaimed Property Law;
i. Transfers as a result of failure to pay property taxes;
j. "Transfers or exchanges to or from any government entity."

TIMING OF DISCLOSURE AND RIGHT TO CANCEL (CIVIL CODE SECTION 1102.2):

a. In the case of a sale, the disclosures to the buyer shall be made "as soon as practicable before transfer of title."
b. "In the case of transfer by a Real Property Sales Contract, (Installment Land Sales Contract) ... or, by a lease together with an option to purchase, or ground lease coupled with improvements, as soon as practical before ... the making or acceptance of an offer."

"If any disclosure, or any material amendment of any disclosure, required to be made by this article, is delivered after the execution of an offer to purchase, the transferee shall have three days after delivery in person or five days after delivery by deposit in the mail, to terminate his or her offer by delivery of a written notice of termination to the transferor or the transferor's agent."

SUBSTITUTED DISCLOSURES: (CIVIL CODE SECTION 1102.4)

a. Neither the transferor nor any listing or selling agent shall be liable for any error, inaccuracy, or omission of any information delivered pursuant to this article if the error, inaccuracy, or omission was not within the personal knowledge of the transferor or that listing or selling agent, was based on information timely provided by public agencies or by other persons providing information as specified in subdivision (c) that is required to be disclosed pursuant to this article, and ordinary care was exercised in obtaining and transmitting it.
b. The delivery of any information required to be disclosed by this article to a prospective transferee by a public agency or other person providing information required to be disclosed pursuant to this article shall be deemed to comply with the requirements of this article and shall relieve the transferor or any listing or selling agent of any further duty under this article with respect to that item of information.

... of a report or opinion prepared by a licensed engineer ...   ... operator, contractor,

---

Be careful how you answer the questions in Part C (page 57). The questions ask for a "yes" or "no" response. If you don't know the answer, write "unknown." Don't guess. Also, don't make assumptions that you can't validate. Question number three, for instance, asks the seller if additions, modifications, and repairs were made without necessary permits. Do you know if the family room added by the previous owner was done with permits? If you have a copy of the permits and the final inspection was signed off by the city, answer yes. Otherwise, answer "unknown" or go to the city building department and ask to see a record of all the permits that were taken out on your property. Your real estate agent can help you with this.

Often sellers incorrectly assume that because they hired a contractor to remodel or repair, the work was done with permits.

c. The delivery ...., land surveyor, geologist, structural pest control op......... or other expert, dealing with makers within the scope of the professional's license or expertise, shall be sufficient compliance for application of the exemption provided by subdivision (a) if information is provided to the prospective transferee pursuant to a request therefor, whether written or oral. In responding to such a request, an expert may indicate, in writing, an understanding that the information provided will be used in fulfilling the requirements of Section 1102.6 and, if so, shall indicate the required disclosures, or parts thereof, to which the information being furnished is applicable. Where such a statement is furnished, the expert shall not be responsible for any items of information, or parts thereof, other than those expressly set forth in the statement.

OTHER DISCLOSURE REQUIREMENTS

I   "...Where the seller knows of facts materially affecting the value or desirability of the property which are known or accessible only to him and also knows that such facts are not known to, or within the reach of the diligent attention and observation of the buyer, the seller is under a duty to disclose them to the buyer." Lingsch v. Savage, 213 Cal. App. 2d 729.

II   "Concealment may constitute actionable fraud where seller knows of facts which materially affect desirability of property and seller knows such facts are unknown to buyer." Koch v. Williams, 193 Cal. App. 2d 537, 541.

III   "Deceit may arise from mere nondisclosure." Massei v. Lettunich, 248 Cal. App. 2d 68, 72.

IV   Failure of the seller to fulfill such duty of disclosure constitutes actual fraud. [Civil Code Section 1572(3)]

V   **California Civil Code: §1709. Deceit — Damages** One who willfully deceives another with intent to induce him to alter his position to his injury or risk is liable for any damages which he thereby suffers. **§1710. Elements of Actionable Fraud** A deceit, within the meaning of the last section, is either: (1) The suggestion, as a fact, of that which is not true, by one who does not believe it to be true; (2) The assertion, as a fact, of that which is not true, by one who has no reasonable ground for believing it to be true; (3) The suppression of a fact, by one who is bound to disclose it, or who gives information of other facts which are likely to mislead for want of communication of that fact; or (4) A promise, made without any intention of performing it.

VI   "The maker of a fraudulent misrepresentation (seller) is subject to liability...to another (buyer) who acts in justifiable reliance upon it if the misrepresentation, although not made directly to the other (buyer), and that it will influence his conduct..." [parenthetical material added]. Restatement (2d) of Torts §533.

VII   "The Seller may have an affirmative duty to disclose certain significant facts regarding the condition of his property. It is not enough for the seller to say nothing because he is not asked." California Real Estate Sales Transactions, §12.2, p.463 (Cal. C.E.B. 1967).

VIII   "A buyer who has been defrauded by the seller has the choice of either: (A) Using the seller's fraud as a defense when and if the buyer refuses to follow through with his obligation under the contract; or (B) Using the seller's fraud as a basis for an action for affirmative relief in the form of an action for damages or for recission of the contract."

IX   Exculpatory Clauses: "It is better for the seller to disclose the specific condition than to attempt to exculpate himself against its nondisclosure. In general, the exculpatory (e.g., "as is") clause provides little, if any, protection." California Real Estate Sales Transactions p.483 (Cal. C.E.B. 1967).

[The Above is a general statement of the seller disclosure obligations. Other disclosure may be required].

Sometimes contractors will do a job without obtaining the required permits in order to save time and costs, and to avoid problems with the bureaucracy. Be sure your contractor takes out the necessary permits, has the city do a final inspection, and gives you the originals. Attach copies of any permits you have to the disclosure form.

A word of caution about "in-law" or "granny" units, commonly a second living unit in a single family home. These units are frequently rented out, often in violation of zoning laws. You must disclose the legal status of an in-law unit that's in your home. If you fail to disclosure a zoning violation and the buyer purchases the property foreseeing a steady stream of rental income only to have a neighbor report the infraction to the city after the close of escrow, chances are the buyer will have good cause for taking legal action against you. Don't take chances; complete and accurate disclosure will minimize your future liability.

In addition to completing this two-page form, it's a good idea to attach a sheet to the form explaining repairs or replacements you have made to the property. You can entitle this "Addendum to the Real Estate Transfer Disclosure Statement" and list it under the "Substituted Disclosures" clause of Section I. Briefly list what work was done, why, when, and by whom. Copies of paid receipts and workman's guarantees or warranties can be attached to the disclosure form with your list.

By now you're probably wondering just how much you have to disclose. Should you mention, for instance, that the water pressure drops when two showers are running at the same time? Ask yourself if this is something you'd want to know before you purchased a home.

Sometimes the answers to these questions are not clear. But it's safe to say that if you're asking yourself whether something needs to be disclosed, disclose it. For example, recent legislation requires the disclosure of a death on the property if it occurred within the last three years. Also keep in mind that what you fail to disclose, your neighbor may disclose for you after the close of escrow. Friendly neighbor disclosures are more common than you'd think, and can result in costly settlements for the seller who was less than forthright.

> Leslie Briggs stated in the Real Estate Transfer Disclosure Statement there were no known problems with the roof of her home. During the general building inspection, the buyers' agent asked Leslie the age of the roof and was told that it was less than eight years old. Based on this information and a phone call to a roofer who said the average life of a composition shingle roof is in excess of fifteen years, the buyers removed their inspection contingency without having a separate roof inspection. After the close of escrow, the buyers became chummy with a neighbor who told them Leslie was planning to replace the roof within a year if she stayed in the house. The buyers called in a roofer, who said the roof needed to be replaced before the next winter. The buyers sent a copy of the bid to reroof the house to Leslie along with a letter indicating they expected her to share in the expense. Leslie's attorney advised her to settle with the buyers to avoid a lawsuit.

Disclosure is not something for a seller to fear; failure to disclose has far more serious consequences. And the seller is not the only party who has obligations under the disclosure law. Agent responsibilities are discussed below, and the buyer in a residential real estate transaction has a duty under this law "to exercise reasonable care to protect himself or herself."

The Real Estate Transfer Disclosure Statement requires that both the seller's and buyer's agents complete "reasonably competent and

Subject Property Address _____

C. Are you (Seller) aware of any of the following:

1. Features of the property shared in common with adjoining landowners, such as walls, fences, and driveways. whose use or responsibility for maintenance may have an effect on the subject property. .... ☐ Yes ☐ No
2. Any encroachments, easements or similar matters that may affect your interest in the subject property. .... ☐ Yes ☐ No
3. Room additions, structural modifications, or other alterations or repairs made without necessary permits. .... ☐ Yes ☐ No
4. Room additions, structural modifications, or other alterations or repairs not in compliance with building codes. ...... ☐ Yes ☐ No
5. Landfill (compacted or otherwise) on the property or any portion thereof. .... ☐ Yes ☐ No
6. Any settling from any cause, or slippage, sliding, or other soil problems. .... ☐ Yes ☐ No
7. Flooding, drainage or grading problems. .... ☐ Yes ☐ No
8. Major damage to the property or any of the structures from fire, earthquake, floods, or landslides. .... ☐ Yes ☐ No
9. Any zoning violations, non-conforming uses, violations of "setback" requirements. .... ☐ Yes ☐ No
10. Neighborhood noise problems or other nuisances. .... ☐ Yes ☐ No
11. CC&R's or other deed restrictions or obligations. .... ☐ Yes ☐ No
12. Homeowners' Association which has any authority over the subject property. .... ☐ Yes ☐ No
13. Any "common area" (facilities such as pools, tennis courts, walkways, or other areas co-owned in undivided interest with others). .... ☐ Yes ☐ No
14. Any notices of abatement or citations against the property. .... ☐ Yes ☐ No
15. Any lawsuits against the seller threatening to or affecting this real property. .... ☐ Yes ☐ No

If the answer to any of these is yes, explain. (Attach additional sheets if necessary.): _____

_____

_____

Seller certifies that the information herein is true and correct to the best of the Seller's knowledge as of the date signed by the Seller.

Seller _____ Date _____

Seller _____ Date _____

III

AGENT'S INSPECTION DISCLOSURE

(To be completed only if the seller is represented by an agent in this transaction.)

THE UNDERSIGNED, BASED ON THE ABOVE INQUIRY OF THE SELLER(S) AS TO THE CONDITION OF THE PROPERTY AND BASED ON A REASONABLY COMPETENT AND DILIGENT VISUAL INSPECTION OF THE ACCESSIBLE AREAS OF THE PROPERTY IN CONJUNCTION WITH THAT INQUIRY, STATES THE FOLLOWING:

_____

_____

Agent (Broker

Representing Seller) _____ By _____ Date_____

(Please Print)   (Associate Licensee or Broker-Signature)

IV

AGENT'S IN...

diligent visual" inspections of the "accessible areas of the property." Their findings, which should include disclosure of defects, facts materially affecting the property value, and "red flags," are recorded in Sections III and IV of the disclosure form (with additional sheets attached, when necessary). A red flag is a condition that may indicate an underlying problem, such as plaster cracks, sagging ceilings, cracks in retaining walls, warped doors, sloping floors, standing water, cracked driveways.

Your agent will inform you of the results of the visual inspection and should ask if you have knowledge about any red flag items. This may jog your memory and help you to disclose something you had previously overlooked. Your agent may judge a red flag that you mention to be the sign of a serious problem and recommend that you seek the advice of an appropriate professional before marketing your home.

INSPECTION DISCLOSURE

(To be completed only if the agent who has obtained the offer is other than the agent above.)
THE UNDERSIGNED, BASED ON A REASONABLY COMPETENT AND DILIGENT VISUAL INSPECTION OF THE ACCESSIBLE AREAS OF THE PROPERTY, STATES THE FOLLOWING:

_____
_____
_____

Agent (Broker
obtaining the Offer) _____ By _____ Date_____
               (Please Print)   (Associate Licensee or Broker-Signature)

V

BUYER(S) AND SELLER(S) MAY WISH TO OBTAIN PROFESSIONAL ADVICE AND/OR INSPECTIONS OF THE PROPERTY AND TO PROVIDE FOR APPROPRIATE PROVISIONS IN A CONTRACT BETWEEN BUYER AND SELLER(S) WITH RESPECT TO ANY ADVICE/INSPECTIONS/DEFECTS.

I/WE ACKNOWLEDGE RECEIPT OF A COPY OF THIS STATEMENT.

Seller _____ Date_____   Buyer _____ Date_____

Seller _____ Date_____   Buyer _____ Date_____

Agent (Broker
Representing Seller) _____ By _____ Date_____
             (Please Print)   (Associate Licensee or Broker-Signature)

Agent (Broker
obtaining the Offer) _____ By _____ Date_____
             (Please Print)   (Associate Licensee or Broker-Signature)

A REAL ESTATE BROKER IS QUALIFIED TO ADVISE ON REAL ESTATE. IF YOU DESIRE LEGAL ADVICE, CONSULT YOUR ATTORNEY.

This form is available for use by the entire real estate industry.
The use of this form is not intended to identify the user as a
REALTOR®. REALTOR® is a registered collective membership
mark which may be used only by real estate licensees who are
members of the NATIONAL ASSOCIATION OF REALTORS®
and who subscribe to its Code of Ethics.

To order, contact — California Association of Realtors®
525 S. Virgil Avenue, Los Angeles, California 90020
Copyright© 1986, California Association of Realtors®

┌─────── OFFICE USE ONLY ───────┐
│ Reviewed by Broker or Designee _____ │
│ Date _____ │
└───────────────────────────────┘

EQUAL HOUSING
OPPORTUNITY

SF-Aug-87

REAL ESTATE TRANSFER DISCLOSURE STATEMENT (TDS-14 PAGE 2 OF 2)

Section V of the disclosure form admonishes the buyer and seller to seek professional advice or inspections and provides spaces for principals and agents to sign. Before you sign the bottom of this form, be sure that both agents have completed Sections III and IV. If an agent found nothing worth adding to what's already contained in the disclosure statement, this should be indicated in the space above the agent's signature with the statement that "No additional conditions were noted." Be certain that this space is filled in so you have proof that the agent complied with the requirements of the law.

It is important to complete the Real Estate Transfer Disclosure Statement as soon as possible after the property is listed. The Civil Code dictates that disclosures must be made to the buyer "as soon as practicable before transfer of title," and also contains a right of rescission period to protect the buyer. If the completed disclosure form or any amendment to this form is given to the buyer after the purchase contract is signed, the buyer has three days after personal delivery of the disclosure, or five days after the form is mailed, to terminate the contract by giving written notification of termination to the seller or his or her agent.

Remember that an offer which is made without the benefit of full disclosure may result in a terminated contract, so protect yourself by having your agent make copies of the disclosure form available to all prospective buyers *before* offers are written.

SHOW AND SELL

The primary objective, once your home is listed for sale, is to sell for the highest possible price in the least amount of time. For some sellers, the notion of a relatively quick sale is unsettling. Keep in mind that there is usually an inverse relationship between the length of time a home is on the market and the percentage of list price that is realized when it sells. Generally, the longer the marketing period, the lower the ultimate sales price. The list price will affect the number of days your house remains on the market, not the ultimate selling price. Well-priced homes sell faster and for a higher amount (relative to the list price) than comparable properties that are priced too high. To protect yourself from selling too low in a strong seller's market, insist that your home be exposed before entertaining an offer.

MARKETING YOUR HOME TO REAL ESTATE AGENTS
One of the ways to ensure a profitable and timely sale is to market your home effectively to the local real estate community. To maximize your success with real estate agents, have accurate information about your home readily available, keep your home in top condition, and make it easy to show.

After filling out and signing the various forms associated with listing, you and your agent should sit down and verify the descriptive information to be used in marketing the home. Your agent should prepare a brochure or property information sheet describing the features and amenities of your home. This will help the real estate agents who show your home, since not every agent will know it as intimately as your listing agent does. Sometimes a house has features that are not readily observable, such as an automatic sprinkler system or solar-assisted heating. The brochure or flyer should be something suitable for a buyer to take home as a reminder of what the home has to offer.

The accuracy of the information included in any marketing material, including newspaper advertisements, is *very* important. Pay particular attention to statements made about square footage and lot size, including acreage. The exact square footage in an older home may be difficult to verify, and you should never rely on the previous owner's estimate. It's far better to refer to square footage and acreage in approximate terms. In some cases, using a room count (or the number of bedrooms and baths) is preferable to referring to square footage at all.

Likewise, use caution when referring to the age of the home, the character of the neighborhood (remember, discrimination in housing is illegal), and subdivision feasibility. An illegal in-law unit should not be portrayed in such a way that implies guaranteed rental income. If you converted part of a basement into a "bedroom" without a permit, don't advertise this as an additional bedroom.

Your real estate agent will arrange for the other agents in the office to preview your home soon after it's listed. This is usually your first exposure to the real estate community. Have your home in glowing condition and be a gracious host if you're at home when the agents come through. Brace yourself for this event: many homeowners experience their first pangs of "seller's remorse" when they open their front door to a group of real estate professionals. It's perfectly normal to feel ambivalent about selling.

The next major event is usually an open house for the local real estate community. During the week preceding the open house, your home will be on a list with other new homes for sale in the area. Agents from different real estate offices will caravan from one listing to another in order to preview the new inventory for prospective buyers. It is recommended that you leave the house during the brokers' open house, which will last for several hours. If you have a dog, particularly one that barks at visitors, take the dog with you.

The Perfect Showing

Making a home accessible for agents to show is an essential step toward selling it. For many sellers this is the hardest part of the marketing process, so don't be surprised if you feel resentful of the showing activity. Even though buying and selling homes is a business, it can also be a very emotional experience.

It's important that you and your agent establish an easy procedure for showing your home. The simplest plan, from the selling agent's perspective, is to have a lockbox on or near the front door. Lockbox use varies from area to area, so take guidance from your agent on this matter. If most homes for sale have lockboxes, so should yours.

The least desirable showing arrangement is one that requires the listing agent to accompany the prospective buyer and selling agent on the showing. This should be avoided, if possible, for two reasons. Buyers usually feel less inhibited if they can preview a new listing with their own agent. There's a lot of psychology involved in buying a new home, and it's important for a buyer to feel at ease, particularly when viewing a home for the first time.

The other point to consider is that coordinating schedules for a showing which requires two agents and a buyer might be difficult, particularly if you've listed with a successful agent who has a busy calendar. The harder it is to show a house, the less it will be shown.

It's critical to your marketing success to keep the house very clean. Light is very important. Open drapes, even if you normally prefer a more private atmosphere. Leave lights on in dark rooms and hallways and keep the house temperature at a comfortable level, especially if you're selling a vacant house in the middle of winter. Show off areas that might be missed by buyers or agents, such as large walk-in closets (leave a door ajar), attic storage, or a basement access.

Fresh flowers brighten the decor. A pleasant aroma is inviting, but don't go overboard. Turn television sets off and the radio down. If you are a smoker, empty ashtrays and air out the house before showings. While the house is on the market, try to smoke as little as possible inside or confine the activity to one room. Avoid cooking foods that leave strong lingering odors.

When an agent calls to make an appointment to show your home, be courteous and congenial. Don't get a reputation for being an uncooperative seller by refusing showings. Word travels fast through local real estate communities. If you're rude to agents and refuse to accommodate requests for showings, agents will shy away from showing your home at all.

Plan to leave the house when it's being shown. If that's out of the question, make yourself scarce. *Never* follow the real estate agent and a buyer around. This almost always guarantees a fruitless showing.

Mr. and Mrs. Simmons, for example, had owned their home for over thirty years when they decided to list it for sale and move to a retirement community. Mrs. Simmons was sure real estate agents would be unable to properly show her home unless she personally assisted, so the house was shown only by appointment with Mrs. Simmons; not even Mr. Simmons could be entrusted with the task. Mrs. Simmons hovered over each and every buyer pointing out the obvious, and refused to let agents conduct showings in a professional manner. The house never did sell and was withdrawn from the market at the end of the listing period.

Buyers are usually reluctant to say anything negative about a house in front of the seller. They're also less likely to look in closets and linger long enough to appreciate the house than they would be if left alone. It's natural to be curious about buyers' reactions to your home; the appropriate way to find out is to ask your agent.

Try to arrange showing appointments so that you don't have too many different groups of people coming at once. The last thing you want is for your spacious home to appear crowded. It's particularly important to stagger appointments if you are selling a smaller home. Likewise, if you have a large family, plan to leave with the children during showings or send them outside to play. Try to present an environment that's free of distractions. While your home is on the market, make arrangements for your children to get together with friends at their homes, not yours.

Be sure to get a business card from each agent who shows your home. You should find an agent's card on a dining room or kitchen table if the house has been shown in your absence. It's fine to answer agents' and buyers' questions, but avoid discussing the price, the terms of the sale, or the particulars of any offers. These questions should be referred to your agent.

OPEN HOUSES

Sunday open houses are an integral part of marketing residential real estate. Many sellers question their effectiveness, and some refuse to have their house held open to the public at all. From a marketing standpoint, however, a Sunday open house is a good idea for a home that is newly listed. It allows real estate agents who have previewed the home on the broker's caravan to bring or send their prospective buyers through.

A common seller complaint is that neighbors make up the biggest percentage of people who frequent Sunday open homes. While it's true that some people, who themselves are not looking for a new home, do frequent open houses, this is not necessarily a bad thing. Some neighbors, certainly, are simply curious to see what homes in the neighborhood are selling for. But others are keeping their eyes open for friends who'd like to move into the area.

Another misconception is that open houses are dangerous. The theory is that they provide potential burglars with an opportunity to examine the house before breaking into it. While there may be a small increased risk of theft when your home is listed for sale, statistically the odds are against it. It is a good idea, though, to put valuables away, particularly expensive breakable items that might be knocked over by a small child. If you are overly concerned, ask your agent if there have been any theft problems in the area recently.

Disgruntled sellers sometimes complain that an agent spent time during their open house selling another house to buyers who came through. Bear in mind that an open house will draw an assorted group of buyers with different housing needs and requirements, and if the house is open to the public, it's open to anyone who wants to take a look.

How often to hold your home open to the public is something for you and your agent to decide. This is best done at the time of the listing so that there are no misunderstandings later. A house should not be held open too frequently, as this can give an impression of desperation and cause the house to become shopworn. Once every three weeks should be sufficient.

Try to remain flexible and avoid making dogmatic decisions about Sunday open houses. If houses are selling quickly and your house is priced right, you can probably sell it without showing it to the public. In slow markets, particularly if there are a lot of homes like yours on the market that aren't selling, you should have open houses periodically.

SELLING A TENANT-OCCUPIED PROPERTY

It's no wonder that sellers often have difficulties marketing tenant-occupied properties. Tenants who don't want to move might tell prospective buyers horror stories about the property (which may or may not be true) in the hopes that the house won't sell. Tenants can also make it difficult for a property to be shown by not permitting a lockbox, insisting on twenty-four-hour notice before the property can be shown (which is usually within their rights), or refusing to allow agents to show the property at convenient times. Another problem is the tenant who lets the property get so run-down that there's no possibility of a good showing, even if an agent is successful in making an appointment.

Owners who have maintained a good relationship with their tenants will probably not experience such problems. To ensure cooperation from tenants, it's a good idea to offer them some kind of compensation for having to endure the marketing process. One possibility would be a rent reduction for each month that the home is on the market, payable to the tenant *after* the property is sold. If renters object to being disturbed during certain hours, set up an acceptable showing schedule and have your agent include this in the Multiple Listing Service information.

Sellers who encounter truly obstinate tenants should have occasional Sunday open houses so that agents can bring their prospective buyers through the property. If tenants have made the house difficult to show and you've finally made arrangements that are agreeable to them for a public open house, have your agent circulate a flyer through-out the real estate community to let agents know they will be able to show the house without encountering a confrontation by the tenants.

THE NITTY GRITTY OF ADVERTISING

What's in an ad? Usually not a lot of information, just enough to make the phone ring at the real estate office. This is precisely the aim of a well-written real estate ad. It's intended to give readers enough in-formation to pique their curiosity, but not so much that they can decide not to bother following up on it.

The marketing proposal you requested from the several agents you interviewed before listing your home for sale should contain detailed information about the company's advertising program, describ-ing where the company places ads and how often you can expect to see your home advertised. A color photograph of the exterior of your home should be displayed in the window of your real estate broker's office. While it's not often that someone buys a house from a picture in the window, this has been known to happen. The general rule as far as marketing exposure is concerned is that no stone should be left unturned.

COPING WITH HAVING YOUR HOME ON THE MARKET

Saying your home is on the market is a bit of a misnomer, since when your home is for sale, your whole life's on display. Dealing with the uncertainty of when your home will sell, the seemingly endless dis-ruptions from showings or, even worse, no showings at all, is nerve-racking. There are steps you can take to make life easier.

Keeping the home in impeccable order is the biggest ordeal, par-ticularly for a working family with children. Divide the labor and write up a schedule of when tasks are to be completed. Hire cleaning help every week or so, and buy extra cleaning supplies. Close off rooms that aren't used much when the house isn't being shown. Pack away knickknacks: they gather dust, add clutter, and could be broken during the showing process.

Scheduling a vacation soon after you put your home on the market is not a bad idea, because you'll need the rest after fixing the house up for sale. If this isn't possible, try taking a long weekend at some point during the marketing phase so that you can relax and get away from it all.

Many sellers get understandably upset when the showing process doesn't work just right. The first rule to remember is *never* to set your-self up to wait for agents and their buyers. If your home has a lockbox, you can leave whenever you like and agents can let themselves in.

The problem usually arises when the seller of a house with no lock-box has something come up and needs to leave at precisely the time the agent and buyer are due to arrive, but they're late. To avoid this type of scenario, ask the agent to pick up your house key at the listing office.

Occasionally, prospective buyers will be so excited about your home that they will ignore the "do not disturb occupant" sign and knock on your front door requesting to see the house. Keep a stack of your agent's business cards on hand for such occasions. You should never, no matter how desperate you are to sell your house, let anyone in unaccompanied by a real estate agent. Be polite, hand the buyers one of your agent's cards, and ask them to call your real estate office to make an appointment.

Monitoring the Marketing Activity

Sellers can assist with the sale of their homes; in return, they should expect to be kept up to date by their agents on the progress of the marketing efforts. Ask your agent to give you information after a real estate office tours your home. Do the agents have any recommendations regarding the condition of the property? What do they think of the list price? Some listing agents make it a practice to collect price estimates from each agent who previews a new listing. If this is common practice in your area, ask to see the office sale price average and remember: the rule of thumb is to be listed within 5 percent of the expected selling price.

Many people balk at the idea of a price reduction early in the marketing program. If a price modification is needed, make it as soon as possible, while your home is still fresh in the minds of the agents. A price reduction three months later, when the real estate community has forgotten your property, won't have quite the effect, so make a correction early to ensure that your initial market impact is not lost.

Ask your agent to request selling price estimates (also referred to as REVs, or Realtors' Estimates of Value) from the agents who attend the broker's open house. Your agent should provide you with the range of selling price estimates along with the average of all of the REVs collected.

In addition to following up on the individual showings and reporting comments from prospective buyers and their agents, your agent should keep you apprised of homes that have recently sold in your area (the most recent comparable sales), new listings in your neighborhood (your competition), as well as relevant changes in current market conditions (interest rate fluctuations or changes in supply and demand). Generally, the more buyers and the lower the availability of housing, the quicker the sale and the higher the sales price.

WHAT TO DO IF YOUR HOME ISN'T SELLING

If your home is sitting stale on the market, you'll need to adjust the list price. Coordinate a price modification with a second brokers' open house and be sure your agent advertises the event to the real estate community. It's not easy to entice agents back to look at a house for a second time, but an agent who advertises a deli lunch, along with a new "priced to sell" list price, is likely to have a terrific turnout.

Make your home easier to show. If showings have been difficult to arrange, change procedures. If agents have plenty of houses to show and sales activity is slow, it stands to reason that the homes that will be shown the most are the ones that have easiest access.

Consider making courtesy keys available at various reliable real estate offices if your home is not on lockbox and it's not located close to your listing office. A courtesy key is a key that your listing agent makes available to cooperating brokers in order to facilitate showings of your home.

Ask your agent if there are any improvements you can make to the physical condition of your property. If agents have complained repeatedly that the colors in your living room and dining room are too overwhelming, consider repainting in a neutral color. Any major changes of this sort should be completed prior to your second brokers' caravan. Consider having a Sunday open house if you haven't had one. Ask your agent to circulate a flyer announcing the event.

Occasionally, a house that should be selling doesn't because the agent is not doing an effective job of marketing. Any change in your marketing program should be announced to the entire real estate community, either by way of the Multiple Listing Service or with a separate flyer to local real estate agents. Relevant information includes a reduced list price, new showing arrangements, cosmetic modifications to the property, or an open house announcement.

Sellers who are not satisfied with the quality of service they're receiving at the end of the listing period—particularly if their feelings of dissatisfaction have been communicated directly to the agent—should find a reliable replacement agent at that time.

CHAPTER 6

FINDING YOUR DREAM HOME

Looking for a new home can be the most enjoyable part of your real estate experience. Take a pad and pen with you on house hunting trips so you can make notes, and refer back to your list of desirable features from time to time to help stay on track.

Whenever possible, leave small children with a sitter or friend. Buyers find it distracting to look at a house, especially for the first time, accompanied by youngsters. Minimize exhaustion and confusion by previewing no more than four or five houses at one time. If you're purchasing a home with someone else, set up an initial house tour with your agent at a time when both of you can attend. It won't take long for a good agent to understand your likes and dislikes. After this, one of you can do the house screening if it's inconvenient for both to go.

THE FOUR CANONS OF REAL ESTATE

There is almost consensus within the residential real estate industry that the most important factor affecting the value of a property is its location. Your aim should be to find a home that suits your needs and is located in the best neighborhood you can afford. Homes located in the most desirable neighborhoods hold their value better and appreciate more than homes located in marginal areas. If you can't afford to buy in the prime communities, find a home that's adjacent to one of these areas. The peripheral neighborhoods often experience good appreciation if the general economy of the area is on the upswing.

The other variable to keep in mind is where, within a given neighborhood, a home is situated. A home on a busy street corner may be difficult to sell when you decide to move again, as may a home that's subject to freeway noise, is in the path of noxious odors from a nearby chemical plant, or is located too close to commercial establishments. If you fall in love with a house that suffers from a location defect, be sure you get it for a good price relative to the value of other homes in the neighborhood. Also bear in mind that if you sell, you'll probably need to make a price accommodation for the next buyer and it may take a bit longer for you to sell.

The second general guideline to consider in making a home purchase is that the most expensive home on the block is not the best investment. Conversely, the least expensive home is usually a better investment, with certain qualifications. The cheapest home may also be one that requires a lot of work, and if the house is very small, with no potential for expansion, your opportunities to improve its value are limited. A safe bet is a moderately sized and priced home surrounded by more expensive homes. The pricier homes in the neighborhood tend to pull the surrounding property values up.

A corollary to the second guideline is: don't overimprove for the neighborhood. If you're considering a home that will need extensive remodeling in order to make it suitable for your family, determine improvement costs and investigate property values in the neighborhood carefully before you buy. Turning the beast on the block into the beauty may not make sense if there's no chance of recovering your investment on resale. The top price a buyer will pay for a home is usually determined by the prices similar homes in the area have recently sold for.

Finally, it usually makes sense to buy the most expensive house you can afford. It's prudent to stretch a little and buy a more expensive home if it will suit your long-term needs and eliminate the necessity of an interim move. The new tax laws certainly favor buying a home at the top of your affordability range and mortgaging it to the hilt in order to maximize your tax write-off. This sort of tax planning, however, does not make sense for everyone.

Buyers obtaining adjustable-rate financing are smart to set aside cash reserves to cover unanticipated increases in mortgage interest rates. This is particularly important for buyers who are living on a fixed income.

Be cautious in your expectations for the future. Buyers who make the decision to buy the most expensive home they can based on the promise of future salary increases or with the hope that home prices will appreciate may suffer serious disappointment if there is an economic downturn.

LENDER PREQUALIFICATION

Before you actually start looking for a new home, make certain you have determined your affordable price range correctly. Ask your agent to refer you to a good lender or mortgage broker for the purpose of getting "lender prequalified." It's important to take care of this detail at the beginning of your search. Have the lender explain the various financing options open to you and find out the benefits and drawbacks of fifteen-year versus thirty-year financing, become familiar with the difference between fixed and adjustable mortgages, and be sure you understand the new convertible home loans. All too often, buyers don't explore the options available to them until an offer they've made to buy has been accepted. Those who have researched the financing alternatives in advance will be that much ahead of the game.

In a seller's market, the buyers who have been prequalified are at an advantage. Ask your lender or mortgage broker to put the range of loan amounts you can qualify for in writing. In a multiple offer situation involving several full-price offers, a seller is going to be the most impressed with an offer from buyers who include written verification that they are prequalified for a loan.

EVALUATING NEIGHBORHOODS

You are buying more than a roof over your head when you purchase a new home—you are buying into a neighborhood the character of which will have a direct impact on your day-to-day life. Your goal is to select a neighborhood that offers qualities compatible with your family's lifestyle. Although selecting a community is somewhat subjective, there are certain quantifiable features to evaluate in making your decision.

Affordability will naturally narrow the choices. Once you've determined which areas you can afford, the two most important considerations are proximity to your place of work and the quality of local schools if you have children.

Commute time is a common concern, so if you'll be driving, take test drives to work during rush hour from the various neighborhoods you're considering. Ask friends at work who live in these areas how they cope with commuting. Car pooling and public transportation are options to be investigated.

Home buyers with school-age children must find out where the closest schools are. Will the children be able to walk to school? If not, is local transportation available, or will you have to drive them? Visit the local school, meet with a counselor or the principal, and visit a class. Ask to see state test scores, inquire about extracurricular activities and special programs, and be sure to verify school district street boundaries. When researching a senior high school, determine what percentage of the students go on to college and which colleges they attend.

Find out who your new neighbors would be by going to meet some of the locals in person. Don't be surprised if your agent is hesitant to make generalizations about the make-up of the neighborhood, however, as discussion of the racial, religious, or ethnic composition of an area is illegal.

Outdoors and sports-minded individuals will be interested in the proximity to parks, lakes, beaches, and recreational facilities. Cultural buffs will need to investigate the availability and location of libraries, art museums, and theaters. The weather may be important to you, or if you're short of time, one-stop shopping may be high on your priority list. Is there one place where you can go on a Saturday morning to take care of the weekly chores? Families with an older relative living in may need to be near a major health care facility.

Most home buyers are concerned about how safe and stable a neighborhood is. Do some investigation on your own. After you've seen a home you like, drive by it during several different times of the day and night to get a sense of the neighborhood. Any agent with an ounce of sense will drive you to a house using the most scenic route. Find the least scenic and see if you still like the looks of the neighborhood. If the houses on the block of the house you admire are perfectly groomed but the yards look shabby several blocks away, do some further investigating.

Too many "for sale" signs in an area may indicate that a neighborhood is deteriorating. There is, however, an odd phenomenon that occurs periodically in the real estate business. Not a single house will be listed in an area for months; then all of a sudden, for no special reason, several homes on one block are put up for sale at the same time. If a lot of homes are for sale in a neighborhood you are considering, ask your agent to find out if this is simply a quirk or a trend to be concerned about.

Call the local police department and inquire about the incidence of crime. Some police departments provide statistics by street on crimes over the past year. Others have census tract information compiled by the category of the crime: burglary, assault, etc.

Additional considerations that may be relevant are: What percentage of the local residences are rented? Are the streets busy or quiet? Are there hazardous traffic patterns? Are there local leash laws for pets? Are religious centers located nearby? What is the availability of daycare centers? Are the local utilities public? Is there adequate street lighting? Is the neighborhood located in a local flood or hazard zone? Are there unreasonable homeowner's association restrictions?

THE ANATOMY OF A DREAM HOME

Houses have character, and it's usually this subjective quality that draws a buyer to one home over another. Feeling comfortable in a home is an important prerequisite to buying it. A home is, after all, your personal haven from the outside world. Savor the moment you walk into a new listing, after weeks or months of looking, and say to yourself: "This is it!" Indulge yourself in the joy of the moment; then step back and face reality. Pull out your notebook and scrutinize the list of features you're looking for and make sure that the home at least meets your "absolute" requirements. If it fits the bill, there are a few more exercises you should perform, before submitting an offer. Take a realistic look at the decor. Are you paying extra for someone else's good taste or decorating expertise? Will your furniture substitute satisfactorily for the seller's? What will it cost you to hire a decorator to recreate the ambiance you've fallen in love with?

After you've taken an objective look at the house, conduct a pre-purchase inspection with the help of your agent. A friend who is knowledgeable about housing would be a suitable assistant in this process. This is not a formal inspection, which requires hired professionals, but a step in determining whether you are willing to spend the time and money involved in making an offer.

The first item to consider is the general layout, also known as the floor plan. Ideally a home should have areas appropriate for gatherings as well as those conducive to private activities. Family and living rooms should be located at a distance from bedrooms, particularly if the bedrooms are to be used by infants or students who need quiet for studying. If members of the family are involved in hobbies or crafts, there should be spaces away from the main family living areas for these endeavors.

The "flow" of a floor plan is very important. A layout that gives access to the primary rooms from a central hall is the best arrangement. The living room, particularly, should not be a room that must be passed through in order to reach other rooms. A house that allows for easy circulation is important for buyers who have children.

Because the kitchen is the focal point of most households, be sure it's well laid out, with a sufficiently large eating area and, ideally, a separate access to the outside. The work space should be set up so that the appliances and counters are located near one another.

Room size and storage space requirements vary from one buyer to the next. Bear in mind that too little storage, with no possibility of improving the situation, always poses a problem. Be sure that rooms are large enough to accommodate your furniture by taking measurements of large pieces of furniture and checking for fit at the new house.

Also take a moment and consider the home from the standpoint of its resale qualities. Features that are most in demand are spacious rooms, kitchens with eating areas, formal dining rooms, direct access from the kitchen to the dining room and from the garage to the house (ideally to the kitchen), a driveway that provides easy access to the street, adequate parking area, level entry to a private yard, sunny exposure, at least one bathroom on each level, convenient washer and dryer locations, a fireplace in the living room, a formal entry hall (with a coat closet), sufficient electrical outlets, and central air conditioning in warm climates.

Pay attention to maintenance considerations. If the house has a pool, determine whether you have the time to clean it and, if not, whether you can afford to pay someone else to do the job. Trees over a pool will make the upkeep even more difficult.

Remember that large yards require a lot of work. Sometimes a small but secluded yard, away from neighbors, can convey the feeling of a large yard for much less work. Find out if the house is insulated and ask the owner for copies of recent utility bills to determine how much these tend to run during average and high expense months.

Have your agent obtain a copy of the seller's Real Estate Transfer Disclosure Statement as well as copies of any existing reports. After reviewing these documents, take one last tour around and through the premises, this time with an eye to determining the general condition of the property.

One of the primary causes of structural defects in houses is water. Watch for signs of excessive moisture. The first rule of home maintenance is to be certain that all water is directed away from the house. Porches and patios should drain away from the foundation and rainwater should be collected in gutters that empty into downspouts connected to drainpipes which take the water away from the building. If this is not possible, the water should at least not collect in puddles next to the house as this can cause the soil underneath a portion of foundation to become saturated and, ultimately, to drop or settle. Some settling is routine and can be expected, particularly in older homes. Every effort should be made, however, to improve the drainage in and around a house to avoid future problems.

Evidence of standing water should be investigated by a qualified professional. Water that collects in a basement area may indicate a need for a drainage system (which can be expensive). If you are buying during the dry season, look for stains on the basement floor or on foundation walls, as these are signs that water may have been present in the past. Other conditions that may be indicative of a drainage problem are large cracks in the soil or basement floor, cracks in the foundation, or erosion channels in the dirt underneath the house. A house with a sump pump, usually located in the basement, most certainly has excessive water under the house, at least periodically.

Look for signs of moisture entry inside the house. Water stains on window sills and around doors suggest that they may not be watertight, and stains on ceilings and walls, or peeling paint and wallpaper, may be a sign that the roof needs repair.

Examine the exterior condition of the roof. Moss growing on a wood shake or shingle roof is not a good sign. A house with three layers of roofing, and evidence of moss and deterioration below the surface layer, should be investigated by a qualified roofer. An old roof that is one layer thick can usually be repaired by simply roofing over the existing surface, whereas a leaky roof that is already several layers thick will be more complicated to repair. Check the gutter and downspout system for voids, rust, and deterioration. If trees overhang the roof, you will need to have gutters and downspouts routinely cleaned and serviced.

Check the fireplace and chimney from inside and out. Cracks inside can mean that the firebox needs work; a chimney that leans away from the house may also signal a problem.

Check the condition of fences and gates around the property. Is the landscaping well maintained, or will you need to consider redoing it in the near future?

Test the water pressure. Turn on the shower and sink faucets, and flush the toilet at the same time. Be aware that the electrical system may need upgrading if there are too few outlets and extension cords running everywhere.

Find out the age of appliances, furnace, and hot water heater. If all the major systems are old, find out if the seller is providing a home protection plan to the buyer.

Look for signs of settling problems from the interior of the house. Do the windowpanes on a set of french doors line up properly? Or does one door hang much lower than the other? If so, this might indicate a foundation problem. Do floors slope? Open and close doors and windows to see if they stick. Are doors and windows warped? Scrutinize doorframes from the opposite side of a room. Are the tops of the doors parallel with the floor? Are the sides of the doorjambs parallel with adjacent vertical walls?

Doors, floors, and windows that are out of plumb can indicate structural problems or poor workmanship; they can also simply signify routine settling. Hardwood floors that squeak and buckle are not nailed properly. Wallpaper patterns that don't line up at the seams are usually the result of shoddy craftsmanship, although a sagging floor (indicative of a possible structural problem) could also be the cause.

The purpose of your pre-purchase inspection is to find out if there are glaring and significant defects that you are certain you can't live with. Examine the property carefully, but don't take too long to make up your mind if buyers are waiting in line to make offers. Your cursory inspection should not be done in lieu of hiring qualified professional inspectors. If you decide to make an offer, make it contingent upon obtaining all inspections you feel are necessary to protect yourself.

Only a licensed contractor, engineer, or roofer can tell you whether a flaw is normal, considering environmental conditions and the age of the house, or whether it is something to be concerned about. Inspections that are done in addition to those that the seller has already ordered are customarily at the buyer's expense. The cost is generally in the range of $200, but if soils reports are involved, you may be looking at an out-of-pocket expense of over $1,000. Extra inspections are worth every penny if they make you feel secure about the integrity of a home, or if they prove that the home is not a good investment.

Buying a Newly Constructed Home

In considering whether to buy a newly constructed home, determine first the reputation of the builder. New roofs can leak, just like old ones. Does the builder have a reputation for responding to calls from buyers when unsuspected defects appear? Is the problem then remedied quickly and without undue hassle? Contractors' and manufacturers' warranties apply to newly constructed homes; contact a real estate attorney or the state contractor's licensing agency for the answers to questions about the builder's liability for defects.

Ask to see other homes the builder has constructed to check out the quality of the workmanship. Be sure to talk to the homeowners and investigate the builder's reputation with lenders and material suppliers. You will have difficulty getting a builder to remedy defects if the company files for bankruptcy or goes out of business after you purchase the home. Check at the county courthouse to see if any suits have been filed against the builder. The local Better Business Bureau and the Contractors' State License Board can tell you if they have received complaints about the builder.

There are definite advantages to buying a newly constructed home. New homes are energy efficient, and anticipation of lower utility costs may enable you to afford a more expensive home. And because new homes are built to modern code requirements, you won't face the prospect of remedying code violations as you often would with older homes. New homes are usually easier to maintain than older homes and are generally equipped with modern amenities. If you purchase in a planned community development, your new home may entitle you to use recreational facilities such as a swimming pool, golf course, or tennis courts.

One drawback of new homes is that they often lack distinctiveness. This can be due to the absence of mature landscaping, a common problem in new developments. It can also reflect the fact that new homes are frequently smaller than older homes, and their locations are sometimes not the best. Beware of the hidden costs of buying a new home; window coverings and landscaping, for instance, are often not included. If this is the case, don't forget to add these costs to the purchase price.

Don't fall in love with a designer decorated model and assume that this is what you'll get at the close of escrow. If you are buying in a tract development, ask to see a sample home that hasn't been decorated for sale and find out what's included in the purchase price. How many of the classy upgrades displayed in the model do you have to pay extra for? Is the carpet in the model of the same grade as that included in the purchase price? What about the light fixtures— are they included in the price or do you pay extra? Do you have any choice in the finishing details?

Some builders will allow a buyer to select certain finishing details, such as floor coverings, cabinets, paint and tile quality and color, finish hardware, and light fixtures. Be sure that all modifications or upgrades are put in writing and signed by both the buyer and builder. This agreement should specify how much additions will cost, when they'll be paid for, and what credits the buyer will receive for deletions. Keep in mind that if houses in a development are selling well, there may be no opportunity for a buyer to negotiate the purchase price, aside from settling on finishing details and upgrades.

One way to protect yourself if the builder is to complete some of the finishing details after the close of escrow is by paying half the cost ahead of time and the other half upon completion of the work. Another possibility is to agree that a portion of the builder's proceeds from the sale will be held in an escrow account to be released when the work is completed.

Complete a final inspection of a new home at least a week before the close of escrow. Take a note pad with you and make a list, commonly called a "punch" list, of items the builder is to complete prior to the close of escrow or within a reasonable amount of time thereafter. Make the punch list a part of your purchase contract and get the builder to sign it. Do not accept a cash settlement from the builder at the close of escrow in lieu of an agreement to complete the items on your list, and don't trust a builder who denies you reasonable access to the property to complete any inspections you deem necessary.

You may be restricted in your choice of lenders when purchasing a new home in a planned development. A builder will often buy commitments from a specific lender in advance, and then make using that lender for the new purchase mortgage a condition of the sale. Likewise, builders of large projects will usually have their own staff of sales agents and a specific sales contract designed for use by these agents. If this is the case, you will not be allowed representation by your own outside agent, so you may want to pay your agent a consulting fee or hire a real estate attorney to review the sales contract to be sure you're adequately protected.

Be aware that lenders usually will not provide a purchase mortgage to an individual who is buying a unit within a tract housing project until a certain percentage of the whole project is sold. If a development is not selling well, you may not be able to obtain the loan you need to purchase and move in. Keep this in mind if you are selling your current home in order to buy one in a new development; you may want to make the sale contingent upon obtaining a firm loan commitment.

BUYING AN OLDER HOME

One benefit of purchasing an existing home is that you are buying into an established neighborhood. The schools may be better than in newer areas, tree-lined streets are commonplace, and yards are usually landscaped. Older neighborhoods are often centrally located, offering good access to freeways, places of employment, theaters, entertainment, cultural activities, and shopping centers.

The major appeal of an older home is its architectural uniqueness. Established areas usually contain a mix of styles, so buyers who are influenced by "curb appeal" (what a house looks like from the street) are usually attracted to older homes. Often these homes are characterized by a high level of craftsmanship, spacious rooms, hardwood floors, high ceilings, built-in bookcases, leaded or stained glass windows, and distinctive moldings that cannot be found in newly constructed homes. Existing homes also usually come equipped with window coverings and light fixtures.

An older home *may* be less expensive than a new home, but this will depend on its general condition. Low energy efficiency is costly, as is the expense of insulating. Maintenance may be higher on an older home if major components such as the roof, kitchen appliances, furnace, and hot water heater have not been replaced recently, so be sure to have a home protection plan to cover the major systems in place at the close of escrow.

Older homes were not built to modern building code requirements, and one consequence of this is that they may not be able to withstand the shock of a major earthquake as well as new houses. If this concerns you, contact a contractor who specializes in equipping older homes to better withstand earthquakes.

BUYING A FIXER-UPPER

Plenty has been written about the great profits to be reaped from buying a dilapidated home, slapping on a fresh coat of paint, and reselling it mere months later for a handsome mark-up. Turning the ugliest house on the block into a jewel may sound like easy money; it's not.

First, you must be able to distinguish a house with profit potential from a lousy investment. Cosmetic repairs can be relatively inexpensive and usually pay back double their cost. But the expense of correcting major structural defects might not add a penny to the market value of a home and could conceivably run a project into the red.

Evaluating the floor plan is critical. A good basic layout with a hideous decor is a great combination in a fixer-upper home. A minimal investment may well turn such a house around. A house with a maze of rooms, on the other hand, has a defective floor plan that no amount of paint and paper will remedy.

Check the major components of the house very carefully. Hire a professional inspector and, if you are anticipating a major renovation which will entail moving walls, consult with an architect before you buy to be sure that it is feasible.

Location is vitally important to the success of a fix-up project. You should buy in the best neighborhood you can afford and make certain that you won't be overimproving for the area. Consult your real estate agent and check the comparable sales in the neighborhood carefully before committing to the project.

> Luke Friedman learned his first renovation lesson the hard way. He bought the smallest and least expensive house he could find in an affluent neighborhood, installed a new kitchen and bathroom, and gave the house a cosmetic face lift. When the refurbished house went back on the market, it was priced lower than any other house in the area. It was also still the smallest house on the block. The house sat on the market for nine months and finally sold only after numerous price reductions, leaving Luke with a sizable tax write-off and no profit. If Luke had done his homework first, he would have discovered that buyers for homes in this particular neighborhood were looking for large family homes, not compact homes on postage stamp lots.

Financing the renovation is a major consideration. Often the costs will have to be paid in cash. It will be easier to obtain a loan if you intend to occupy the home; however, it is unrealistic to expect you and your family to live in a home that will be a construction zone for a period of time.

Asking a seller to carry the financing is a possibility if the property is free of other liens and if the seller has been unable to sell for all cash. Sometimes a seller who won't carry a first loan will carry a small second, say for 10 percent of the purchase price. The buyer obtains the new first loan and pays the seller the major portion of the purchase price at the close of escrow (90 percent in this case). The balance is paid to the seller in a relatively short period of time when the buyer has finished the fix-up work and sells the home.

Financing the purchase of a fixer-upper with a new adjustable rate mortgage that is assumable by a subsequent buyer makes good sense. The interest rate will be lower than on a fixed rate loan and, if financing is difficult to obtain by the time the renovator is ready to sell, there will be a loan in place on the property that can be taken over by a qualified buyer.

An unsecured line of credit can be used to pay for the fix-up work if the buyer qualifies. This indebtedness does not have to be paid back when the house is sold since it isn't secured as a lien against the house, and the interest on the loan may be tax deductible as a cost of doing business.

Successful renovators have used the lease option as a way to finance a fix-up project. The buyer gives the seller a relatively small amount of cash to apply toward a predetermined purchase price and then leases the property from the seller for a specified period of time. During the lease period, the buyer fixes up the property; then, when the project is done, the buyer exercises the option, completes the purchase, and immediately sells the house to another buyer for a profit.

There is some risk to the buyer because title to the property remains in the seller's name during the lease period. The buyer is paying to fix up someone else's property, so it's imperative to check a preliminary title report very carefully before entering into this sort of agreement. Further protection is obtained by recording the lease so that it will have priority over future liens the seller may secure against the property. Also, the buyer cannot use a secured line of credit to finance the rehabilitation work since the property will still be in the seller's name during the fix-up period. Another problem with lease options is that few sellers are agreeable to selling for anything less than all cash in a strong seller's market.

Whether you lease option or purchase a fixer-upper outright, the cost of leasing or owning the property during the rehabilitation period must be considered in calculating the profit potential. This is particularly true if you will not be occupying the property. Experienced renovators will tell you that fix-up projects generally cost more and take longer than anticipated, so figure an extra amount into the budget to cover for cost overruns.

Novices should carefully consider whether they are temperamentally suited to be successful renovators. Fix-up projects must be carefully supervised to keep them on time and close to budget. The renovator must have a critical eye, be attentive to details, have an ability to organize, and be able to deal effectively with total chaos and endless frustration.

In planning your renovation, keep in mind that kitchens, bathrooms, and storage spaces are important to today's home buyers. The kitchen/family room combination is particularly desirable and can often be created in an older home by knocking out the walls that separate the kitchen from a breakfast room or maid's room. A spacious master bedroom suite with a private bath and large walk-in closet is also attractive to most buyers.

A home with a large termite problem might provide a good fix-up opportunity, but it's important to evaluate what sort of work is required ahead of time. If a bathroom floor, walls, and shower are rotted and the termite report calls for replacing them, a buyer might be wise to negotiate a credit from the seller for the dollar amount required to complete these repairs. Since termite estimates are usually on the high side compared to a contractor's cost, the credit might pay for a whole new bathroom. Make certain that the lender will allow escrow to close without a termite clearance if new financing is a part of the transaction.

Curb appeal is important, so plan on improving the landscaping and front entry. Stick to neutral color schemes and put a little extra into less expensive items, such as light fixtures, hardware (doorknobs, light switch plates, cabinet pulls and knobs), and bathroom plumbing fixtures. Quality sells a home, and extra attention to detail will build you a good reputation, which is important if you intend to rehabilitate more properties in the area.

BUYING A TOWN HOUSE OR CONDOMINIUM

An ideal compromise for the individual who desires the tax benefits of home ownership without the cost and trouble of home maintenance is a condominium or town house. When you buy into a town house or condominium complex, you purchase a specific unit which you own individually. In addition, you share in the ownership of common areas, such as hallways, elevators, exterior grounds, pools, tennis courts, or club house.

Condominium ownership is not for everyone, since you must be agreeable to living in close proximity to your neighbors and, in some cases, to sacrificing privacy. The tradeoff is low maintenance and a secure lifestyle.

Location is critical in determining the value of the investment and the potential for appreciation. Some well-located and well-managed condo projects demonstrate a good history of appreciation; many more, however, have not appreciated much, if at all, in recent years. The detached residence is currently more in demand than condominiums or town houses, but this will probably change in the years ahead as the population ages, creating a larger demand for low-maintenance living environments.

In evaluating a condo development, find out what percentage of the units are owner-occupied as opposed to tenant-occupied. The more owner occupants, the better. Owners usually demand a higher caliber of management and maintenance, since they have an investment in the condition of the project. Sometimes a high percentage of renters indicates that the original developer was unable to sell the project when it was new. Find out how many of the units are still owned by the original developer. Some lenders won't approve new mortgages for buyers purchasing into condo developments with a large percentage of renters.

A monthly maintenance fee is charged to the individual owners in a condo development. Find out how much this fee is and what expenses it covers. It usually includes garbage collection, maintenance of exterior grounds, homeowners' insurance, and sometimes exterior maintenance of individual units. Pay particular attention to the insurance coverage that's provided for the association, as this usually does not include coverage for your personal possessions or for damage to the interior of your unit. It probably won't include a personal liability rider, either.

Other important questions regarding the maintenance fee are: How often has it been raised in the past? Are there any anticipated increases in the near future? How much of a reserve does the homeowner's association maintain to cover the cost of repairs to common areas such as pools and tennis courts? Is the homeowner's association involved in any litigation against the builder for structural defects? If the association loses and cannot recover the cost to repair defects, what is the potential amount that individual owners will pay to remedy the problems? Find out how many homeowners are delinquent in making their monthly maintenance dues payments. A high percentage of delinquencies might indicate dissatisfaction with the management of the association. Be aware, by the way, that homeowner's dues projections listed at new construction sites are sometimes unrealistically low. If so, anticipate that they will go up in the future and budget for this increase. Also be aware that your association dues are not tax-deductible.

Read the CC&R's (Covenants, Conditions, and Restrictions) and bylaws of the homeowner's association carefully. One drawback of living in a planned community development is that you do not have unrestricted ownership privileges. The CC&R's may prohibit pets and may also include remodeling, rental, and resale restrictions.

Have a building inspector assess the general quality of construction and examine the common facilities for any major structural defects that could result in future assessments against the homeowner's association. A termite inspection of the individual unit is also recommended.

Investigate the parking and additional storage situations thoroughly. Will you have an assigned parking place or is parking on a "first come, first serve" basis?

California law prohibits homeowners' associations from charging exorbitant transfer fees. Prior to this ruling, fees as high as $2,000 were charged for transfers. The new law limits fees to the actual cost of changing the association's records plus the cost of sending the required notices to prospective buyers. Double-check to be sure you're not being unlawfully overcharged.

BUYING FORECLOSURES

You *may* get an incredibly good deal by buying a home that a lender has taken back from an owner who stopped making mortgage payments. Such a distressed sale property is acquired by the lender through foreclosure proceedings against the defaulting borrower and is referred to as an REO, which is the industry jargon for "real estate owned."

Lending institutions often offer attractive prices, terms, and financing to prospective buyers in an attempt to sell excess REO properties. Whether or not such a deal makes sense for you depends on several factors; be aware that evaluating an REO requires more care than is necessary in other potential purchase situations.

Make sure that the price is truly a bargain. Owners who can't support the mortgage payments usually won't let a property go into foreclosure unless the remaining balance owed to the lender is close to or more than the market value of the property. If the current value of the house had actually been in excess of the loan amount, the owners would probably have sold the property themselves, thereby recouping some or all of their equity investment and avoiding a damaged credit rating.

Check property values in the neighborhood carefully. Also, find out what similar homes in the area were selling for six months ago to be sure that you're not buying into a neighborhood where property values are declining.

REO's are often sold in their "as is" condition, and you probably will not have the benefit of reviewing a Real Estate Transfer Disclosure Statement. Make sure you see the property yourself before purchasing and hire professional inspectors because many distressed sale properties are also in poor physical condition.

Insist that the lender provide you with clear title to the property, and purchase title insurance to protect yourself. Owners who let mortgage payments slide might have had other debts they couldn't handle, so make certain that you will have no liability to the previous owner's creditors.

On the bright side, if you do find an REO that meets your specifications, the lender may be willing to provide you with attractive financing, sometimes at lower interest rates. You may even receive assistance with some of your closing costs.

Lenders are often not aggressive in marketing their REO properties. If this sort of property intrigues you, call lenders directly and talk to the person in charge of REO's. Another source is the federal government, which has over 60,000 repossessed houses for sale; the Federal Housing Administration (FHA) and Veterans Administration (VA) periodically announce the availability of these properties, usually in newspaper ads. For the best results, call your local Board of Realtors and ask for a recommendation of an agent who specializes in foreclosures.

Many repossessed properties are tenant-occupied, in which case it's wise to make your purchase conditioned on the lender delivering the property to you vacant. Otherwise you might be faced with having to evict a tenant who is unwilling to leave the premises.

Another word of caution: if you are purchasing a property from a seller who's in the midst of a bankruptcy proceeding, be sure to consult with an expert, such as a real estate professional with experience working on bankruptcies and foreclosures or a knowledgeable real estate attorney.

BUYING A PROBATE PROPERTY

Generally speaking, a probate sale refers to a property that's being sold because the owner is deceased and the sale is necessary to settle the estate. More specifically, a probate sale is one in which the sale of the property must be confirmed in a court of law, either by a judge or by a probate commissioner.

California state law requires that a probate property be advertised according to statute provisions. Any offer that's accepted must be for at least 90 percent of the property's court-appraised value. Following acceptance, a court date is set so that the sale can be confirmed. Any interested buyer can attend this court hearing, at which time the property is offered for open bidding before the sale is approved.

A buyer interested in bidding in court must make a minimal starting bid, the formula for which is set by probate law. The overbid must be for at least 10 percent of the first $10,000 of the initial buyer's bid plus 5 percent of the remaining balance; otherwise it won't be considered by the court. For instance, if the first buyer's accepted offer was $250,000, the minimal acceptable overbid would be $263,000 (10 percent of $10,000 is $1,000; 5 percent of $240,000 is $12,000; the total is $13,000 which, when added to the initial bid of $250,000, equals $263,000). Overbidders, as well as initial bidders, should be prepared with a cashier's check in hand. Subsequent overbid increments are set at the discretion of the court.

Probate properties are usually sold "as is," a condition provided by law to protect the heirs, who may have no first-hand knowledge about the property. Additionally, any offers made must be contingency-free. This means that financing, inspection, and any other contingencies must be satisfied before the court date. The law also requires the buyer of a probate property to make a deposit to the estate equal to 10 percent of the purchase price.

Buyers often shy away from listings that require court confirmation because they don't like the idea of not knowing until they've gone to court whether or not they can have the home. Those involved in a purchase requiring court confirmation may want to make the sale of their current house contingent upon that confirmation, or at least make arrangements to rent it back in case they get overbid in court.

Until recently, all estate sales routinely required court confirmation. The process was simplified in 1985, when state laws changed to allow for the sale of estate properties without court confirmation under certain conditions. Consult with an attorney if you are buying or selling an estate property to determine the most advantageous way to proceed. Buyers don't like the court confirmation process because it aggravates moving anxiety. It may be an unavoidable necessity, however, in cases when an estate is being divided among disputing beneficiary factions.

BECOMING AN EXPERT ON PRICES

Buyers who have done a lot of looking have the benefit of knowing more about current market values than they might realize. Ask yourself how the house you are considering measures up to other homes in the area. Ask your agent to find out how much homes you considered but ruled out ended up selling for, because the sale price of comparable homes is the true indicator of current market value, not the list price.

If you feel unfamiliar with local property values, have your agent prepare a comparative market analysis of a home you're interested in before you make an offer. This doesn't have to be as complete a market analysis as one an agent prepares for prospective sellers who are attempting to set the list price on their home. It can be as simple as a computer print-out of multiple listing information on similar homes that have been sold recently. Also ask for information regarding other properties being offered for sale in the neighborhood. Compare the amenities and list price of these properties with those of your home of choice.

Look to the multiple listing statistics for guidance in determining your offer price. In addition to sale price information, investigate how long the neighboring properties were on the market and how close the final sale price was to the initial list price. In addition, find out how long the subject property has been on the market. Have there been other offers? Why were they rejected? Is there any flexibility in the price? A listing agent cannot divulge that the seller will accept less than the asking price unless the seller has given express permission for the agent to do so. If the agent is unsure about what the seller will accept, it may be because the agent doesn't know or has been advised not to say.

Often a buyer will want to know what a seller paid for the property, how long ago, and what improvements have been completed during the current ownership. County property ownership records will indicate the length of ownership. And it's usually possible to figure out what the seller paid for a property, even if the seller won't divulge this information. In California, when a property transfers title from one owner to the next, the seller pays a documentary transfer tax, the amount of which is stamped on the face of the grant deed when it is recorded. These documents are part of the public record. The tax is equal to $1.10 per thousand dollars of transfer price. Divide the amount of the tax paid by 1.1 and multiply this figure by $1,000 to arrive at the approximate sale price at the time of transfer. For example, a documentary tax of $110, divided by 1.1, equals $100. Multiply this figure by $1,000 for an indicated sale price of $100,000. This figure may not be accurate if the seller carried financing for the buyer, in which case the figure may reflect the sale price minus the amount of seller financing.

When sufficient comparable sales data is not available, a buyer will often look at the seller's original purchase price and add to this allowances for price appreciation during the seller's period of ownership (your realtor should be able to provide rough approximations), as well as increases in value attributable to the seller's improvements to the property. This method of evaluating property value is approximate, at best, since it does not take local market conditions into account.

In a seller's market, the comparable sales figures may be out of date and analyzing average price appreciation to determine what the house "should" be worth may be irrelevant. Conversely, in a sour market, yesterday's comparable sales may indicate a value higher than what similar properties are worth today. Investigate what kind of residential real estate market you're in, and gear your offer accordingly.

Many buyers wonder if they should hire a licensed appraiser to complete an evaluation of a property before an offer is made. Most good real estate agents can provide you with all the relevant data you need to make an intelligent decision, and it won't cost you a dime extra.

NEGOTIATING THE PURCHASE CONTRACT

In California, a real estate purchase contract must be in writing in order to be enforceable. Gone are the days of one-page purchase agreements; today's real estate contracts are at least four pages long and encompass terms and conditions that were rarely considered a decade ago. Once accepted by the seller, the agreement becomes a legally binding contract, so be sure that it's drafted carefully and accurately reflects the terms of the transaction. In some states a real estate purchase agreement must be prepared by an attorney; in California, however, licensed real estate agents are permitted to complete standard form purchase agreements.

THE REAL ESTATE PURCHASE CONTRACT AND RECEIPT FOR DEPOSIT

The more familiar buyers and sellers are with the standard form purchase agreement, the easier it will be for them to draft and review agreements with their agents. The sample contract included in this book is a standardized California Association of Realtors form. Although individual company forms will deviate from this standard form somewhat, most purchase contracts used in the state contain the same basic elements.

The first blank at the top of this form is for the name of the city in which the contract is written. This is followed by a space for the date. It's important to fill in the date the contract is drafted, since any addenda or counteroffers to the contract will refer to the original contract date.

Below is a space for the full name(s) of the buyer(s), followed by the amount of the earnest money, or good faith, deposit. The amount of the initial deposit is negotiable, and customary deposit amounts vary from one area to another. Check one of the four boxes below the deposit amount to indicate the form of the deposit. The deposit is usually payable either to a real estate company trust account or to a title-escrow company. The next space is for the purchase price the

REAL ESTATE PURCHASE CONTRACT AND RECEIPT FOR DEPOSIT
(LONG FORM — WITH FINANCING CLAUSES)
THIS IS MORE THAN A RECEIPT FOR MONEY. IT IS INTENDED TO BE A LEGALLY BINDING CONTRACT. READ IT CAREFULLY.
CALIFORNIA ASSOCIATION OF REALTORS® (CAR) STANDARD FORM

_____, California, _____, 19_____

Received from _____

herein called Buyer, the sum of _____ Dollars $ _____

evidenced by ☐ cash, ☐ cashier's check, ☐ personal check or ☐ _____, payable to _____

_____, to be held uncashed until acceptance of this offer as deposit on account of purchase price of

_____ Dollars $ _____

for the purchase of property, situated in _____, County of_____ California,

described as follows: _____

1. FINANCING: The obtaining of Buyer's financing is a contingency of this agreement.

    A. DEPOSIT upon acceptance, to be deposited into _____ $ _____

    B. INCREASED DEPOSIT within_____ days of Seller's acceptance to be deposited into_____ $ _____

    C. BALANCE OF DOWN PAYMENT to be deposited into_____ on or before _____ $ _____

    D. Buyer to apply, qualify for and obtain a NEW FIRST LOAN in the amount of .... $ _____

        payable monthly at approximately $_____ including interest at origination not to exceed

        _____ %, ☐ fixed rate, ☐ other _____ all due_____ years from date of

        origination. Loan fee not to exceed _____ Seller agrees to pay a maximum of_____

        FHA/VA discount points. Additional terms_____

        _____ .

    E. Buyer ☐ to assume, ☐ to take title subject to an EXISTING FIRST LOAN with an approximate balance of ... $_____

        in favor of_____ payable monthly at $_____ including interest

        at_____% ☐ fixed rate, ☐ other _____ .

        Fees not to exceed_____ . Disposition of impound account _____ .

        Additional Terms _____ .

    F. Buyer to execute a NOTE SECURED BY a ☐ first, ☐ second, ☐ third DEED OF TRUST in the amount of $ _____

        IN FAVOR OF SELLER payable monthly at $_____ ☐ or more, including interest at_____% all due

        _____ years from date of origination, ☐ or upon sale or transfer of subject property. A late charge of

        _____ shall be due on any installment not paid within_____ days of the due date.

        ☐ Deed of Trust to contain a request for notice of default or sale for the benefit of Seller. Buyer ☐ will, ☐ will not

        execute a request for notice of delinquency. Additional terms_____

        _____ .

    G. Buyer☐ to assume, ☐ to take title subject to an EXISTING SECOND LOAN with an approximate balance of . $_____

        in favor of_____ payable monthly at $_____ including interest

        at_____% ☐ fixed rate, ☐ other _____ . Buyer fees not to exceed _____ .

        Additional terms _____

    H. Buyer to apply, qualify for and obtain a NEW SECOND LOAN in the amount of .... $ _____

        payable monthly at approximately $_____ including interest at origination not to exceed

        _____% ☐ fixed rate, ☐ other_____

        _____, all due_____ years from date of origination. Buyer's loan fee not to exceed_____ .

        ____ Terms _____

buyers are offering, followed by the city and county the property is located in and the property description, usually given as either the street address or the assessor's parcel number or both.

The financing section of the contract specifies the manner in which the buyers plan to finance the purchase. It also states that the buyers' ability to obtain financing is a contingency of the purchase agreement. This means that if the buyers are unable, after using diligent and good faith efforts (see Item J) to obtain the financing proposed in the contract, they are not obligated to complete the purchase and their deposit will be refunded.

Item A in the financing section refers to the earnest money deposit. If the deposit is to be increased prior to the close of escrow, the amount and date of increase are entered at Item B. An increased deposit is often

Additional

I. In the event Buyer assumes or takes title subject to an existing loan, Seller shall provide Buyer with copies of applicable notes and Deeds of Trust. A loan may contain a number of features which affect the loan, such as interest rate changes, monthly payment changes, balloon payments, etc. Buyer shall be allowed_____calendar days after receipt of such copies to notify Seller in writing of disapproval. FAILURE TO NOTIFY SELLER SHALL CONCLUSIVELY BE CONSIDERED APPROVAL. Buyer's approval shall not be unreasonably withheld. Difference in existing loan balances shall be adjusted in ☐ Cash, ☐ Other_____

J. Buyer agrees to act diligently and in good faith to obtain all applicable financing. _____

K. ADDITIONAL FINANCING TERMS:_____

L. TOTAL PURCHASE PRICE . . . . $_____

2. OCCUPANCY: Buyer ☐ does, ☐ does not intend to occupy subject property as Buyer's primary residence.

3. SUPPLEMENTS: The ATTACHED supplements are incorporated herein:
☐ Interim Occupancy Agreement (CAR FORM IOA-11)   ☐ _____
☐ Residential Lease Agreement after Sale (CAR FORM RLAS-11)   ☐ _____
☐ VA and FHA Amendments (CAR FORM VA/FHA-11)   ☐ _____

Buyer and Seller acknowledge receipt of copy of this page, which constitutes Page 1 of _____ Pages.
Buyer's Initials (_____) (_____)   Seller's Initials (_____) (_____)

OFFICE USE ONLY
Reviewed by Broker or Designee_____
Date _____

SF-Oct-87

REAL ESTATE PURCHASE CONTRACT AND RECEIPT FOR DEPOSIT (DI F-14 PAGE 1 OF 4)

made upon removal of all contingencies. Until that time, the buyer's deposit money is refundable if contingencies cannot be satisfied. The Balance of Down Payment (Item C) is deposited on or before the "close of escrow" (often abbreviated as COE). The balance of the down payment should be equal to the total cash down minus the deposit amount, since deposits are ordinarily applied toward the total purchase price. Items D through K specify the additional financing terms buyers are proposing to complete the purchase; only the relevant clauses should be filled in.

Some buyers object to providing specific financing terms such as the interest rate and loan fee and would rather state simply: "terms acceptable to buyer." Most attorneys, however, feel this is not advisable since if a dispute were to arise between the buyers and sellers, a judge might rule the contract to be unenforceable due to the vagueness of its terms. Under Additional Terms in this section, buyers may want to enter, for example, "No prepayment penalty," to indicate their unwillingness to accept a loan that contains a penalty for early prepayment.

Buyers making an offer contingent upon taking over an existing first or second loan (Items E and G) would be wise to determine the existing lender's policy regarding takeovers before they make an offer. Many existing loans, particularly fixed rate loans, have enforceable due on sale clauses, and there may be a risk that the lender will call the loan due, and even start foreclosure proceedings, if the property transfers to a new buyer and the existing loan is not paid off at that time.

Some existing loans, particularly the newer adjustable rate mortgages, can be assumed by a subsequent buyer, but only on certain terms and conditions. Usually the buyers must be creditworthy and must make formal application to assume the loan. Also, fees are often involved, and terms of the original loan may change when it is assumed by the new buyer.

Item F is completed if the buyer is requesting the seller to carry all or a portion of the financing. If the "or more" box following the monthly payment space is checked, this indicates that the buyer can pay more than the amount due in any given month without penalty. In this case, a "prepayment penalty" is not part of the note, and the loan can be paid off in full at any time.

In California, when an "arranger" of credit is part of a transaction in which the seller carries financing for the buyer, the Civil Code Sections 2956–2967 require that a Seller Financing Disclosure form be completed giving full disclosure of the financing terms to the buyers and sellers involved in the sale. A real estate broker representing buyers or sellers in such a property transfer is considered an "arranger" of credit. Either under the Additional Terms portion of Item F or under Section 3, entitled Supplements, note should be made that a Seller Financing Disclosure form is to be incorporated into the purchase agreement.

Item H is filled in only if the buyer is applying for a new second loan. This might be a financing condition if the buyer is assuming an existing first loan with a relatively low balance, or if the seller is carrying the first loan and the buyer needs to finance the difference between the amount of that loan plus the down payment and the purchase price.

Item I applies when the buyer is proposing to take over an existing loan secured against the property. A space is provided to enter the number of days the buyer has to approve the applicable loan documentation. Any discrepancy between the assumed remaining loan balance (usually based on the seller's records) and the actual remaining loan balance (which must the verified with the lender) is usually adjusted in "cash" from the buyer. An "other" option would be for the seller to carry back the amount of the difference. In the space following this section, insert a clause that stipulates buyer's approval of the lender's "statement of condition" of the loan to be a contingency of the contract. A "statement of condition" confirms the remaining loan balance and indicates whether the sellers are current in their mortgage payments. If they aren't, the buyer should insist that the sellers bring the loan current as a condition of the purchase.

A word about the sentence in Section I that states, "Failure to notify seller shall conclusively be considered approval." This statement appears repeatedly throughout the CAR purchase contract. There is some disagreement in the industry as to whether it's preferable to have a contingency be deemed approved if the buyer does not disapprove of it in writing, or whether it's better to have all contingencies approved or disapproved in writing. Many professionals agree that there is greater certainty that the buyers are satisfied with a contingency if they inform the seller of this fact in writing. Sellers who feel more comfortable with written approval of contingencies should have their agent strike the above phrase wherever it appears in the contract and under Other Terms and Conditions (Item 22 on page four of the contract) insert, "All contingencies to be approved or disapproved in writing by buyer."

Under Additional Financing Terms (Item K), add a clause that states the buyer will have a fixed period of time to obtain the necessary financing commitments. Thirty days is usually adequate unless the real estate market is particularly active, in which case it may take longer to process a loan. Additional provisions might be added under this section, such as, "Seller to pay any prepayment penalties charged by lenders on existing loans that seller is paying off at close of escrow." A buyer making an offer in a competitive bidding, or multiple offer, situation might add, "Buyer to be lender prequalified within five days of acceptance and buyer to submit a completed loan application within three days of acceptance." An addendum can be attached to the contract if the space provided is not sufficient. Use the space provided to reference the addendum, stating, for instance, "See Addendum A attached and made a part hereof."

The total amount of the purchase price is filled in at the bottom of the financing section (Item L). Double check to be sure that the deposit, cash down payment, and loan amount equal the purchase price.

In the Occupancy section, check the appropriate box to indicate if the property will be occupied as the buyer's primary residence. Lenders offer different financing programs for owner-occupied versus non-owner-occupied properties. Since the lender will require a copy of the accepted contract, it's important that one of these boxes is checked.

The Supplements section at the bottom of page one allows for the incorporation of additional relevant forms into the contract. An Interim Occupancy Agreement should be included if the buyer wants to occupy the property prior to the close of escrow, or a Residential Lease Agreement After Sale is incorporated when the seller is to retain possession of the property after the close of escrow. If the buyer is applying for VA or FHA financing, the box next to VA and FHA Amendments should be checked. These amendments state that the buyer will not be obliged to complete the purchase if the property is not appraised at the purchase price.

Enter a "4" in the Acknowledgement phrase underneath the Supplements section to indicate that this is page one of four pages. The buyer initials the appropriate space at the bottom of this page, and the property address is filled in at the top of page two.

The name of the title or escrow company is entered on the first line of the Escrow section. The escrow company is usually chosen by the buyer, but this can also be a negotiable item. Buyers who are selling a home and want to have escrow on the old and new homes close simultaneously should use the same escrow company for both transactions. If the two properties are not located in the same county, it may be difficult to accomplish a simultaneous close; in this case, make sure that the escrow on the old home closes a day or so before the escrow on the new home. This is critical if the proceeds from the sale of the old home are to provide the down payment for the purchase of the new home. If a real estate broker involved in the transaction has a financial interest in the escrow or title company, this must be disclosed in writing in the purchase agreement.

Escrow procedures differ somewhat in Southern and Northern California. In Southern California, it is customary for the buyer and seller to deliver escrow instructions to the escrow holder soon after the seller's acceptance, say within five days. In Northern California, escrow instructions are usually not given to the escrow holder until sometime within the last few weeks prior to closing. Who pays the escrow fee varies from county to county.

The Title section is intended to protect the buyer in the event the seller is unable to deliver clear title to the property. A specific number of days is filled in for the buyer to review the preliminary title report. It is incumbent upon the buyer to disapprove of any unacceptable title matter in writing. Again, customs differ between counties as to who pays for the preliminary title report and title insurance policy.

Normally, Prorations covers any property taxes, homeowner's

association dues, bonds or assessments, or rents that are prorated to "the day of recordation of the deed." The appropriate box is checked to indicate who pays for bonds or assessments currently levied against the property (such as a sewer bond). The county transfer tax ($1.10 per thousand dollars) is normally a seller expense. Spaces are provided for any additional transfer fee, such as a city transfer tax, and for the manner in which this fee is to be paid (by buyer, seller, or split between the two).

Read carefully the bold print regarding property reassessment and the sentences that follow, because property taxes almost certainly will be higher after the change of ownership. The supplemental tax bill will probably not arrive promptly after close of escrow, but when it does it will be retroactive to the date the deed was recorded.

The Possession clause specifies when occupancy of the property is to be delivered to the buyer. Sellers often do not feel comfortable moving out until they are certain that escrow has closed. Sometimes the buyer will allow the seller a courtesy day or two to move free of charge. If the seller is going to remain in possession for a longer period of time after the close of escrow, it is customary for the seller to compensate the buyer by paying rent. This is usually equal to the total of the buyer's principal, interest, taxes and insurance (PITI), prorated on a per diem basis.

When sellers have made it a condition of the listing that they be able to rent the property back for a period of time, this can be detailed in the "or" space of the possession clause. For instance, such a condition might read, "Sellers have option to rent back property for up to sixty days after close of escrow, at a cost equal to buyer's PITI, prorated on a per diem basis. Sellers to give buyer written notice thirty days prior to vacating." If more space is required, an addendum can be attached to the contract (referenced by "See Addendum B attached and made a part hereof"). The buyer and seller should make a "Residential Lease Agreement After Sale" a part of the contract.

Vesting indicates how title will be held by the buyer at the close of escrow. This decision should not be made lightly, especially when purchasing a property with another person, since the manner of holding title has legal and tax significance and should be discussed with the appropriate advisors. Buyers who are undecided at the time the offer is made should write, "Vesting to follow." A real estate agent is not qualified to give advice on these matters.

The Liquidated Damages clause is a source of confusion for many buyers and sellers of residential real estate in California. This bold type clause must be either separately initialed by both the buyers and sellers or left completely uninitialed for the purchase agreement to

Subject Property Address _____

4. ESCROW: Buyer and Seller shall deliver signed instructions to_____ the escrow holder, within _____calendar days from Seller's acceptance which shall provide for closing within_____ calendar days from Seller's acceptance. Escrow fees to be paid as follows: _____
_____

5. TITLE: Title is to be free of liens, encumbrances, easements, restrictions, rights and conditions of record or known to Seller, other than the following: (a) Current property taxes, (b) covenants, conditions, restrictions, and public utility easements of record, if any, provided the same do not adversely affect the continued use of the property for the purposes for which it is presently being used, unless reasonably disapproved by Buyer in writing within _____ calendar days of receipt of a current preliminary report furnished at_____ expense, and (c) _____
Seller shall furnish Buyer at _____ expense a standard California Land Title Association policy issued by _____ Company, showing title vested in Buyer subject only to the above. If Seller is unwilling or unable to eliminate any title matter disapproved by Buyer as above, Buyer may terminate this agreement. If Seller fails to deliver title as above, Buyer may terminate this agreement; in either case, the deposit shall be returned to Buyer.

6. PRORATIONS: Property taxes, payments on bonds and assessments assumed by Buyer, interest, rents, association dues, premiums on insurance acceptable to Buyer, and _____ shall be paid current and prorated as of: ☐ the day of recordation of the deed; or ☐ _____ . Bonds or assessments now a lien shall be ☐ paid current by Seller, payments not yet due to be assumed by Buyer; or ☐ paid in full by Seller, including payments not yet due; or ☐ _____ . County Transfer tax shall be paid by _____ . The _____ transfer tax or transfer fee shall be paid by _____ . **PROPERTY WILL BE REASSESSED UPON CHANGE OF OWNERSHIP. THIS WILL AFFECT THE TAXES TO BE PAID.** A Supplemental tax bill will be issued, which shall be paid as follows: (a) for periods after close of escrow, by Buyer (or by final acquiring party if part of an exchange), and (b) for periods prior to close of escrow, by Seller. **TAX BILLS ISSUED AFTER CLOSE OF ESCROW SHALL BE HANDLED DIRECTLY BETWEEN BUYER AND SELLER.**

7. POSSESSION: Possession and occupancy shall be delivered to Buyer, ☐ on close of escrow, or ☐ not later than _____ days after close of escrow, or ☐ _____ .

8. VESTING: Unless otherwise designated in the escrow instructions of Buyer, title shall vest as follows: _____
_____

(The manner of taking title may have significant legal and tax consequences. Therefore, give this matter serious consideration.)

9. MULTIPLE LISTING SERVICE: If Broker is a Participant of a Board multiple listing service ("MLS"), the Broker is authorized to report the sale, its price, terms, and financing for the publication, dissemination, information, and use of the authorized Board members, MLS Participants and Subscribers.

10. LIQUIDATED DAMAGES: If Buyer fails to complete said purchase as herein provided by reason of any default of Buyer, Seller shall be released from obligation to sell the property to Buyer and may proceed against Buyer upon any claim or remedy which he/she may have in law or equity; provided, however, that by placing their initials here Buyer: (   ) Seller: (   ) agree that Seller shall retain the deposit as liquidated damages. If the described property is a dwelling with no more than four units, one of which the Buyer intends to occupy as his/her residence, Seller shall retain as liquidated damages the deposit actually paid, or an amount therefrom, not more than 3% of the purchase price and promptly return any excess to Buyer. Buyer and Seller agree to execute a similar liquidated damages provision, such as California Association of Realtors® Receipt for Increased Deposit (RID-11), for any increased deposits. (Funds deposited in trust accounts or in escrow are not released automatically in the event of a dispute. Release of funds requires written agreement of the parties or adjudication.)
ATION: If the only controversy or claim between the parties ari_____ Buyer's deposit, such
at the election of the parti_____ with

be considered ratified. If one party agrees to the clause and the other does not there is no contract. What the clause means when initialed is that the seller is willing to accept the buyer's deposit as liquidated damages if the buyer defaults. A default occurs when a buyer fails to go through with a purchase agreement for reasons the contract does not allow for. The recourse a seller has against a buyer if the clause is *not* initialed is to sue the buyer for actual damages or to sue for specific performance (to perform under the terms of the contract).

In California, the law limits the amount of liquidated damages, in cases when the clause is initialed, to 3 percent of the purchase price. It is difficult to determine in advance whether this amount will be sufficient to cover the actual damages a seller would suffer if the buyer defaults. Also, be aware that even if both buyer and seller initial the

11. AR̶B̶I̶T̶̶ ̶̶̶̶̶̶̶̶̶̶ ses out of or relates to the disposition of the controversy or claim s̶h̶a̶l̶l̶ a̶t̶ t̶h̶e̶ ̶̶̶̶̶̶ parties be decided by arbitration. Such arbitration shall be determined in accordance with the Rules of the American Arbitration Association, and judgment upon the award rendered by the Arbitrator(s) may be entered in any court having jurisdiction thereof. The provisions of Code of Civil Procedure Section 1283.05 shall be applicable to such arbitration.

12. ATTORNEY'S FEES: In any action or proceeding arising out of this agreement, the prevailing party shall be entitled to reasonable attorney's fees and costs.

13. KEYS: Seller shall, when possession is available to Buyer, provide keys and/or means to operate all property locks, and alarms, if any.

14. PERSONAL PROPERTY: The following items of personal property, free of liens and without warranty of condition, are included: ____
_____
_____

15. FIXTURES: All permanently installed fixtures and fittings that are attached to the property or for which special openings have been made are included in the purchase price, including electrical, light, plumbing and heating fixtures, built-in appliances, screens, awnings, shutters, all window coverings, attached floor coverings, T.V. antennas, air cooler or conditioner, garage door openers and controls, attached fireplace equipment, mailbox, trees and shrubs, and _____ except_____ .

16. SMOKE DETECTOR(S): Approved smoke detector(s) shall be installed as required by law, at the expense of ☐ Buyer, ☐ Seller.

17. TRANSFER DISCLOSURE: Unless exempt, Transferor (Seller), shall comply with Civil Code Sections 1102 et seq., by providing Transferee (Buyer) with a Real Estate Transfer Disclosure Statement: a) ☐ Buyer has received and read a Real Estate Transfer Disclosure Statement; or b) ☐ Seller shall provide Buyer with a Real Estate Transfer Disclosure Statement within _____ calendar days of Seller's acceptance after which Buyer shall have three (3) days after delivery to Buyer, in person, or five (5) days after delivery by deposit in the mail, to terminate this agreement by delivery of a written notice of termination to Seller or Seller's Agent.

18. TAX WITHHOLDING: Under the Foreign Investment in Real Property Tax Act (FIRPTA), IRC 1445, *every* Buyer of U.S. real property *must*, unless an exemption applies, deduct and withhold from Seller's proceeds ten percent (10%) of the gross sales price. The primary exemptions are: No withholding is required if (a) Seller provides Buyer with an affidavit under penalty of perjury, that Seller is not a "foreign person," or (b) Seller provides Buyer with a "qualifying statement" issued by the Internal Revenue Service, or (c) if Buyer purchases real property for use as a residence and the purchase price is $300,000.00 or less and if Buyer or a member of Buyer's family has definite plans to reside at the property for at least 50% of the number of days it is in use during each of the first two twelve-months periods after transfer. Seller and Buyer agree to execute and deliver as directed, any instrument, affidavit and statement, or to perform any act reasonably necessary to carry out the provisions of FIRPTA and regulations promulgated thereunder.

19. ENTIRE CONTRACT: Time is of the essence. All prior agreements between the parties are incorporated in this agreement which constitutes the entire contract. Its terms are intended by the parties as a final expression of their agreement with respect to such terms as are included herein and may not be contradicted by evidence of any prior agreement or contemporaneous oral agreement. The parties further intend that this agreement constitutes the complete and exclusive statement of its terms and that no extrinsic evidence whatsoever may be introduced in any judicial or arbitration proceeding, if any, involving this agreement.

Buyer and Seller acknowledge receipt of copy of this page, which constitutes Page 2 of____ Pages.

Buyer's Initials (_____) (_____)   Seller's Initials (_____) (_____)

```
┌──────── OFFICE USE ONLY ────────┐
│ Reviewed by Broker or Designee ___ ___ │
│ Date ___ │
└─────────────────────────────────┘
```
EQUAL HOUSING OPPORTUNITY
SF-Oct-87

REAL ESTATE PURCHASE CONTRACT AND RECEIPT FOR DEPOSIT (DLF-14 PAGE 2 OF 4)

clause, the release of deposit money held in escrow is never automatic and always requires the agreement of both parties in writing.

Professional advice on whether to initial the liquidated damages clause can only be obtained by consulting with an attorney. If the clause is initialed by the buyer and seller and there is to be an increase made to the deposit, a separate form, called a Receipt for Increased Deposit (California Association of Realtors form RID-11), which restates the liquidated damages provision, must accompany the increased deposit and be signed by both buyer and seller in order for the liquidated damages clause to apply to the full amount of both the deposit and the increase.

Under Personal Property, list unattached items that are included in the sale, such as freestanding kitchen appliances, a fireplace screen, and swimming pool equipment. Refrigerators, freezers, washers, and dryers are sometimes included. Buyers usually ask for what they want; sellers can always say no, in the form of a counteroffer, if they need

Subject Property Address _____

20. CAPTIONS: The captions in this agreement are for convenience of reference only and are not intended as part of this agreement.

21. ADDITIONAL TERMS AND CONDITIONS:
ONLY THE FOLLOWING PARAGRAPHS A THROUGH J *WHEN INITIALED BY BOTH BUYER AND SELLER* ARE INCORPORATED IN THIS AGREEMENT.

Buyer's Initials   Seller's Initials

_____ / _____   _____ / _____   **A. PHYSICAL INSPECTION:** Within _____ calendar days after Seller's acceptance Buyer shall have the right, at Buyer's expense, to select a licensed contractor(s) or other qualified professional(s), to inspect and investigate the subject property, including but not limited to structural, plumbing, heating, electrical, built-in appliances, roof, soils, foundation, mechanical systems, pool, pool heater, pool filter, air conditioner, if any, possible environmental hazards such as asbestos, formaldehyde, radon gas and other substances / products. Buyer shall keep the subject property free and clear of any liens, indemnify and hold Seller harmless from all liability, claims, demands, damages or costs, and repair all damages to the property arising from the inspections. All claimed defects concerning the condition of the property that adversely affect the continued use of the property for the purposes for which it is presently being used shall be in writing, supported by written reports, if any, and delivered to Seller within_____ calendar days after Seller's acceptance. Buyer shall furnish Seller copies, at no cost, of all reports concerning the property obtained by Buyer. When such reports disclose conditions or information unsatisfactory to the Buyer, which the Seller is unwilling or unable to correct, Buyer may cancel this agreement. Seller shall make the premises available for all inspections. BUYER'S FAILURE TO NOTIFY SELLER SHALL CONCLUSIVELY BE CONSIDERED APPROVAL.

Buyer's Initials   Seller's Initials

_____ / _____   _____ / _____   **B. GEOLOGICAL INSPECTION:** Within _____ calendar days after Seller's acceptance, Buyer shall have the right at Buyer's expense, to select a qualified professional to make tests, surveys, or other studies of the subject property. Buyer shall keep the subject property free and clear of any liens, indemnify and hold Seller harmless from all liability, claims, demands, damages or costs, and repair all damages to the property arising from the tests, surveys, or studies. All claimed defects concerning the condition of the property that adversely affect the continued use of the property for the purposes for which it is presently being used shall be in writing, supported by written reports, if any, and delivered to Seller within _____ calendar days after Seller's acceptance. Buyer shall furnish Seller copies, at no cost, of all reports concerning the property obtained by Buyer. When such reports disclose conditions or information unsatisfactory to the Buyer, which the Seller is unwilling or unable to correct, Buyer may cancel this agreement. Seller shall make the premises available for all inspections. BUYER'S FAILURE TO NOTIFY SELLER SHALL CONCLUSIVELY BE CONSIDERED APPROVAL.

Buyer's Initials   Seller's Initials

_____ / _____   _____ / _____   **C. CONDITION OF PROPERTY:** Seller warrants, through the date possession is made available to Buyer: (1) property and improvements thereon, including landscaping, grounds and pool/spa, if any, shall be maintained in the same condition as upon the date of Seller's acceptance; (2) the roof is free of all known leaks and that water, sewer, plumbing, heating, air conditioning, if any, and electrical systems and all built-in appliances are operative, (3) _____ .

Buyer's Initials   Seller's Initials

_____ / _____   _____ / _____   **D. SELLER REPRESENTATION:** Seller warrants that Seller has no knowledge of any notice of violations of City, County, State, Federal, Building, Zoning, Fire, Health Codes or ordinances, or other governmental regulation filed or issued against the property. This warranty shall be effective until the date of close of escrow.

to take the items requested with them. Beware of the seller who wants to include old freestanding appliances in order to avoid having to move them. The buyer should specify, in writing, that the seller remove unwanted items from the property by close of escrow.

Fixtures includes all items permanently attached to the property as opposed to personal property, which is moveable. If you are buying a house that has a pool, write pool heater and filter in the space provided for additional fixtures. Fixtures excluded from the sale are listed after "except."

Smoke detectors are required by California state law. If they are not already in place and operative at the time an offer to purchase is made, they must be installed by close of escrow at buyer's or seller's expense. The appropriate box in the Smoke Detector section is checked

Buyer's Initials   Seller's Initials

___/___   ___/___   **E. PEST CONTROL:** Within_____ calendar days from the date of Seller's acceptance Seller shall furnish Buyer, at the expense of ☐ Buyer, ☐ Seller, a current written report of an inspection by_____
_____ , a licensed Structural Pest Control Operator, of the main building and all structures on the property, except_____ .

If no infestation or infection by wood destroying pests or organisms is found, the report shall include a written "Certification" as provided in Business and Professions Code 8519(a) that on the date of inspection "no evidence of active infestation or infection was found."

All work recommended in said report to repair damage caused by infestation or infection by wood-destroying pests or organisms found, including leaking shower stalls and replacing of tiles removed for repairs, and all work to correct conditions that cause such infestation or infection shall be done at the expense of Seller.

Funds for work to be performed shall be held in escrow and disbursed upon receipt of written Certification as provided in Business and Professions Code 8519(b) that the property "is now free of evidence of active infestation or infection".

Buyer agrees that any work to correct conditions usually deemed likely to lead to infestation or infection by wood-destroying pests or organisms, but where no evidence of existing infestation or infection is found with respect to such conditions is NOT the responsibility of Seller, and that such work shall be done only if requested by Buyer and then at the expense of Buyer.

If inspection of inaccessible areas is recommended by the report, Buyer has the option of accepting and approving the report or requesting further inspection be made at the Buyer's expense. If further inspection is made and infestation, infection, or damage is found, repair of such damage and all work to correct conditions that caused such infestation or infection and the cost of entry and closing of the inaccessible areas shall be at the expense of Seller. If no infestation, infection, or damage is found, the cost of entry and closing of the inaccessible areas shall be at the expense of Buyer.

Other_____
_____ .

Buyer's Initials   Seller's Initials

___/___   ___/___   **F. FLOOD HAZARD AREA DISCLOSURE:** Buyer is informed that subject property is situated in a "Special Flood Hazard Area" as set forth on a Federal Emergency Management Agency (FEMA) "Flood Insurance Rate Map (FIRM) or "Flood Hazard Boundary Map" (FHBM). The law provides that, as a condition of obtaining financing on most structures located in a "Special Flood Hazard Area," lenders require flood insurance where the property or its attachments are security for a loan.

The extent of coverage and the cost may vary. For further information consult the lender or insurance carrier. No representation or recommendation is made by the Seller and the Brokers in this transaction as to the legal effect or economic consequences of the National Flood Insurance Program and related legislation.

Buyer and Seller acknowledge receipt of copy of this page, which constitutes Page 3 of_____ Pages.

Buyer's Initials (_____) (_____)   Seller's Initials (_____) (_____)

┌─── OFFICE USE ONLY ───┐
Reviewed by Broker or Designee _____
Date_____

EQUAL HOUSING OPPORTUNITY
SF-Oct-87

REAL ESTATE PURCHASE CONTRACT AND RECEIPT FOR DEPOSIT (DLF-14 PAGE 3 OF 4)

to indicate who will pay for them.

The Transfer Disclosure section refers to the Real Estate Transfer Disclosure Statement that a seller, unless exempt, must provide a buyer in order to comply with Civil Code requirements. If the buyer has received and read a fully completed disclosure statement (including agent inspections), the form should be dated and signed by the buyer and box "a" should be checked on the purchase agreement. Box "b" is checked if the buyer has not received a completed seller disclosure form by the time the offer is written. Fill in the number of days the seller has to provide the buyer with this completed form.

At the bottom of the page, a "4" is entered in the blank included in the acknowledgement clause to indicate that this is page two of four pages. Buyers and sellers initial the appropriate spaces below and the property address is filled in at the top of page three.

Additional Terms and Conditions includes paragraphs A through J which, when initialed by both buyer and seller, are incorporated into the contract. As with the liquidated damages clause, buyer and seller must both either initial or not initial each clause in order to have a valid agreement.

The Physical Inspection clause entitles a buyer to have the property inspected by qualified professionals within a specified number of calendar days after the seller's acceptance. These inspections are done at the buyer's expense. If defects that will affect the continued use of the property are discovered and the buyer is unwilling to accept the property unless the seller corrects them, the buyer must notify the seller of this in writing within a specified amount of time. If the seller is unwilling or unable to correct defects claimed by the buyer, the buyer may cancel the agreement and have the deposit refunded.

The Geological Inspection clause is similar to the Physical Inspection clause. Sometimes buyers will initial both at the time an offer is made and then waive the geological inspection clause if the physical inspections do not reveal a need to pay for additional, and often costly, geological inspections. In areas of known soil instability, a geological inspection is a must.

In the Condition of Property clause, the seller (1) warrants that the property will be in the same condition at the date of buyer's possession as it is at the time of seller's acceptance, and (2) vows to deliver the property to the buyer with a roof that is free of known leaks and with operative mechanical systems. In the blank space that follows (3), it's wise to fill in: "All debris and items of personal property not included in the purchase will be removed from the premises and the property will be in broom clean condition at date of possession." A buyer may want to request that the seller replace all cracked and broken windows before the close of escrow; such a stipulation can be included in an addendum.

Most buyers will want the Seller Representation clause initialed; in it, the sellers warrant that they have no knowledge of any notice of code violations filed or issued against the property.

The Pest Control clause should specify within how many days of acceptance a report will be furnished, who will pay for the report, who the licensed structural pest control operator will be, and if any structures on the property are to be excepted, such as a detached garage or tool shed. Read this entire clause carefully: it details what the buyer's and seller's responsibilities will be with respect to existing infestation and infection by wood destroying organisms, as opposed to conditions deemed likely to lead to infestation or infection in the future. It clearly states how further inspection of inaccessible areas is to be handled if recommended in the pest control report.

The Other section of the Pest Control clause can be used to propose alternatives such as, "Buyer waives the right to have a pest control inspection," or, "Buyer accepts seller's existing pest control report completed by [a specific termite company], on [a specific date]; seller to pay for work recommended in this report." The buyer might be willing to take the property in "as is" condition with respect to pest control work, subject to reviewing and approving a current pest control report. If the buyer or buyer's agent is concerned that the lender will require a termite clearance by close of escrow, which is quite common, enter, "Seller to provide termite clearance by close of escrow" in the space provided.

The Flood Hazard Area Disclosure clause should be initialed if the property is located in a Special Flood Hazard Area, in which case the buyer's lender will require flood insurance. For more information about flood hazard zones, contact the Federal Emergency Management Agency (FEMA), 10101 Senate Drive, Lanham, MD 20706, (800) 638-6620.

The buyer and seller initial the bottom of the page, which is page three of four, and the property address is entered at the top of page four.

The Special Studies Zone Disclosure clause is initialed if the property is situated in a Special Studies (earthquake fault) Zone, in which case the construction of "any structure for human occupancy may be subject to the findings of a geologic report prepared by a geologist registered in the State of California." The buyer is allowed a specified number of calendar days to make further inquiries and may cancel the purchase agreement if the inquiries reveal unsatisfactory conditions that the seller is unable or unwilling to correct. For more information about Special Studies Zones, contact the California Department of Conservation's Division of Mines and Geology, (213) 620-3560 or (916) 445-5716.

The Energy Conservation Retrofit clause is initialed if required by local ordinance, and the appropriate box is checked to indicate whether the buyer or seller will be responsible for compliance.

The Home Protection Plan clause informs the buyer and seller that home protection plans are available and that they may provide additional protection. Buyers and sellers should direct any questions they might have about coverage directly to the protection plan company. The appropriate box is checked to indicate who is paying for the plan; the amount to be paid is entered in the space provided. If the company name is not known at contract time, enter "to follow" in that space. The waiver box is checked if a protection plan is not to be made a part of the contract.

Clause J is initialed when the buyer is purchasing a condominium or PUD (planned unit development). Spaces are provided for disclos-

Subject Property Address _____

Buyer's Initials   Seller's Initials

_____ / _____ **G. SPECIAL STUDIES ZONE DISCLOSURE:** Buyer is informed that subject property is situated in a Special Studies Zone as designated under Sections 2621-2625, inclusive, of the California Public Resources Code; and, as such, the construction or development on this property of any structure for human occupancy may be subject to the findings of a geologic report prepared by a geologist registered in the State of California, unless such a report is waived by the City or County under the terms of that act.

Buyer is allowed _____ calendar days from the date of Seller's acceptance to make further inquiries at appropriate governmental agencies concerning the use of the subject property under the terms of the Special Studies Zone Act and local building, zoning, fire, health and safety codes. When such inquiries disclose conditions or information unsatisfactory to the Buyer, which the Seller is unwilling or unable to correct, Buyer may cancel this agreement. BUYER'S FAILURE TO NOTIFY SELLER SHALL CONCLUSIVELY BE CONSIDERED APPROVAL.

Buyer's Initials   Seller's Initials

_____ / _____ **H. ENERGY CONSERVATION RETROFIT:** If local ordinance requires that the property be brought in compliance with minimum energy Conservation Standards as a condition of sale or transfer, ☐ Buyer, ☐ Seller shall comply with and pay for these requirements. Where permitted by law, Seller may, if obligated hereunder, satisfy the obligation by authorizing escrow to credit Buyer with sufficient funds to cover the cost of such retrofit.

Buyer's Initials   Seller's Initials

_____ / _____ **I. HOME PROTECTION PLAN:** Buyer and Seller have been informed that Home Protection Plans are available. Such plans may provide additional protection and benefit to a Seller or Buyer. California Association of Realtors® and the Broker(s) in this transaction do not endorse or approve any particular company or program:

a) ☐ A Buyer's coverage Home Protection Plan to be issued by _____
Company, at a cost not to exceed $ _____ , to be paid by ☐ Seller, ☐ Buyer; or

b) ☐ Buyer and Seller elect not to purchase a Home Protection Plan.

Buyer's Initials   Seller's Initials

_____ / _____ **J. CONDOMINIUM/P.U.D.:** The subject of this transaction is a condominium/planned unit development (P.U.D.) designated as unit _____ and _____ parking space(s) and an undivided _____ interest in all community areas, and _____ . The current monthly assessment charge by the homeowner's association or other governing body(s) is $ _____ . As soon as practicable, Seller shall provide Buyer with copies of covenants, conditions and restrictions, articles of incorporation, by-laws, current rules and regulations, most current financial statements, and any other documents as required by law. Seller shall disclose in writing any known pending special assessment, claims, or litigation to Buyer. Buyer shall be allowed _____ calendar days from receipt to review these documents. If such documents disclose conditions or information unsatisfactory to Buyer, Buyer may cancel this agreement. BUYER'S FAILURE TO NOTIFY SELLER SHALL CONCLUSIVELY BE CONSIDERED APPROVAL.

22. OTHER TERMS AND CONDITIONS: _____

_____
_____

ing the unit number, the number of parking spaces included, and the amount of the monthly homeowner's association dues. A number of days is entered in the appropriate space for the buyer to read and approve copies of the CC&Rs (Covenants, Conditions and Restrictions), as well as the articles of incorporation, bylaws, rules and regulations, and financing statements. Pending assessments, claims, or litigation against the seller are to be disclosed to the buyer. If the documents disclose conditions unsatisfactory to the buyer, the buyer has the right to cancel the purchase agreement.

An Arbitration Notice clause will appear in some purchase agreements that offer binding arbitration as an option to buyers and sellers as a method of resolving disputes. Like the Liquidated Damages clause, the Arbitration Notice clause appears in bold print and must either be separately initialed by both buyer and seller or left uninitialed in order for the contract to be binding. CAR standard contracts that contain the Arbitration Notice provision will present contract clauses

---

23. AGENCY CONFIRMATION: The following agency relationship(s) are hereby confirmed for this transaction:
LISTING AGENT: _____ is the agent of (check one):
    ☐ the Seller exclusively; or ☐ both the Buyer and Seller
SELLING AGENT: _____ (If not the same as Listing Agent) is the agent of (check one):
    ☐ the Buyer exclusively; or ☐ the Seller exclusively; or ☐ both the Buyer and Seller.

24. AMENDMENTS: This agreement may not be amended, modified, altered or changed in any respect whatsoever except by a further agreement in writing executed by Buyer and Seller.

25. OFFER: This constitutes an offer to purchase the described property. Unless acceptance is signed by Seller and the signed copy delivered in person or by mail to Buyer, or to _____ who is authorized to receive it, in person or by mail at the address below, within _____ calendar days of the date hereof, this offer shall be deemed revoked and the deposit shall be returned. Buyer has read and acknowledges receipt of a copy of this offer.

REAL ESTATE BROKER_____   BUYER _____
By _____   BUYER _____
Address _____   Address _____

Telephone _____   Telephone _____

ACCEPTANCE

The undersigned Seller accepts and agrees to sell the property on the above terms and conditions and agrees to the above confirmation of agency relationships. Seller agrees to pay to Broker(s) _____

compensation for services as follows:_____ .

Payable: (a) On recordation of the deed or other evidence of title, or (b) if completion of sale is prevented by default of Seller, upon Seller's default, or (c) if completion of sale is prevented by default of Buyer, only if and when Seller collects damages from Buyer, by suit or otherwise, and then in an amount not less than one-half of the damages recovered, but not to exceed the above fee, after first deducting title and escrow expenses and the expenses of collection, if any. Seller shall execute and deliver an escrow instruction irrevocably assigning the compensation for service in an amount equal to the compensation agreed to above. In any action or proceeding between Broker(s) and Seller arising out of this agreement, the prevailing party shall be entitled to reasonable attorneys fees and costs. The undersigned has read and acknowledges receipt of a copy of this agreement and authorizes Broker(s) to deliver a signed copy to Buyer.

Date_____ Telephone_____   SELLER_____
Address _____
_____   SELLER_____
Real Estate Broker(s) agree to the foregoing.

Broker _____ By _____ Date_____

Broker _____ By _____ Date_____

This form is available for use by the entire real estate industry. The use of this form is not intended to identify the user as a REALTOR®. REALTOR® is a registered collective membership mark which may be used only by real estate licensees who are members of the NATIONAL ASSOCIATION OF REALTORS® and who subscribe to its Code of Ethics.

Page 4 of_____ Pages.

OFFICE USE ONLY
Reviewed by Broker or Designee _____
Date _____

EQUAL HOUSING OPPORTUNITY
SF-Oct-87

REAL ESTATE PURCHASE CONTRACT AND RECEIPT FOR DEPOSIT (DLF-14 PAGE 4 OF 4)

---

in slightly different order than they appear in the sample CAR contract in this book.

Other Terms and Conditions provides space for incorporating additional provisions into the contract. If the space provided is not sufficient, attach an addendum. If the buyer or seller is a real estate agent licensed in the state of California, this fact would be disclosed here, as would a contingency requiring that the offer be approved by the buyer's attorney or tax advisor. If a buyer is concerned about the cost of heating a large home built before energy code requirements went into effect, a contingency in this section might call for access to the seller's utility bills for the past year. An agreement about repairs the seller is to make, a buyer's request to complete a final walk-through inspection, or a notice that the property is in probate and sale is subject to court confirmation would be included in this section.

Buyers purchasing a tenant-occupied property will want to request that the property be vacant at the close of escrow, while those making an offer on a property where tenants will retain possession will want to request that any tenant deposits be turned over at the closing; either request would be made in Other Terms and Conditions. The proration clause (Item 6 of this purchase agreement) provides for rents to be prorated. A buyer should also condition the offer upon the seller providing written verification from the appropriate local government authority regarding the legality of the rental unit(s).

Local ordinances that must be complied with upon the transfer of title or that may restrict the rights of property owners should be included in "Other Terms and Conditions" with a provision stating who is to be responsible for compliance. Perhaps the buyer's offer is contingent upon the sale or successful closing of another property; such contingencies would be included here. A contingency requiring a buyer to qualify for "swing financing" should be here in wording similar to that used to describe the loan contingencies disclosed in the Financing section of the purchase agreement. Include the loan amount and term, interest rate, and fees involved, as well as a time period within which the buyer must qualify.

Consult your real estate agent, attorney, or tax advisor to be certain that you haven't overlooked any pertinent contingencies or conditions that should be made a part of the purchase agreement. Leaving terms of the contract, such as closing and possession dates, open for future negotiation can invite trouble.

The Agency Confirmation section provides space for the listing and selling agents to identify themselves and to indicate whom they are representing in the transaction. The Agency Disclosure form should be reviewed and signed by the buyer and seller as soon as is practicable *prior* to entering into a real estate contract.

The Offer section gives the number of days the seller has to sign acceptance and return the purchase agreement to the buyer or the buyer's representative. If the seller fails to accept within this period, the offer is deemed to be revoked and the deposit is returned unless the buyer agrees to grant the seller an extension. While it's understandable that buyers want a response to their offer as soon as possible, it may be unrealistic to request an answer from the seller upon presentation of the offer.

The buyer signs below this section only after reading and understanding the entire contract, including all of the fine print. If you don't understand a part of the contract and your real estate agent cannot satisfactorily explain it to you, consult a real estate attorney *before* signing the contract. Also, be certain that the terms of the contract accurately reflect your intentions and capabilities. Once the purchase agreement is signed by all parties, it becomes a legally binding contract and penalties for noncompliance may be severe.

After you've reviewed and signed the contract, have your agent complete a Buyer's Cost Sheet for you. This will give you an approximation of what costs you will pay in addition to the down payment amount required to close the escrow. Be certain before you enter into a binding agreement that you will be able to perform under the terms and conditions of the contract.

Finally, you should receive copies of each document you sign in the course of a real estate transaction: the agency disclosure form, copies of each page of the purchase agreement that you submit to the seller, copies of real estate transaction disclosure forms, and anything else you sign that will be made a part of the contract. Dedicate a file to your real estate acquisition: the paperwork may seem cumbersome, but it's intended to protect you.

PRESENTING THE OFFER

The manner in which an offer to purchase is presented to a seller varies from area to area. Regardless of local custom, however, it is always preferable to have the offer presented in person by the buyer's agent. Buyers should not attend the presentation as their presence might deter the sellers from asking questions and airing objections about the offer.

Sellers will often want to know the offering price in advance of the formal presentation of the offer, but there are several good reasons why it's better to wait to hear an offer presented in its totality. The primary reason is that, in a dual agency situation, a potential conflict of interest is created if the listing agent has advance knowledge of another buyer's offer. Another reason for waiting is that there is more to an offer than the price, and hearing a low initial bid can prejudice the seller against listening to the rest of the offer. A low offer from a qualified buyer that can be negotiated is far better than a full price offer from a buyer who can't qualify.

The presentation occurs in private, ideally in the conference room at the listing agent's office. The buyer's agent presents and reviews the offer thoroughly with the seller and the seller's agent. In addition, the buyer's agent should inform the seller of the buyer's financial capacity to perform under the terms of the contract. If the buyer has been prequalified by a lender, a letter confirming this should accompany the offer. Relevant financial information that the buyer's agent should have on hand at the presentation includes the buyer's occupation, the length of time the buyer has been employed in that occupation, the buyer's annual gross income, and the amount of any long-term outstanding debts. With this information, the seller and the seller's agent can determine if the buyer is qualified to obtain the financing terms proposed in the contract. Sellers, by the way, should never hear an offer without having their agent present.

After the offer is presented and all questions answered to satisfaction, the buyer's agent should be excused so that the offer can be discussed by the selling party in private. At this point, the seller's agent should prepare a "Seller's Net Sheet" to indicate the amount of cash proceeds that will be realized if the offer is accepted.

Given the complexity of real estate purchase contracts, it is rare that a seller will accept an offer exactly as it's written. Keep in mind that virtually everything in a purchase agreement is negotiable, including the form of the purchase contract itself. If the offer is written on an overly simplistic form that doesn't cover the items included in the CAR purchase agreement, your agent can rewrite it on the appropriate form.

Whenever possible, respond to the buyer's offer as soon as possible. An offer to purchase can be withdrawn at any time prior to the moment that the seller's signed acceptance is delivered back to the buyer. Keep in mind that buyers are most enthusiastic about a house at the time they make an offer, so if you keep a buyer waiting the initial eagerness may wear off. Use the buyer's excitement to your own advantage, but be sure you consider your response carefully before making a formal counteroffer. Once the contract is signed by all parties, it's difficult if not impossible to change the terms.

Any counteroffer should be made in writing. Oral offers and counteroffers are virtually worthless, since a real estate contract must be in writing to be enforceable. A seller's agent is legally required to present all offers, even the most ridiculously low, to the seller. You don't have to accept or even counter an offer if you don't want to, but your agent must present it to you.

Buying and selling long distance requires a slightly different procedure. If it is not feasible to coordinate an in-person presentation soon after the buyer's offer is written, a phone presentation should be arranged. The buyer's and seller's agents make a conference call to the seller and present the offer, as if the seller were present; the seller then wires acceptance or the terms of a counteroffer. Related paperwork is express mailed to the seller for signature.

REVIEWING THE OFFER
The sellers and their agent need to weigh the pros and cons of an offer

carefully. Some offers are clean and straightforward; others that are sloppily written may only require a little reworking to make them perfectly acceptable. This is the time for the sellers to determine which terms they can live with and which require modification.

Starting at the top of the contract, make sure you know who is making an offer to purchase your home and that all buyers have signed the contract. Beware of the phrase "and/or assignee" or "and/or nominee," next to a buyer's name. Insist that the nominee or assignee be named within a certain number of days following acceptance and that that party signs the original purchase agreement. Likewise, if a husband and wife are making an offer to purchase and only one of them has signed the contract, write into a counteroffer that the other party must sign within a day or two of acceptance.

A seller can request an increase in the deposit amount if the buyer's initial deposit is too low. There is no rule as to what amount is adequate. One percent of the purchase price is an average good faith deposit, but local custom will dictate how much is considered reasonable. A long close of escrow, particularly when at the buyer's request, should be accompanied by a substantial deposit. An increased deposit may be requested upon acceptance, several days after acceptance, or upon removal of all contingencies.

An offer accompanied with a deposit in the form of a promissory note rather than a personal or cashier's check should be countered with a provision that the note be replaced with a check within a day or two of acceptance. A promissory note is simply a promise to pay. A check, which is cashed by the escrow holder, is a more secure deposit.

The purchase price is probably the most frequently countered item in a purchase agreement. Many times the first offer is the best one a seller will receive, yet it may also be well below what the seller feels is reasonable. In evaluating an offer, there are a number of important factors to take into account in addition to the price. An offer from a qualified buyer with cash in the bank who can close escrow quickly may be worth more to a seller than a higher offer requiring a long close that is contingent upon the sale of another home. On the other hand, if your agent concurs that the offer is on the low side, try to get a sense from the buyer's agent during the presentation of whether there's any flexibility in the buyer's price. If you think the buyer or buyer's agent is unfamiliar with local property values, ask your agent to provide a list of comparable sales to justify your price.

When considering the amount of the cash down payment, it is safe to say that the more cash down, the better. A loan for 90 percent of the purchase price will, in most cases, be more difficult for a buyer to obtain than will a loan for 80 percent or less. A lender feels more secure about making a loan when a larger cash down payment is involved. This does not mean that a seller should refuse an offer from a buyer who needs to qualify for a 90 percent loan. There are plenty of well-qualified buyers with substantial incomes who are unable to accumulate large cash down payments, often because a good portion of their income goes to taxes. As a seller, you must keep in mind that the lender qualifying procedure will be more rigorous than it would be if the buyer were able to make a large cash down payment. Make certain in advance that the buyer can qualify for the proposed loan and that there are good comparable sales in the neighborhood to justify the purchase price to the lender's appraiser. Remember, if the house is appraised at less than the purchase price, a buyer applying for a 90 percent loan is unlikely to have the additional cash on hand to make up the difference.

Be certain that the interest rate and loan fee stated in the offer are readily available. If interest rates are heading upward or if the loan fee the buyer is proposing is on the low side (1 percent of the loan amount rather than 1.5 or 2 percent), include in a counteroffer a request that the buyer accept a loan with a higher interest rate or larger loan fee if necessary. It is not advisable to counter that a buyer accept the "best prevailing interest rate," as a judge could interpret this phrase to be too vague to enforce should interest rates soar and the buyer fail to complete the purchase.

Normally the buyer chooses the lender for the new first loan. Sometimes, however, a seller may want to have some say in that choice. During periods of unstable interest rates, for instance, a seller may be wise to counter that the buyer seek financing from a lender who will "lock in" an interest rate upon or soon after application. If rates rise, the buyer has the lender's promise to charge the lower rate, provided that the loan is approved and closes within a specified period of time.

Sellers who have a prepayment penalty on their loan need to find out whether it may be waived if the buyer finances the home purchase through the same lender. This could result in a substantial savings to the sellers and, therefore, a lower purchase price for the buyers.

Ninety percent financing usually requires that the buyer and the property qualify for Private Mortgage Insurance (PMI), to protect the lender in case of default. PMI qualification can be a different process, although some lenders self-insure their 90 percent loans. Loan approval is usually easier to obtain from lenders that handle the entire process internally. If the buyer appears to be marginally qualified, you might counter that the buyer obtain financing through a "portfolio" lender who is less likely to be unreasonably rigorous in qualifying the buyer.

It is unwise for a seller to be overly restrictive about the buyer's choice of lender; after all, it is the buyer who has to live with the new first loan, not the seller. A seller should never insist that the buyer obtain the new loan from a lender that the seller has a financial interest in.

Sometimes a buyer takes over an existing loan instead of obtaining a new one; in these situations, the seller will commonly prefer that the buyer formally assume the loan rather than take title "subject to" the existing loan. When the buyer formally assumes the loan, the lender looks primarily to the assuming borrower for payment and only secondarily to the original borrower. With a "subject to" transfer, the seller may still be primarily responsible for payment. A "subject to" transfer may also involve an additional risk to the buyer, since most lenders will only permit an existing loan to be taken over through formal assumption and could start foreclosure proceedings following a "subject to" transfer if the note contains a valid "due on sale clause."

Sellers who carry back a note as part of the purchase price usually want to make a late charge part of the agreement. A late fee of 6 percent of the payment due is customarily charged if payment is not received within ten days of the due date. Likewise, a seller will want the buyer to provide a request for notice of default or sale and a request for notice of delinquency, both of which can be arranged through the title company.

The interest rate on an owner-carry loan is negotiable. Ask your agent to check with a mortgage broker to determine the current rate on institutional first (or second) loans. Seller financing is usually a little less expensive than conventional financing, and loan fees typically are not charged. The interest rate on a seller-carry loan will also be influenced by current treasury bill and certificate of deposit rates. Sellers are usually not willing to carry a loan for a lower return than they could earn if their money was invested elsewhere.

Imputed interest rates are charged by the IRS if sellers carry back a note at too low an interest rate; in this case, sellers could be taxed on income they haven't received. Installment sale rules have changed several times in recent years, so have current information and understand the tax ramifications before entering into a legally binding contract.

Under the Additional Financing Terms section of the purchase agreement, make certain a clause is included stating a time period within which the buyer is to qualify for the new loan or assume any existing loans. If such a clause is not part of the offer, include it in a counteroffer. In addition, it is advisable to request that the buyer submit a loan application within five days of acceptance (to ensure that the loan will be approved on time) and provide a letter confirming lender prequalification within seven to ten days of acceptance. If the buyer is making an all-cash offer with no loan contingency, request verification of the source of funds within five to ten days of acceptance. If parents are providing all or part of the financing, ask them to verify their intent and ability to participate in writing, since it's not uncommon for buyers to think they can count on their parents for extra cash when in fact the parents have no desire to assist.

The Escrow section of the contract should specifically name the escrow company to be used for the transaction. If the buyer's offer to purchase merely states "a reputable title/escrow company," include the name of a specific company in the counteroffer. The close of escrow date may require adjustment, depending on the buyer's situation and on how much the buyer and the buyer's agent knew about the seller's needs before drafting the offer.

The Possession and Occupancy section may need fine tuning, particularly if the buyer is selling a house and the seller is purchasing another home that's occupied. Occupancy dates will have to be staggered to allow each homeowner time to move out of the old home and into the new one. For instance, if you've agreed to give the seller of the home you're purchasing two days after close of escrow to move but you can't close that escrow until the one on your current home closes, then you will need to ask the buyer to allow you to stay in possession of your current home for at least three days after it closes (and this will give you just one day to move). Sellers who stay in possession after the close need to keep their insurance in effect. The new buyer's insurance will cover the dwelling in case of fire, but it will not cover the seller's personal possessions. A "Residential Lease Agreement After Sale" should be made a part of the contract.

Occasionally a seller vacates a house before the close of escrow. This is quite common if the seller has been transferred. A buyer making an offer on a vacant home may request to take possession before the transfer of title, but there are potential problems with early possession, not the least of which is that the buyer may fall out of love with the home and move out before the closing. A seller who permits a buyer to take early occupancy should insist that the buyer carry insurance and that an Interim Occupancy Agreement be part of contract.

It is never advisable for a seller to grant permission for a buyer to do cosmetic or structural work to a house prior to the closing. The buyer may think it's a good idea to do fix-up work while the house is empty, but if the escrow never closes for some unanticipated reason, the buyer will have paid to improve the seller's property. If the escrow doesn't close, the seller may be stuck with putting a half-painted house (or one that's painted atrociously) back on the market.

Personal property that's included in the sale should be sold "as is" if it's old or no longer under a manufacturer's warranty. Any known defects should be disclosed in writing to the buyer.

Offers to purchase are often written hastily and without complete information. For instance, the buyer may not know which appliances are included in the sale and which fixtures are excluded. Don't be offended by a request you can't live with—counter it.

Sellers who exclude light fixtures will often offer to provide the buyer with substitutes. Another alternative is to offer a credit in escrow, and let the buyer take responsibility for selecting and replacing the fixtures after closing.

A reminder on the Transfer Disclosure: The buyer has three days after personal delivery of this document to terminate the contract (five days if mailed). Complete the disclosure form and deliver it to the buyer's agent as soon as possible to avoid any last minute hang-ups in the transaction. Any serious defect that you do not intend to correct before the close of escrow should be listed separately in the purchase agreement or counteroffer.

Physical inspections of the property are a necessary part of any real estate transaction. Sellers are advised to keep in mind that a property that has been well inspected during the course of the sale is less likely to be the source of a legal dispute afterwards. Encourage the buyer to complete all inspections deemed necessary, but request completion within a reasonable amount of time (within ten to fourteen days of acceptance). If the purchase agreement does not include a clause stating that all contingencies will be removed in writing, add this to the counteroffer if it makes you feel more comfortable.

The Condition of the Property clause includes a seller's warranty regarding the property. Any known defects that will not be corrected by the close of escrow should be disclosed in writing, both in this portion of the purchase contract or counteroffer and in the Transfer Disclosure statement. It should be expressly stated in both documents that the seller does not warrant the condition of any such defective item. Some purchase agreements contain a provision stating that the seller will replace all cracked and broken glass, including shower enclosures, prior to close of escrow. If this is the case and you do not intend to replace all cracked glass (for instance, a tiny crack in a stained glass pane), include this in writing in a counteroffer.

Likewise, a warranty is a part of the Seller Representation clause (Item 21-D). A seller who has knowledge that any notice of the code, ordinance, or regulation violations listed in this clause has been filed against the property should disclose this in writing in a counteroffer and in the Transfer Disclosure statement.

Sellers who have obtained a pre-sale pest control report should ask the buyer to accept that report within several days. If the buyer insists on ordering a termite report, the sellers should limit their liability for pest control corrective work to the amount stipulated in the first report. When the sellers do not have a current pest control report at the time an offer to purchase is made, they should counter with a provision that the sellers will read and approve the new pest control report within several days of receiving it. Alternatively, sellers can limit their liability for pest control work to a specific amount, with any amount over this limit subject to future negotiation.

The Flood Hazard Area Disclosure, Special Studies Zone Disclosure, and Energy Conservation Retrofit clauses should be included in the contract if they apply. If any of these have been initialed and they don't apply, counter that the appropriate clause be deleted from the contract. Agents, particularly if they are working outside of their regular area, may not be aware of local ordinances or the location of flood hazard and special study zones.

If the new Arbitration Notice is not included in the purchase contract, you may want to counter that the Arbitration Supplement-Addendum be made a part of the contract (CAR standard form ARB-11).

Other Terms and Conditions could include a contingency for the buyer's attorney or tax advisor to approve the contract. Such a contingency should be satisfied within a short period of time (within five days of acceptance). If the buyer has requested a final walk-through inspection prior to the close of escrow, be sure that the contingency is specific and doesn't give the buyer a way out of the contract at the last minute. The final walk-through should be for the express purpose of assuring the buyer that the property has been maintained in the same condition it was in when the offer to purchase was made. If the seller agreed in the purchase contract to complete work on the property by close of escrow, the final walk-through serves to verify that the work is complete. This final inspection should be completed a specific number of days before the closing, and the buyer's approval should not be unreasonably withheld. The seller should have the opportunity to correct any defects that become apparent during the walk-through before the closing.

An offer to purchase that is contingent upon the sale of another property should include a release clause to protect the seller. The time period on the release clause is negotiable, but seventy-two hours is customary. The release clause states that until the buyer removes the contingent sale contingency from the contract, the seller will continue to offer the property for sale. When the seller receives another acceptable offer, it will be accepted in back-up position, and the seller will notify the first buyer in writing that the contingent sale contingency must be removed within seventy-two hours. If the buyer is unable or unwilling to do this, the first contract becomes null and void and the back-up offer is elevated to primary position by written notification from the seller to the second buyer.

In addition to the release clause, a contingent sale offer should define time periods for two specific areas of performance. The first is the time period for the buyer's property to sell. The second is for the close of escrow. By stating a date within which the other property is to be sold, the sellers retain more control. If, at the end of this time period, the buyer's home is not sold, the sellers can either void the contract or grant an extension. Sellers can also request that their agent approve the list price of the buyer's property and that the property be listed (ideally including multiple listing exposure) within five or seven days of acceptance.

The Agent Confirmation clause can be countered, if necessary. The buyer's agent will usually call the sellers' agent before writing an offer to find out what sort of agency relationship the sellers have with the agent. If this information was not available in advance and the agency relationships checked on the offer are not accurate, the correct information can be included in a counteroffer.

COUNTEROFFERS

A counteroffer should be made in writing, on a separate form, such as the one included in this chapter. This is preferable to modifying and initialing items on the original contract. The sellers' agent will make a notation at the bottom of the original purchase agreement, above the sellers' acceptance signature, indicating that "a counteroffer is attached and made a part of the contract." When the sellers sign the purchase agreement, they are accepting the buyer's terms and conditions except those that are modified in the counteroffer.

The date of the original offer, the property address, and the names of the buyers and sellers should appear at the top of the counteroffer. The individual items to be modified are listed in the body of the counteroffer, with each change numbered and made in reference to a specific item on the original offer.

Any change requested to the terms proposed in the original offer creates a new offer that requires acceptance by the other party. The counteroffer is not legally binding and can be withdrawn by the party making it at any time up until it's signed by the other party and the signed acceptance is delivered back to the party making the counteroffer. A specific time period for acceptance should be stipulated in

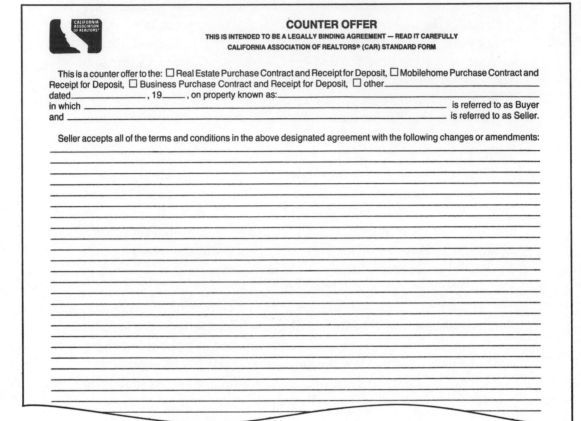

COUNTER OFFER

THIS IS INTENDED TO BE A LEGALLY BINDING AGREEMENT — READ IT CAREFULLY

CALIFORNIA ASSOCIATION OF REALTORS® (CAR) STANDARD FORM

This is a counter offer to the: ☐ Real Estate Purchase Contract and Receipt for Deposit, ☐ Mobilehome Purchase Contract and Receipt for Deposit, ☐ Business Purchase Contract and Receipt for Deposit, ☐ other_____
dated_____ , 19_____ , on property known as:_____
in which _____ is referred to as Buyer
and _____ is referred to as Seller.

Seller accepts all of the terms and conditions in the above designated agreement with the following changes or amendments:

the counteroffer, after which the counter will become null and void if it's not accepted. Twenty-four hours is usually sufficient, unless the other party is out of town or somehow unable to respond within that time.

Until a counteroffer is signed by the buyer and delivered back to the seller, the seller can accept another offer. The delivery aspect is very important. A buyer's signature is not binding on a counteroffer until the signed counter is *delivered* back to the seller. To avoid any confusion, it's best to make specific arrangements to have the delivery made to the seller in person. It is also a good idea to have the seller sign for receipt of the ratified counteroffer so that there is no misunderstanding about whose offer takes priority should another offer be presented during the time that a counteroffer is outstanding.

There is no limit to how many times buyers and sellers can counter back and forth. If there's more than one counteroffer, number each one and note at the bottom, above the acceptance section, that counter-

The Seller reserves the right to continue to offer the herein described property for sale and accept any offer acceptable to Seller at anytime prior to personal receipt by Seller or _____ , Seller's authorized agent, of a copy of this counter offer, duly accepted and signed by Buyer. Unless this counter offer is accepted in this manner on or before _____ , 19_____ at_____ AM/PM, it shall be deemed revoked and deposit shall be returned to the Buyer, Seller's acceptance of another offer shall revoke this counter offer.
Receipt of a copy hereof is hereby acknowledged.

Dated _____ 19_____   Seller_____

Time _____   Seller_____

☐ The undersigned Buyer hereby accepts the above counter offer, or
☐ The undersigned Buyer hereby accepts the above counter offer with the following changes or amendments:
_____
_____
_____
_____
_____

Unless the above is accepted on or before _____ , 19_____ at _____ AM/PM, it shall be deemed revoked.
Receipt of a copy hereof is hereby acknowledged.

Dated _____ 19_____   Buyer _____

Time _____   Buyer _____

Receipt of signed copy on_____ , 19_____ at _____ AM/PM, by Seller_____
or Seller's authorized Agent_____ is acknowledged.   (Initials)
                              (Initials)

Seller accepts Buyer's changes or amendments to Seller's counter offer and agrees to sell on the above terms and conditions.

Dated _____ 19_____   Seller_____

Time _____   Seller_____

NO REPRESENTATION IS MADE AS TO THE LEGAL VALIDITY OF ANY PROVISION OR THE ADEQUACY OF ANY PROVISION IN ANY SPECIFIC TRANSACTION. A REAL ESTATE BROKER IS THE PERSON QUALIFIED TO ADVISE ON REAL ESTATE AND ON BUSINESS TRANSACTIONS. IF YOU DESIRE LEGAL ADVISE CONSULT YOUR ATTORNEY.

This form is available for use by the entire real estate industry.
The use of this form is not intended to identify the user as a
REALTOR®. REALTOR® is a registered collective membership
mark which may be used only by real estate licensees who are
members of the NATIONAL ASSOCIATION OF REALTORS®
and who subscribe to its Code of Ethics.

To order contact — California Association of Realtors®
525 So. Virgil Ave., Los Angeles, California 90020
Copyright© 1986, California Association of Realtors®

CO-14

OFFICE USE ONLY

Reviewed by Broker or Designee _____

DATE_____

EQUAL HOUSING
OPPORTUNITY

SF-A7-SF

offer number two (three, four, etc.) is attached and made a part of the contract.

Sellers often wonder whether it's worthwhile to counter an offer that seems ridiculously low. It is advisable to make a counteroffer to any offer from qualified buyers, even one that's on the low side. Some people need to bargain, or at least be able to justify to themselves that they tried, in order to feel good about their home purchase.

NEGOTIATION STRATEGIES
Consummating a real estate transaction depends on maintaining open communication between the buyer, the seller, and their respective agents. Contrary to the old school of thought which advocated adversarial negotiations based on attempts by each party to extract major

concessions from the other, the current consensus is that a spirit of honest and enthusiastic cooperation usually yields the best results.

This doesn't mean that a buyer shouldn't try to obtain a property for the lowest price possible. And sellers will certainly want to sell for the highest price obtainable. Although it may seem that buyers and sellers have conflicting interests, at least as far as the purchase price is concerned, both parties are definitely working toward the common goal of completing a house sale.

Some buyers and sellers have an aversion to bargaining and use a take it or leave it approach. Principals who are so inclined need to have their agents talk with those of the other party to determine if this straightforward approach will receive a positive reception. Some buyers and sellers feel a need to test the other party to see if there's any flexibility in price. If the sellers' agents feel their clients will counter any offer that's for less than the list price, the buyers are better off offering less than their best price initially so that they have some room for upward movement when the sellers counter back with a higher price. That is unless there are several competing offers, in which case sincere buyers should make their very best offer at the outset.

The most important part of the negotiation process is to keep the momentum going. Lethargy or game-playing on the part of either party can result in a stalled transaction. If, after several rounds of counter-offers, it looks as if the buyers and sellers are stuck at prices that aren't too far apart, one approach that often works is to "split the difference" between the last two prices proposed. Settling on a compromise price can make both parties feel they're coming out ahead.

Don't expect the agents to know what price the other party will accept. Buyers and sellers frequently don't know themselves what price they'll be willing to accept until they're well into the negotiation process. There's much more to selling a house than agreeing on price, and often the other components of the purchase contract will be so desirable that a party will accept a price higher or lower than even they anticipated. For example, suppose the buyers and sellers haven't reached agreement on price and the sellers let it be known that they might make a price concession if the buyers agree to close escrow quickly. If the buyers are able to meet this condition, a deal can be made at a price that might be quite a bit lower than the sellers' list price.

During your negotiations, remember that buying and selling homes, unlike other business transactions, can be a very emotional process. If you have the opportunity to meet the other party in person before an agreement is finalized, be polite and diplomatic but avoid engaging in direct dialogue about the purchase contract, as this is best left to the agents who will act as your intermediaries.

Making Your Home More Affordable

A low offer may indicate that the buyers cannot afford to pay more, no matter how much they love the house. There are several ways that willing buyers and sellers can work together for a successful transaction in this situation.

A buyer with mechanical skills, for instance, might be willing to purchase the property in "as is" condition with respect to termite work (after reading and approving a pest control report, that is), thereby inducing the sellers, who would normally be paying for this work, to reduce the purchase price by the amount it would have cost them.

A seller can offer to pay all or a portion of the buyer's non-recurring closing costs if the buyer is short on cash but otherwise qualified financially. These costs include such items as loan origination fees, title insurance and escrow fees (in areas where the buyer customarily pays for these), and transfer taxes. The lender will need to agree, since cash credits from the seller to the buyer are sometimes not permitted, particularly if the buyer is to receive cash at the close of escrow. Be sure to check with the lender in advance to avoid any last minute surprises. Also be aware that even if the lender does permit the seller to pay for the buyer's non-recurring closing costs, the lender's appraiser might deem this to be a price concession on the part of the seller and adjust the purchase price accordingly.

Some lenders offer buydown programs which permit a seller to pay a fee to the lender in return for a reduction in the buyer's interest rate on the new home loan for a certain number of years. This makes it easier for the buyer to qualify for the loan, since the initial monthly payments are discounted.

Seller financing is another way to make a home more affordable. Sellers who do not need all the cash proceeds from the sale of their home might offer to carry a first or second loan for the buyer. It is important that seller-assisted financing not inflate the value of the property if the buyer is obtaining a new first loan as a part of the purchase. For instance, if the fair market value of the home is $250,000 and you agree to sell for $260,000 including a seller carry-back second of $30,000, you may run into trouble when the lender of the new first loan is unable to appraise the property for the sale price. If the purchase price is justifiable, you should have no problem.

Multiple and Back-Up Offers

Sellers who list their homes during strong real estate markets may experience the good fortune of receiving multiple offers. Custom varies from area to area as to how multiple offers are presented to the sellers, but they should be handled in such a way as to ensure fairness to all parties and to protect the sellers from inadvertently selling the property to more than one buyer.

The preferred custom is to notify the sellers and each buyer's agent that there are multiple offers. The sellers' agent should refrain from reviewing the terms of each offer before the presentation to ensure confidentiality and fair dealing. If the sellers' listing agent has written an offer for a prospective buyer, the agent's broker should step in to represent the sellers so that the listing agent is not privy to other buyers' offers.

Offers should be presented to the sellers and their agent in private by each buyer's agent. After hearing all offers, the sellers and their agent can confer privately to determine the appropriate course of action.

Since there is only one house to sell and several willing buyers, it's advisable to counter only one offer in writing. Sellers who insist on countering more than one offer should rank them in order of priority and notify each buyer in writing that multiple written counters are being made. For instance, "This is counteroffer B, which is made subject to the collapse of counteroffer A."

Sellers listing a home in an active market, particularly if prices are increasing rapidly, should ensure that they get good market exposure before accepting any offer to purchase. It may be advisable to let the Realtors know, when the property goes on the market, that offers will not be heard for several days (a specific date should be set). This will give agents an opportunity to show the home to their buyers and will maximize the sellers' chances of receiving multiple offers. Multiple offers don't always materialize at the same time, and the first buyer to make an offer is not necessarily the one who will end up with an acceptance.

Joyce Wong saw a house she loved on a Saturday morning and made an offer through her agent for less than the asking price. Since the house was new on the market and Joyce was the first buyer to see it, the sellers countered at full price. Joyce countered the sellers' counter at a compromise price and gave the sellers until Sunday night to decide. A second buyer walked through the open house Sunday afternoon, fell in love with the home, and wrote a full-price offer on the spot. The sellers accepted the second offer and notified Joyce that they rejected her counteroffer. Joyce was furious because she felt the sellers should have given her another opportunity to reconsider before even entertaining another offer. The sellers were under no obligation to do so, since Joyce had rejected their counter. Had Joyce signed the sellers' counter, the house would have been hers.

A back-up offer is an offer that's accepted subject to the collapse of the offer in primary position. It may be one of a number of multiple offers, or it may be an offer that's presented after the seller has already accepted another offer. Remember, *all* offers must be presented to the seller. A back-up offer is negotiated just as if it were a primary offer, but the purchase agreement must contain a clause specifying that it is a back-up offer and subject to the collapse of the primary offer. There is no limit to how many back-up offers you can have, but they must be numbered in order of priority so that there's no confusion or dispute on the part of the buyers. In fairness to the buyers, a back-up offer should contain a provision allowing withdrawal from back-up position at any time prior to written notification of elevation to first position. The buyer's notification of withdrawal should be in writing.

WHEN IS A HOME SOLD?

After the seller has accepted an offer to purchase, the escrow period begins. During this period, which can vary anywhere from two weeks to three months or more (forty-five to sixty days is customary), the property is said to have a pending sale. It is not technically sold until title transfers to the new buyer at the close of escrow.

It is advisable for a seller to continue to show the property to prospective buyers in the hopes of generating a back-up offer, at least until inspection and buyer's loan prequalification contingencies have been satisfied. When another buyer's agent calls about the home, the seller should inform the agent that an offer has been accepted but that there are contingencies and the property is available for showing. A seller who has accepted an offer contingent upon the sale of another property should encourage showings until the other property has sold and the buyers have removed that contingency.

Many sellers make the mistake of telling prospective buyers or their agents that their home is sold when in fact they are still in the midst of negotiating a purchase contract. A sale is not pending until the purchase agreement and all counteroffers have been fully signed and accepted by all parties involved. Rumors spread fast within the real estate community, and the last thing sellers want is to have local agents think their home is sold when it's not.

CONTRACT CONTINGENCIES

A clause stating that "time is of the essence" is a part of most residential real estate purchase agreements. If it doesn't exist in the preprinted contract it can be added in an addendum or counteroffer (see paragraph number nineteen of the CAR Real Estate Purchase Contract and

Receipt for Deposit). This phrase means that the parties agree that timely performance is an important part of the agreement.

All contingencies in the purchase agreement should have time periods, specified in writing, within which they are to be approved or disapproved by the buyer or seller. Confusion often arises concerning precisely what date a contingency is to be removed from the contract. To arrive at the correct date, do not count the acceptance date as day one; day one is the day following the acceptance date. Do count the last day (day ten, for instance, if a contingency is to be removed ten days following acceptance). If the final day falls on a Sunday or government holiday, the contingency removal is due the following day. It's preferable to use calendar days, rather than business or working days, for contingency time periods. Ask your agent to prepare a summary of the contract contingency dates and forward a copy to the other agent to ensure that everyone involved in the transaction is operating on the same time schedule.

Ideally, all contingencies (and waivers of contingencies) should be removed from the contract in writing. If this condition is not a part of your contract and you have any question regarding the status of a contingency, ask your agent to address your concern in a letter or inquiry to the other party or agent. If written approval or disapproval of contingencies is a part of your contract and a contingency is due but has not yet been removed, have your agent notify the other party in writing that either the contingency should be removed or a reasonable extension requested within twenty-four hours.

COPING WITH BUYER'S AND SELLER'S REMORSE

Buyers and sellers may experience a peculiar reaction during the course of a real estate transaction. It's called remorse, and it usually sets in just after you've entered into a purchase agreement. The best thing to do if you start feeling you've made the wrong decision is to realize that this sort of an emotional reaction is natural and will pass.

Some sellers suffer a psychological jolt the first time they see a "for sale" sign in front of their home. Or they feel resentful when they find a stack of Realtors' cards on the coffee table. This is understandable, since your home is both your haven and an extension of your identity. The selling process can seem like an intrusion on sacred territory.

Buyers' remorse can set in as early as the first time buyers see a house they really want to buy. Don't be surprised if you hear yourself saying, "I'm really not interested in this house," even though you've looked for months and have finally found the home of your dreams.

CONTINGENCY REMOVAL

CALIFORNIA ASSOCIATION OF REALTORS® (CAR) STANDARD FORM

This addendum is a part of the Real Estate Purchase Contract and Receipt for Deposit dated _____

between _____ (Buyer)

and _____ (Seller)

regarding the real property described and _____

_____

The undersigned, hereby waives the following condition(s) _____

_____

_____

_____

_____

and agrees to purchase the property in accordance with all the other terms and conditions.

The undersigned acknowledges receipt of a copy hereof.

DATED: _____

BUYER _____

BUYER _____

RECEIPT BY SELLER

Receipt of a copy of the above waiver is hereby acknowledged.

DATED: _____

SELLER _____

SELLER _____

OFFICE USE ONLY

Reviewed by Broker or Designee _____

Date _____

SF-Jan-88

FORM CRCR-11

A skillful and experienced agent will recognize early signs of remorse and be able to help you through a period of indecision without making you feel pressured.

TERMITE INSPECTIONS, REPORTS, AND REPAIRS

LET'S TALK TERMITE

Obtaining a Structural Pest Control Report, better known as a termite report, is one of the most universally disliked, but necessary, aspects of a residential real estate transaction. Buyers and sellers have expressed dissatisfaction with the termite inspection process in California because frequently the company that inspects a property and issues the report is the same company that performs the required corrective work.

There is a common misconception that a termite report is concerned only with determining whether a property is infested with termites. In fact, a termite report documents the presence or absence of infestation or infection by any wood destroying organisms, including dry rot, fungus, beetles, and other wood pests, as well as termites.

California state law does not require that a termite report be completed when a home is sold, but most lenders require a report before they will approve a new loan. And many lenders insist that corrective work specified in the report be completed before the close of escrow. Termite reports have, therefore, become an integral part of a home sale in California, and it's generally thought to be good protection for the buyer to require that the property be inspected by a licensed structural pest control operator and that corrective work be completed as part of the property transfer agreement.

Deciding when to order the report is a subject of debate. A seller listing an older home is advised to have the property inspected by a licensed structural pest control operator prior to listing or as soon after as possible. A caution regarding the pre-sale inspection, however, is that it can become outdated if the home doesn't sell within a reasonable period of time. Ask the termite inspector to put in writing how long the report and price estimates are good for and what the cost of a reinspection report would be.

In most parts of the state, it's customary for a buyer to ask the seller to pay for or complete structural pest control corrective work as part of the property sale agreement. Sellers who order a pre-sale inspection report can make this a part of the purchase agreement and ask the buyers to accept it. If the buyers elect to obtain their own structural pest control report on the property, the sellers will at least have a report that can be referred to in the contract and can limit their liability to the amount stated in the original report.

Sellers who do not order a pre-sale report are advised to make their acceptance of an offer contingent upon approving a report within several days of receiving one. Sellers who agree to provide a buyer with a termite clearance (a certification that the property is free and clear of infestation) without having a concrete dollar amount for required repair work are signing the equivalent of a blank check. Be sure to confirm and approve the amount required for structural pest control work before you agree to pay for the work.

Termite inspectors and companies are licensed by the state of California, which means that their activities are subject to specific rules and regulations. In addition, state law requires the seller or the seller's agent to provide the buyer with a copy of a termite report on the property "as soon as practicable" before close of escrow. Legislation regarding the termite inspection industry is constantly being amended to reflect current consumer needs, and the Structural Pest Control Board is available to hear consumer complaints.

How to Select a Reputable Termite Company

Selecting the right termite company is a bit like choosing the right real estate agent. If you were pleased with the company that inspected your home when you purchased it, call them to complete a pre-sale inspection report. Be wary of using an out-of-the-area company that might not be familiar with local conditions. Once you've settled on a company, call the Structural Pest Control Board in Sacramento, which will look up background information on companies, including complaint history, free of charge.

When you call to order an inspection, specifically request that the termite report differentiate between wood destroying infestation, infection, and damage that *currently exists* in the house, as opposed to conditions *deemed likely* to lead to structural pest control problems in the future. If the termite inspection company does routine structural pest control repair work, ask for an itemized repair estimate. This will be important should you decide to have other contractors complete the termite repair work. You may, in this case, need to have the original termite inspection company return to reinspect the property after the corrective work has been completed. If the original termite inspection company gave cost estimates as a part of the original inspection or thereafter, this company is required by law to complete a reinspection of the property, even if they do not perform the corrective work, as long as the reinspection is ordered within four months of the original inspection. The company can charge no more for the reinspection than was charged for the original inspection.

How to Read a Termite Report

There are four basic parts to a termite inspection report. The first is a code section itemizing structural pest control problems. The nine categories of the code are: S – Subterranean Termites, K – Dry-wood Termites, F – Fungus or Dry Rot, B – Beetles-Other Wood Pests, FG – Faulty Grade Levels, EC – Earth-wood Contacts, Z – Dampwood Termites, SL – Shower Leaks, CD – Cellulose Debris, EM – Excessive Moisture Condition, IA – Inaccessible Areas, and FI – Further Inspection Recommended. Next to each code is a box which is checked if the problem was found at the property.

The second part of the report lists which areas of the structure were inspected. This is usually followed by a statement noting where on the structure the inspector posted an inspection tag and whether other structural pest control tags (dated within the last two years) were found.

A licensed pest control operator is required by law to post an inspection tag (and a completion tag, if the company does the repair work). The tags are posted either at the entrance to the attic or subarea or in the garage and will include the name of the inspection company, the date of the inspection, and a statement that the tag is not to be removed.

The third part of the inspection report consists of a diagram of the structure and a narrative description of the findings and recommendations for correcting the structural pest control defects. Each numbered or lettered finding in the narrative description will be noted on the diagram in the approximate location where the condition was found. A termite company will customarily not inspect inaccessible areas (for instance, areas behind finished walls) that do not show any outward signs of infestation or infection.

Finally, if the inspection company is in the business of correcting structural pest control defects, an itemized cost estimate of recommended repairs should be included as a part of the report. If an itemized cost estimate is not automatically included, request it. Each numbered item from the narrative description and diagram will have a corresponding price quote for correcting the problem.

Call the inspector who examined the property for a complete

explanation if you have any questions. Watch out for statements that say "if additional damage is found during the course of completing corrective work, a supplemental bill will be issued." An itemization of the costs of repair work should be complete and not open-ended. Insist that the termite company quote you a firm price before you authorize any work.

Sometimes a termite company will find defects but suggest that another type of tradesperson (such as a plumber or tiler) do the work. The report may suggest that the homeowner consult the appropriate tradespeople for bids. Until you have obtained a bid for this work, you will not know the full extent of your termite liability.

WHO PAYS FOR WHAT?

The person obtaining the inspection report usually pays the cost of the initial inspection, although one party can agree to reimburse the other if this is negotiated as a part of the purchase agreement. Termite companies often require payment for the inspection before issuing a written report. The cost of an inspection and report varies, but usually ranges from $100 to $130 for a structure of 3,000 square feet or less.

The seller usually pays to correct both the conditions that led to and the damage caused by active infestation and infection. The buyer usually takes responsibility for any work recommended to correct conditions that are deemed likely to lead to infestation or infection in the future. The rationale behind this sharing of responsibility is that sellers should be liable for correcting problems that developed during their period of ownership and buyers should take care of problems that may develop after purchase.

INACCESSIBLE AREAS AND FURTHER INSPECTIONS

A recommendation for further inspection signifies that the termite report is not complete. It's advisable, in most cases, to obtain a complete inspection, because if a further inspection is not ordered at the time it's recommended, the termite company won't take responsibility for subsequent damage or infestation that might be discovered in the uninspected area.

The CAR Purchase Contract and Receipt for Deposit makes a specific suggestion on how the payment for further inspections should be handled if they are recommended in the termite report (see Section 21-E of the CAR Purchase Contract included in Chapter 7). If the buyer requests that the further inspection be made, it's done at the buyer's expense. If infestation, infection, or damage is discovered, the seller pays to correct the condition plus the cost of entering and closing the inaccessible areas. If no infestation, infection, or damage is found, the buyer pays the cost of entering and closing the areas.

A seller should require that a buyer deposit funds with the termite company to cover opening and closing inaccessible areas before the additional inspections are ordered. If the transaction is terminated, the seller could otherwise have difficulty collecting this money directly from the buyer. Also, it should be a condition of the purchase agreement that both buyers and sellers read and approve all termite reports that were not available at the time the purchase contract was negotiated, including supplemental reports issued following inspections of inaccessible areas.

A word of caution about the recommendation for further inspections. A termite inspector will not automatically complete a further inspection, as it will usually involve defacing a homeowner's property to some extent. The inspector will want the homeowner's permission first, which is understandable. However, if the owner is at home during the inspection, the inspector should inform the owner that further inspections are indicated and explain what will be involved. If the owner authorizes the work on the spot and the inspector does not need specialized equipment to complete the further inspection, it should be done at that time. A further inspection which requires the inspector to return to the property on a separate occasion will usually involve an additional fee. A seller who is home during the initial inspection and is not informed that further inspections are necessary should discuss this with the termite company if the subsequent inspection report includes recommendations for further inspections which will only be completed by request and at additional expense.

THE PROS AND CONS OF GETTING A SECOND TERMITE REPORT

There are several reasons why a buyer or seller might want to obtain a second, or even third, termite report. A buyer could have had a previous bad experience with the termite company that has issued a current report on the seller's home. Or the buyer may have been advised to get a second opinion, regardless of who completed an inspection report for the seller. The sellers could question the accuracy of the first report, in which case they might ask a second company to inspect the home.

When ordering an additional report, keep in mind that all termite reports obtained during the past two years must be delivered to the buyer, even any that you dispute. Full disclosure is required by law, and it's good practice for sellers to make all termite reports, no matter how old, available to buyers.

Also, be aware that the termite inspection process is somewhat subjective. One inspector may believe that a damaged piece of wood is still serviceable, while another might call for its complete replacement. Nonetheless, two termite reports on the same house should reflect similar findings regarding the presence of structural pest control damage, infestation, and infection. Large discrepancies need to be brought to the attention of the companies that completed the reports.

When sellers have an existing report and the buyers obtain a second opinion that reveals additional damage which was not itemized in the first report, the sellers should meet with their initial inspector at the property. Similarly, sellers who purchased their home within the last year and were issued a termite clearance at that time should have a serious discussion with their termite company if a new inspection report reveals a large amount of pest control damage that could not possibly have occurred within one year. Termite inspectors are licensed by the state of California and if a licensed structural pest control operator did not complete the job according to the law, the cost of remedying the problem should not be the homeowner's responsibility. Call the Pest Control Board or a knowledgeable real estate attorney if you are concerned about damage that might have been overlooked. Although consumers are entitled to expect some consistency between the findings of two or more current termite reports on the same home, the recommendations on how to correct the defects will often vary from one company to the next, as will cost estimates for repairs.

Structural pest control reports become a part of the public record, and anyone can obtain copies of inspection reports and notices of completion that were filed on a property within the past two years by making a written request to the Structural Pest Control Board and paying a nominal fee.

How to Interpret Primary and Secondary Recommendations
Often a single termite report will contain both a primary and a secondary recommendation for how to remedy a specific problem. The primary recommendation is the preferred method of repair; however, the secondary recommendation will be adequate for the purpose of issuing a notice of completion stating that the property is free and clear of active infestation.

Consult with an independent licensed contractor to determine if the primary recommendation is realistic or if it's an overassessment of what's necessary. A secondary recommendation, on the other hand, may be satisfactory in terms of obtaining a termite clearance but might not be a long-term solution to a pest control problem.

Normally, the primary recommendation is the more expensive; however, buyers should be aware that a secondary recommendation may require additional repairs in the future (at the buyer's expense), whereas a primary recommendation will often be a permanent solution to the problem. For instance, a wood retaining wall with earth-to-wood contact might exhibit some fungus damage but still be serviceable if chemical treatment is administered. In this case, chemical treatment would be a secondary recommendation.

The primary recommendation would be to tear out the existing wall and install an engineered concrete retaining wall in its place. This solution would effectively remove the earth-to-wood contact as well as take care of the existing infestation problem. The cost differential between these two procedures is significant. Whether primary or secondary recommendations are accepted can become a negotiable issue between buyers and sellers.

> Sam and Teresa Watkins accepted a secondary recommendation to treat a fungus-damaged deck chemically when they purchased their home. Less than a year later, Sam was transferred out of state and the home had to be sold. The buyers made an offer conditioned upon Sam and Teresa's providing a current termite report and a pest control clearance. The new termite report called for total replacement of the deck, as it was now damaged beyond repair; no secondary recommendation was made. Sam Watkins complained to the termite inspector but to no avail. The chemical treatment had arrested the fungus deterioration but scattered pockets of dry rot were now evident throughout the deck, including the support posts. The only way for Sam and Teresa to provide a clearance for the buyers was to have the deck torn down and rebuilt at considerable expense.

SCHEDULING TERMITE WORK

Scheduling termite repair work requires that the seller (and buyer, if there is a pending sale on the property) sign a Work Authorization form. Normally the termite company will bill the escrow company if there is a pending sale and will receive payment from the seller's proceeds at or after the close of escrow. If the job is sizable (in excess of $5,000, or so), however, the termite company may require partial payment in advance.

It's important in active markets to schedule termite inspections and repairs well in advance so the work can be completed by close of escrow. This is particularly true if a termite clearance is a requirement of the buyer's lender. Some lenders will permit escrow to close without the termite work being completed. The lender will usually make it a condition of closing that the termite work be completed within ninety days following the close date. In addition, the lender may require that excess funds be left in an escrow account until the termite work is finished (usually one and one-half or two times the cost of the repair work). The rationale behind this requirement is that if extra money is held, the termite work will be completed in a timely fashion. It's usually the seller who is required to leave the extra money in escrow pending completion of termite work on the property, although this is also negotiable.

One advantage to having termite work completed after the close of escrow is that, while there is some inconvenience in having work done on a home after taking possession, at least then the buyer is in a position to supervise the work. After all, the buyer has to live with the termite company's work in the future, not the seller.

> Fran Goldberg and her sister Carol bought an older house that needed a lot of work. They negotiated to have the seller pay for the termite work, which was considerable, and since the seller had already vacated the property, they scheduled the work to be done before the close of escrow. Imagine how devastated Fran and Carol were when their Realtor took them by the house to measure for drapes and they discovered the termite contractors had demolished the wrong bathroom: the only decent room in the house. The termite company did take responsibility for their mistake and retiled the bathroom, but there was no way to salvage the irreplaceable vintage tile.

HAVING TERMITE WORK COMPLETED BY OTHER CONTRACTORS
Occasionally a seller will prefer to contract termite work out to other professionals rather than have the termite company complete the required repairs. This can result in a savings to the seller. Sometimes the company that issues the inspection report is not in the business of repairing structural pest defects. In active markets, the termite company that performs the initial inspection on the property may be too busy to complete the repair work prior to close of escrow. Sometimes a termite company known for performing competent inspections does not have a good reputation for the quality of their repair work. In either case, a homeowner might prefer to use other contractors to complete the repairs.

Contractors should provide the homeowner with firm written bids for the work to be performed and obtain city building permits when necessary. All permits taken out to correct structural pest control defects should be signed off by the city building inspector before the contractors are paid. The homeowner will want to keep copies of all permits on file. After the work is completed, the homeowner needs to have the property reinspected by a licensed pest control operator in order for a notice of completion to be issued.

Occasionally, sellers will complete items on a termite report that do not require special expertise. One repair that's frequently performed by homeowners is removal of cellulose debris, which is nothing more than scraps or pieces of wood found in the substructure of the building. Cellulose debris is of concern to termite inspectors since it can provide a nesting site for termites. Homeowners will often hire a handyman to complete other recommended repairs that do not require the skill of a licensed contractor or building permits.

One benefit of hiring a termite company or licensed contractor to complete structural pest control repair work is that both are licensed by the state. If there is a problem with the corrective work after the close of escrow, the buyer will have recourse against the contractor. Make sure, as a seller, that you are not responsible for correcting future structural pest defects that arise as a result of shoddy work completed by unlicensed contractors. Remember also that even if a homeowner hires licensed contractors to complete termite repairs, only a termite company can apply chemicals for treatment of infestation or infection.

Take special care in selecting a company to complete fumigation of a property. Since tenting a structure can result in damage to the roof, a termite company will usually require that the homeowner sign a hold-harmless clause which states that the termite company will not be held liable for inadvertent damage to the structure or landscaping.

THE NOTICE OF COMPLETION

After the termite company has completed the work authorized by the homeowner, a notice of completion is issued. Formally known as the Standard Notice of Work Completed and Not Completed, this form refers to the original inspection report by number, date, and registration stamp number; it lists the repair recommendations completed by the company (as numbered in the original inspection report), as well as those not completed. The total cost of the repairs will also appear on the notice of completion.

When some of the items are handled by other contractors, the notice of completion should indicate the items, by number, that were "completed by others" in the section entitled Recommendations Not Completed by This Firm. If all the work recommended in the original inspection report has been completed, this should be indicated in a statement that says the property is now free of evidence of active infestation or infection.

Sellers who complete all the recommended structural pest control work themselves will not receive a notice of completion from a termite company. If, however, the termite company that originally inspected the property included repair cost estimates, the seller can order a reinspection report from the same company anytime within four months of the original report.

In order to issue a notice of completion, a termite company must first have issued an inspection report on the property. Keep this in mind if you ask a second termite company for a bid to complete the work recommended in another company's report. If you want the second company to do the work, be sure that company issues its own inspection report on the property. Otherwise, it will not be able to issue a notice of completion when the work is completed.

Some termite companies will guarantee their repair work, usually for a period of one year. They will not, however, guarantee work done by others. This is why it's important for a seller to use a licensed contractor with a good reputation for customer service if some or all of the termite work is to be completed by someone other than the termite company.

After the notice of completion is signed by the buyer and seller, the escrow company releases payment to the termite company. Once in a while, there are excess funds left after the termite company is paid. These funds are normally released to the party who pays for the structural pest control repairs; confirmation of this should be made in writing and signed by both the buyers and the sellers.

HANDLING GRIEVANCES

Occasionally, two termite reports will differ considerably in their findings. Alternatively, a homeowner might take issue with a specific finding contained in an inspection report or dispute a recommendation for correcting a defect or be dissatisfied with the manner in which corrective work was completed. The homeowner's primary recourse is to discuss the matter with the termite inspector or the owner of the termite company. In California, the Structural Pest Control Board regulates all licensed pest control operators. Serious disputes that cannot be settled directly should be brought to the attention of this board. If the board is unable to mediate a complaint, contact the Better Business Bureau or consult a real estate attorney. A two-year statute of limitations applies to all inspection reports and notices of completion. This means that a complaint must be filed with the board within two years of the inspection or notice of completion date. Termite problems that develop after the date of inspection are not the responsibility of the termite inspection company.

PROTECT YOUR INVESTMENT

Prudent homeowners will have their property reinspected by a reliable structural pest control operator every two years so that there are no big surprises in store when it comes time to sell. Pest control problems often cost less to repair if they're detected and remedied in the early stages. The cost of an inspection report is minimal compared to the potential expense of ignoring a major defect.

Many buyers feel it's a waste of money to have a newly constructed home inspected for structural pest infestation. Again, the cost is minimal compared to possible consequences. Be aware that requirements of the Structural Pest Control Act differ from some modern building code requirements.

Even if there is no active infestation, the buyer of a newly constructed home should be made aware of conditions that may lead to infestation problems. Cellulose debris, for instance, is commonly found under new homes. It is also possible that the building materials could have been infested before construction, particularly by dry wood termites. A new construction site could require chemical treatment for the control of subterranean termites that are frequent inhabitants of the soils of Northern California.

CHAPTER 9

PHYSICAL INSPECTIONS

THE PHYSICAL INSPECTION

A physical inspection is always necessary, regardless of how much you think you know about the structural integrity of a house. Even building contractors buying homes for themselves may suffer from myopia when it comes to detecting defects.

Take the case of Randy Capp, a licensed contractor with years of experience building new homes, who purchased an older home to renovate for profit without obtaining an independent inspection. When Randy sold the home, the buyer's inspector recommended that the local utility company check the gas furnace since it appeared to be old and emitted a peculiar odor. The utility company shut the furnace down because it was cracked and leaking hazardous fumes. Randy never personally occupied the home and was unaware of this defective condition but, since he contracted to sell a house equipped with an operative furnace, he was obliged to install a new one before close of escrow at his expense.

Anyone who wants to buy badly enough can develop blinders to virtually any potential house problem. Don't make the mistake of waiving your rights to inspect a property just for the sake of relieving the anxiety of not knowing where you'll be moving to next. You won't be doing the seller a favor, either, if your folly results in a lawsuit regarding defects that might have been discovered ahead of time.

Many buyers think they are protected if a current termite report has been completed on the property. Keep in mind that a termite report is limited to inspection for wood destroying organisms only, and may give little information regarding the condition of the roof, drainage system, and foundation, not to mention the mechanical systems of the home. A general physical inspection is a professional evaluation of the house and its major systems. Although a decade ago general home inspections were completed in less than 2 percent of home sale transactions, they are now done over 90 percent of the time. Home prices have escalated rapidly in California, and defects in any of the major components of a house can be expensive to repair.

Sometimes a termite report will mention conditions that are outside of its specific jurisdiction. For instance, if the termite inspector sees cracks in a foundation, a roof that shows weathering, or a potential drainage problem, a disclaimer may be contained in the report suggesting that the buyer seek the advice of the appropriate professional. Such items should be reviewed by the buyers. Don't, however, count on a termite report to pinpoint problems that are not the direct responsibility of the structural pest control inspector.

Even if you're purchasing a newly constructed home, have it inspected by a general building inspector. One of the difficulties inherent in new homes is that they have not weathered the years, so it's difficult to predict if problems will arise in the future. One advantage of buying an older home is that it has been put to the test of time.

When inspecting a new home, make the plans, soils report, engineering calculations, city inspector reports, and any other relevant documentation available to the building inspector. The inspector's review of these documents should reveal if the home has been properly constructed and if the removal of the inspection contingency needs to be conditioned upon the builder's completing or remedying unacceptable conditions. In addition, have the general building inspector help to complete a punch list of items that the builder must attend to before the close of escrow.

There are rare instances when a buyer will not be able to include a physical inspection contingency in the offer to purchase. Estate (probate) and foreclosure sales are usually "as is" sales and are exempted from the Transfer Disclosure requirement. When purchasing an estate or foreclosure property, it's imperative to have the property thoroughly inspected by both a termite inspector and a general building inspector. In a normal home sale, the physical inspection is usually ordered by the buyer after the purchase offer has been signed by both buyer and seller. If the offer to purchase an estate or foreclosure property must be "as is," without any contingencies, have the property inspected in advance of presenting the purchase contract.

The general inspection clause of the CAR purchase contract states that the inspection is to be done at the buyer's expense. Approval or disapproval of the inspection is at the buyer's discretion, and the buyer agrees to deliver copies of the inspection report to the seller. Implicit in this agreement is the notion that the buyer will not unreasonably withhold the approval of this contingency. What this means is that the buyer will not use the inspection contingency as a way to back out of the contract for reasons other than the existence of defects that the seller is unwilling or unable to remedy.

How to Select a General Building Inspector

Home inspectors are not licensed, although there is movement in California in the direction of licensing. Recently, the home inspection business has been flooded with people who have marginal qualifications. Ideally, the general inspector you select should be either an engineer, an architect, or a contractor. When possible, hire an inspector who belongs to one of the home inspection trade organizations. The California Real Estate Inspection Association (CREIA) sets standards for member firms and, on a national level, the American Society of Home Inspectors (ASHI) has developed formal inspection guidelines and a professional code of ethics for its members. Membership to ASHI is not automatic; proven field experience and technical knowledge about structures and their various systems and appliances are a prerequisite.

General home inspections cost between $150 and $400, depending on the inspector and on whether the inspection includes an oral or a written report. It's generally preferable to have a written inspection report, as this may be helpful if you decide to sell the house. Also, if defects are discovered, a written report will provide documentation of the problem for the seller. An oral representation of a defect may not carry the same weight as a written disclosure, so if you select an inspector who only offers oral reports or whose written reports are extremely expensive, ask if mention of significant defects can be made in writing.

Definitely find an inspector who is knowledgeable about local properties and soil conditions. Don't use an inspector from out of the area, and don't hire an inspector who has a vested interest in the property. If you're buying the house with a contractor, have an independent, impartial contractor complete the inspection. The inspector should not be someone you intend to hire to repair any defects that are found or to complete work on the property at some later date.

The Scope of the General Inspection

Before the inspection begins, establish precisely what is to be included in the inspection. A general building inspection should cover the general site; the surrounding topography; sidewalks and streets adjacent to the property; the house exterior; the roof, downspouts, and gutter system; drainage in and around the house; the foundation, including basements and crawl spaces; the interior walls, floors, windows, and doors; the electrical, plumbing, and heating/cooling systems; the appliances; the attic; visible insulation; patios and decks; the fireplace; the garage; health hazards and code violations.

The buyer should accompany the building inspector if possible. This is perhaps the most important aspect of the home buying process, particularly for first-time buyers. Ask questions freely and request an oral summary of the findings at the end of the inspection. Bring along the seller's Transfer Disclosure, a current termite report, and any other reports you have, and ask the inspector to review them with you. Have the inspector pay particular attention to any red flag items noted by the listing or selling agent in the agent inspection portion of the Transfer Disclosure form. For instance, if an agent mentions that there is a crack in the fireplace, find out if the inspector thinks this is a significant defect and if it warrants further inspection by a specialist. If you're buying a newly constructed home and have not ordered a termite report, ask the building inspector if there are indications that a report should be ordered.

Take a note pad to the inspection. One of the major benefits of a thorough inspection is learning precisely what routine maintenance the home will require. Make notes as you follow the inspector around the property.

Buyers purchasing a home long-distance should arrange for a relative or good friend who lives in the area of the home to attend the inspection. If this is not possible, ask your agent to tape record the inspection and send the tape to you along with the written inspection report.

The ideal inspection is one that's conducted in the seller's absence. Sellers who must be present should not intrude. Sellers can also have their agent follow up on the inspection and report back with a summary of the findings.

Buyers should understand, before they embark on a home inspection, that there will be some defects uncovered in almost any home. Have the inspector distinguish between insignificant flaws and major deficiencies. It is important to put the results of the inspection in perspective. A little bit of settling in an older home may be considered routine; settling in a newly constructed home can indicate a bad foundation pour, which may be relatively insignificant, or improperly compacted fill (soil brought into the site in order to alter the ground level), which could be a major problem.

You will usually need the written report as soon as possible, since inspection contingencies are normally removed within the first two weeks after acceptance of a purchase contract. When you receive the report, don't be alarmed to find that it contains many disclaimers.

Inspectors are well aware of their potential liability, and they usually build qualifications into written reports in order to protect themselves. If there is anything you don't understand in the report, call the inspector immediately and ask for clarification. Qualifications in the report that seem unreasonable should be brought to the inspector's attention. Make notes of any such conversations you have with your inspector and, whenever possible, have the inspector respond to your questions in writing.

WHEN TO ORDER ADDITIONAL INSPECTIONS

Any additional inspection recommended in the general report should be ordered and completed before the inspection contingency is removed from the purchase contract. Detection of a suspected defect that is outside the realm of the inspector's expertise or the presence of a pre-disclosed exception to the inspection report are the types of situations where additional reports will be recommended. For example, the report may suggest that the buyer seek the counsel of a licensed roofer, swimming pool inspector, drainage specialist, or soils expert in order to obtain a professional evaluation. Regardless of whether the recommendation is due to a suspected problem or merely a statement that certain systems have not been inspected conclusively, take the advice and follow through with the recommended reports.

Building code violations mentioned in a written inspection report need to be evaluated carefully. Most older homes do not conform to the current building code since code requirements have changed over the years. Sellers are usually not required to bring an older home up to modern code requirements before they sell, however.

If remodeling work has been done on a property, be aware that it may not have been covered by the required building permits. Owners and contractors often elect to bypass the building code process to avoid dealing with the bureaucracy, to save the cost of the permit, or to avoid a property tax reassessment. Lenders have started requesting verification that remodels were completed with permits in place before they will approve a loan. Ask the sellers to provide you with copies of any building permits on the property. If they don't have any and they're unsure if structural improvements to the property were made with permits, check with the city building department.

Most city building departments will allow a homeowner to take out a permit for work that has already been completed (after the fact, so to speak). Keep in mind that in order to obtain final approval from the city on the already-completed renovation, you may have to open walls to verify that plumbing and electrical work was done according to code requirements.

Some code violations present health or safety hazards and should be corrected. Buyers who plan to remodel a home should be aware that they may be required to correct previous code violations.

When ordering additional inspections on the property, make certain in advance that you will receive a report on the condition of the item in question and not merely a bid to replace it. Roofers, for instance, will often provide an estimate to replace an old roof with a new one with no evaluation at all of the existing roof. Roofs, septic systems, private wells, and swimming pools should always be examined by the appropriate qualified professional. There will usually be an additional charge if the location of the septic tank or well is unknown and needs to be determined as part of the inspection process.

Recently the Federal and California state governments have expressed concern about the possibility of exposure to asbestos in the home. Asbestos has been used as both an insulating and a stiffening component in many products: ceiling tiles, sprayed ceilings, furnace and stove insulation, roofing shingles, exterior siding, patching compounds, textured paints, vinyl floor tiles, vinyl sheet flooring, appliances. Contact an asbestos-certified contractor for more information and a bid for proper asbestos removal or treatment if this is a concern to you. Do not attempt to remove asbestos yourself. Without proper handling, tiny asbestos particles will become airborne, creating a serious health hazard. Whether exposure to undisturbed asbestos is a serious health threat is at this point unknown.

Determining if asbestos is present in a product may require chemical analysis, so don't let someone talk you into an expensive removal job without first determining conclusively that the material in question contains a potentially hazardous amount of asbestos. There is currently no requirement for a seller to provide a buyer with an asbestos-free environment, although there has been a move in this direction in the California legislature. A booklet prepared by the U.S. Consumer Product Safety Commission and the Environmental Protection Agency entitled "Asbestos in the Home" is a good source of further information. It is offered for sale by the Superintendent of Documents, U.S. Government Printing Office, Washington, D.C. 20402.

Risk of exposure to radon gas is a concern to homeowners throughout the country, although it appears to be less of a problem in California than elsewhere. Radon is an invisible, odorless, and potentially deadly gas that is emitted from decaying underground uranium. Radon testing has not been standardized, and there is some concern that radon testing scams will become prevalent. Ask your real estate agent and general building inspector whether radon is a problem in your area. If it is, hire only an Environmental Protection Agency-approved tester.

Contact your state radiation-protection agency for a recommendation, or call the nearest EPA regional office and ask for assistance. California's regional EPA office is located at 1200 Sixth Avenue, Seattle, WA 98101. Three informative booklets are available free of charge from the regional EPA office: "A Citizen's Guide to Radon—What It Is and What to Do About It," "Radon Reduction Methods—A Homeowner's Guide," and "Radon Reduction Techniques for Detached Houses."

Although obtaining additional inspections when they are recommended is critical, it is equally important to the successful completion of purchase agreement negotiations to approve or disapprove of all contract contingencies in a timely fashion. If the general inspector recommends a further inspection that cannot be completed prior to the contingency deadline, it's advisable that you remove the general inspection contingency (if you're satisfied with the overall condition of the property) with the qualification that the contingency is being removed subject to the buyer's receiving a satisfactory report on the part of the property that requires further inspection.

A qualified contingency removal might be worded as follows: "Buyer removes inspection contingency, per paragraph 21-A of the purchase agreement, pending acceptable documentation from the local gas company or a licensed heating contractor that the furnace is operable and in safe working order within ten calendar days." This example is for explanatory purposes only.

An additional inspection by a soils or structural engineer will be expensive, often in excess of $1,000. If you're interested in purchasing the home so long as it is in safe condition, but your budget can't absorb the extra $1,000, you might ask the seller to share the expense of further inspection. Most sellers prefer to help with the cost rather than have a buyer terminate a contract.

Don't make the mistake of not ordering a further inspection on the assumption that the expense of repairing a system that breaks down following the close of escrow will automatically be covered by the home protection plan that you and the seller have agreed to purchase. If the seller is aware of any pre-existing conditions in any of the systems or appliances to be covered by a home protection plan, these need to be disclosed to the home protection company at the time the application is made and will not be covered by the protection plan. The sellers are also required to disclose these defects to the buyers and repair them by close of escrow unless the buyers specifically agree in the purchase agreement to accept the defective items in their "as is" condition.

READING AND APPROVING THE TRANSFER DISCLOSURE STATEMENT

Normally the first order of business after entering into a purchase agreement is for the buyers to read and approve the sellers' Transfer Disclosure Statement regarding material facts relating to the property. The Real Estate Transfer Disclosure Statement must be read and approved by the buyers within three days of receipt if the form is hand delivered, or within five days if it's mailed. Make certain that both the listing and selling agents have completed their written agent inspections.

Any inquiries you have about the disclosure statement should be directed to your agent. Buyers and sellers often wonder why real estate agents are so insistent that the questions that come up during the course of a transaction be handled through the agents. Real estate agents are apprehensive about buyers and sellers talking directly to one another about substantive matters because if a question arises involving a condition that may require a material disclosure, the details of the disclosure should be made in writing. Oral disclosures can lead to problems because they are hard to substantiate. The following is an example of how an oral disclosure can result in a costly dispute after the close of escrow. The Real Estate Transfer Disclosure Statement asks sellers to indicate whether the property has a burglar alarm, but does not require the seller to disclose whether the alarm system is leased or owned. Let's say the buyers ask the sellers directly if the system is owned and the sellers answer that it is. If the system is owned, the owners usually have the option of having the alarm ring at a central monitoring station, in which case they pay a monthly service fee. The buyers in our example decide, after they move in, to disconnect the central hook-up; several days later the alarm company arrives to remove the equipment, which in fact the sellers were leasing on a month-to-month basis. The buyers are outraged because the sellers represented to them that the system was owned, and they insist that the sellers purchase a replacement alarm system for them. Be aware that sellers quite often think they own a system when in fact they are leasing it. If the question of who owned the alarm system had been directed to the agents involved, they could have independently verified with the alarm company whether the system was leased or owned and determined the terms on which it could be transferred to the buyers.

OLD REPORTS AND MAINTENANCE RECORDS
Ask the sellers to provide you with all reports, regardless of age, concerning the property. Obtain copies of work contracts, proposals and invoices, or paid receipts for any major work. If major systems such as the furnace, hot water heater, or roof have been recently replaced, ask for copies of warranties and guarantees, and check with the contractor who performed the work to make sure that warranties are

transferable to a new owner. Request that original building plans be left for the buyer at the close of escrow if they exist. They provide important additional documentation about the house and will prove useful if you remodel in the future.

AMENDMENTS TO THE TRANSFER DISCLOSURE

Any material facts about a home that are discovered in the course of the transaction and that might affect a buyer's decision to purchase or influence the price a buyer would be willing to pay for the property must be disclosed in writing. For instance, if a drainage problem that the sellers were unaware of when they listed the property is discovered during the property inspection process, it must be disclosed to the buyer in the form of an addendum to the Real Estate Transfer Disclosure Statement. Any addendum to the Transfer Disclosure institutes a new right of rescission period (three days from receipt if the addendum is hand delivered, or five days from the date of mailing) during which time the buyer has the right to terminate the contract.

It's important to amend the Transfer Disclosure Statement as soon as possible if a previously undisclosed material defect becomes apparent to the sellers or their real estate agent. If the buyer is unwilling or unable to accept the property with the defective condition, it's better for the sellers to have this knowledge sooner rather than later so that they can begin to negotiate a sale with another buyer. It's by far worse to have a buyer rescind the contract at the last minute, not to mention the fact that failure by the sellers or their agent to disclose a known material fact could have serious legal repercussions.

DEALING WITH DEFECTS: RENEGOTIATE OR TERMINATE?

Reading the inspection report on the home you're purchasing or selling can be disheartening. Defects discovered during the inspection process can be dealt with in several ways. The buyers can accept the property with the disclosed faults or can ask the sellers to correct the conditions. Sometimes sellers will feel the request to correct a problem is frivolous or is simply not within their budget; if this is the case, the buyers and sellers should attempt to negotiate an agreement to share the costs.

Renegotiations are bound to be stressful. The sellers may feel they compromised as much as they could during the initial negotiations. The buyers, on the other hand, may already have stretched their dollar as far as possible. Willing parties to a transaction can usually find a way to work out an equitable resolution if a serious defect is uncovered. Sometimes obtaining a second professional opinion or at least several cost estimates for the recommended repair work is all that's necessary.

Sellers should keep in mind that it takes time to put a house back on the market and it's often difficult to rekindle interest in a property that previous buyers have backed out of purchasing. Sellers who have a back-up buyer waiting in the wings are in an enviable position. However, existing inspection reports must be disclosed to future prospective buyers, so if a serious problem exists, it's likely the new buyers will want to have it fixed. Buyers need to weigh the time and energy that will be involved in finding a suitable replacement home if they choose not to go through with an offer to purchase.

A home protection plan purchased by either buyer or seller at any time before the close of escrow will not require an inspection by protection plan company representatives. If the buyer's general building inspector indicates that the major support systems of the home are old, it might be a good idea to sign up for a protection plan if this is not already a part of the purchase contract. Be sure to request a copy of the protection plan policy before escrow closes to make certain that you are covered where you need to be.

WHY NOT SELL "AS IS"?

Many sellers hope to avoid their disclosure responsibilities by listing a home for sale "as is." Yet selling "as is" provides little protection to the sellers when the phrase is used generally, as a catchall clause. In addition, marketing a home for sale "as is" can have a negative impact on prospective buyers who fear that the sellers may have something to hide.

It is acceptable, however, to sell a home with the stipulation that a certain component of the property or an appliance that's included in the sale is being included in "as is" condition. If you know the roof is leaking and you disclose this to a buyer or if you're including the stove but the oven doesn't work and you've informed the buyer in writing of this defect, then selling the property "as is" with respect to these specific defects is fine as long as both parties agree to this in writing.

The primary reason for not selling with a general "as is" clause is that the provision will probably only apply to defects readily observable by the buyer. A defect that's not visibly apparent is not likely to be covered by an "as is" clause. Also, selling "as is" does not relieve the seller of legal responsibility for disclosing known material defects. Withholding such information could be considered fraudulent in a court of law. It's far better to be straightforward regarding known defects rather than to assume an "as is" clause will provide any protection against a buyer's future claim.

This admonition applies to ordinary residential property transfers. Estate (probate) and foreclosure sales are exempt from the Real Estate Transfer Disclosure requirement, and the California statute dictates that these sales are to be "as is" sales. In both cases, the law protects the seller (usually an heir or a financial institution) who has recently acquired the property through adverse circumstances and may have little or no direct information about it.

Discovering Defects After the Close of Escrow

Keep in mind that homes need continual maintenance to function properly. An older home is bound to have some problems, and even new homes built to modern code requirements are not free of flaws. No matter how thorough the inspection process might be, there's always the possibility that an unanticipated breakdown will occur after the close of escrow.

When, you may be asking yourself, does the sellers' responsibility for their previous home end? Unfortunately, there's no clearcut answer to this question. In California, there's an implied seller's warranty that the house being sold is habitable. Presumably, a habitable home has four walls, doors and windows that work, a functioning furnace and hot water heater, a potable water supply, a sanitary waste system, and a roof that doesn't leak, not to mention a sound foundation. Talk to a real estate attorney if you have any questions regarding what sellers are legally responsible for providing to buyers at the close of escrow.

The buyer's first course of action if a major system fails soon after the close and the home protection company refuses to repair it is to seek an amiable mediation with the sellers. The sooner the buyers make their complaint known to the sellers, the better; statutes of limitation on pursuing such claims do apply. If an inquiry doesn't remedy the problem, the buyers should consider sending a formal written claim to the sellers in care of their real estate agent. When all else fails, consult a real estate attorney.

ALL ABOUT FINANCING

Many people complain that the current mortgage market is an indecipherable maze of ARMs, GPMs, GPAMs, SAMs, SEMs, ROLs, and RNGs. Don't let the variety intimidate you; it's not as complicated as it seems. This chapter will decode and demystify the world of home financing so that you can make a sensible home loan selection.

Over 90 percent of all home purchases are made contingent upon the buyer's ability to obtain the appropriate financing. Until the financing is secured, the sale is pending and can't be closed until the lender issues the funding check (usually for at least 80 percent of the purchase price) and the buyers place the cash necessary to cover the down payment plus closing costs into the escrow account.

SHOPPING FOR A LENDER

A customary financing contingency time period is thirty days following acceptance of the purchase contract. This is usually sufficient time to receive formal approval from the lender, but in active real estate markets, a longer time period may be required. Your ability to remove the financing contingency and close the escrow on time will depend on your efforts during the first few days after you enter into a purchase contract. A completed loan application submitted later than five days after acceptance of the purchase contract stands little chance of being approved within the required thirty-day time period.

The most frequent sources of home purchase financing in California are savings and loan companies, commercial banks, mortgage banks, mortgage brokers, and credit unions. Your real estate agent can provide you with rate sheets from various lenders and can make recommendations. Many real estate firms can help you shop for a home loan by using a computerized service, and major metropolitan newspapers usually print a summary of current home loan rates. Keep in mind that any interest rate figures may be a little out of date if the financing markets are active.

Don't overlook business connections when searching for a lender. Talk with a representative from the bank or savings and loan that handles your personal accounts. Associates of businesses with large commercial accounts can often arrange for better-than-market financing, since the bank considers you a valued customer. Employees of banks are usually offered a preferential interest rate or a discount on the loan origination fees. Credit unions sometimes offer their members exceptional programs.

Contact the lender that holds the loan on your current home: you may be able to get a break in the interest rate or loan fees by financing the new home through the same lender. If there is a prepayment penalty on your existing home loan, request that the penalty be waived if you finance through the same lender.

LENDER COMPARISON CHECK LIST

The following questions will help you find the lenders that can best serve your needs.

1. What type of home loan programs are offered? Some lenders offer only adjustable rate loans, while others have both fixed and adjustable. Some lenders that offer fixed loans provide either a fifteen- or thirty-year variety but not both. Since you may be undecided about the type of loan you want, it's important to keep track of which lenders are offering what loan programs.
2. What is the current interest rate? Although this will vary from one loan to another, adjustables usually have the lowest rates *initially.* And the interest rate on a fifteen-year fixed loan is always lower than that on a thirty-year fixed rate loan.
3. What are the loan origination fees? These will also vary according to the loan but adjustables usually have lower start-up fees than fixed rate loans. Most lenders quote these fees as points, with one point equaling 1 percent of the loan amount. Be sure to ask if there are any additional charges for credit reports, property appraisal, or loan processing, which are often quoted in addition to the points.

   The interest rates and points charged by lenders will vary depending on the demand for money. When there is plenty of money to lend and the demand for financing drops, lenders usually offer lower interest rates and loan origination fees than during periods of high demand.
4. When are the loan origination fees paid? Some lenders require as much as $350 at the time the application is submitted to cover the cost of the appraisal and credit report. Other lenders don't

require a dime until the escrow is closed.

5. Are fees refundable if the loan is not approved?

6. What is the Annual Percentage Rate (APR)? The APR is the actual yearly interest rate paid by the borrower, figuring in the points charged to initiate the loan. When prospective borrowers call lenders for their current interest rates, the lenders will customarily quote only the interest rate on the note, not the APR. By law, the APR must be disclosed to a borrower but not necessarily at the time of the initial inquiry. The APR discloses the real cost of borrowing by adding on the points and by factoring in the assumption that the points will be paid off incrementally over the fifteen- or thirty-year term of the loan. The APR is usually about .5 percent higher than the note rate. There may be tax advantages to some borrowers in paying the points in one lump sum at the time the loan is originated.

7. What are your qualifying ratios? The qualifying ratio represents the relationship between the borrowers' projected PITI payments (principal, interest, taxes, and insurance) and their gross monthly income. Conservatively, lenders like to see the PITI not exceed 30 percent of the borrowers' gross monthly income (28 percent for 90 percent financing). Lenders will sometimes quote ratios in terms of two parameters. They may, for instance, require a $^{30}/_{36}$ ratio, which means the borrowers' PITI figure must not exceed 30 percent of their gross monthly income (housing to income ratio) and their PITI plus other long-term outstanding debts must not exceed 36 percent of their gross monthly income (debt to income ratio).

   Some lenders are more lenient in their qualifying ratios, and generally, the larger the cash down payment the easier the qualifying will be. A lender should be able to tell you over the phone if you'll qualify for a certain loan amount if you specify the amount of your cash down, the size loan you're looking for, your gross income, and the amount of any long-term outstanding debts.

8. Will the loan require Private Mortgage Insurance (PMI)? PMI insures the lender against a default on the part of the borrower; it is often required when the borrower is making a cash down payment of less than 20 percent of the purchase price and usually involves a higher interest rate, larger loan origination fee, and a second loan approval process. If PMI will be required, find out whether the lender will drop the requirement in the future when you have accrued more than 20 percent equity in the property.

9. Will the loan require an impound account? An impound account is held by the lender for the payment of the borrower's property

taxes and fire insurance. The borrower makes monthly payments to this account in addition to the mortgage payments, and the lender then pays the tax and insurance bills as they come due. Loans for more than 80 percent of the purchase price may call for an impound account.

10. When is the interest rate locked in? During times of rising or falling interest rates, this is a critical variable to consider in evaluating a loan program. When lenders lock in rates for a prospective borrower, they are reserving money at a specified interest rate for a given period of time (usually thirty or forty-five days). If rates increase during this period, the borrower's rate is protected as long as the loan is closed in time. Some lenders will lock in a rate when the buyer submits a loan application, others when the loan is approved, and some only at the time that the loan documents are drawn. Get the lock-in commitment in writing and find out whether the lender will honor the commitment if the loan doesn't close on time due to an error by the lender. If interest rates are rising, it may be worthwhile to pay a little extra to secure a rate, but be sure you have the option of taking a lower interest rate should rates drop before your loan documents are drawn.

11. How long will it take to approve the loan? The approval process usually takes from two to four weeks after a completed loan application is submitted.

12. Does loan approval and processing occur locally? Unanticipated delays are most likely to occur if formal approval and documentation must come from a corporate office located outside of the area.

13. Will you give a loan commitment in writing? Many lenders are more than happy to provide oral confirmation of approval but are reluctant to follow up with written confirmation. Insist on it. The commitment should include the interest rate, a summary of the terms of the loan, an itemization of the origination fees, and a date by which the escrow must be closed.

14. Are you a portfolio lender? Portfolio lenders retain most of the loans they make for their own investment purposes. Other lenders make home loans with no intention of keeping them after the escrow closes. These loans are usually sold on the secondary money market to Fannie Mae (Federal National Mortgage Association) or Freddie Mac (Federal Home Mortgage Corporation), two organizations that purchase home loans at a discount to resell to investors. Loans that are targeted for sale to Freddie Mac or Fannie Mae have rigid qualifying criteria and must be packaged for sale according to strict guidelines. The portfolio lender has greater flex-

ibility in qualifying and more latitude in approving buyers.

15. Do your loans have prepayment penalties? A prepayment penalty is a fine charged by the lender for paying the loan off early. There are plenty of loans available that do not have prepayment penalties, so a loan that has one should be extra special. You should feel confident you won't be moving before the prepayment clause expires (usually five years following the note date) before accepting such a loan.

16. Is the loan assumable? Fixed rate loans usually are not, but adjustables often are. If the loan is assumable, will the subsequent buyer need to go through formal loan qualification? Will the loan be assumable on the same terms, or will they change to reflect current market conditions?

17. Will a termite clearance be required by the close of escrow? In a busy real estate market, this may be the determining factor between one loan program and another. If the termite companies are backlogged with work and you have a short close of escrow, it may be impossible for the work to be complete before the close date. Loans that are packaged for sale to Fannie Mae or Freddie Mac usually require a termite clearance before the loan can be sold. Portfolio lenders have more flexibility due to the fact that they set their own guidelines for loan approval. If a clearance is not required by close, how much money will the lender require to remain in the escrow account after closing?

18. Will you permit credits from seller to buyer for repairs? Many lenders will not allow credits at all, which can present a problem if a significant defect was discovered during the property inspection and the buyer and seller negotiated a credit to correct the problem. Sometimes a lender will permit a hold-back pending completion of the repair work, while other lenders might require that the work be completed before the close of escrow, which could delay the transaction. If the seller has agreed to pay part of the buyer's non-recurring closing costs, find out if this is acceptable to the lender. Again, a portfolio lender may have more flexibility.

19. How long have you been in business? Beware of the new lender in town, with the deal of a lifetime, who runs out of money just prior to funding the loan.

20. Will you provide names and phone numbers of recent customers? Follow up by calling several borrowers who have recently obtained a loan from a lender you're seriously considering. Ask if they were satisfied with the service and if the lender delivered the loan as promised. Check with your agent and escrow officer to find out if either has worked previously with the lender. Were they satisfied?

A poorly managed loan company that is understaffed during the peak home buying season may not be able to approve and fund your loan efficiently enough to close escrow on time.

THE PROS AND CONS OF WORKING WITH A MORTGAGE BROKER

Mortgage brokers are intermediaries between borrowers and lenders. They usually have access to a multitude of loan products, and can frequently arrange financing that would not otherwise be available to a home buyer. Many lenders that work with mortgage brokers will not accept loans directly from an individual borrower.

Working with a good mortgage broker can save you time, as a broker can switch you from one loan program to another with relative ease. Let's say you apply for a fixed rate loan, but rates climb so high you no longer qualify for the loan. A broker can pull your loan package from the fixed rate lender and submit it to a lender with a lower interest rate adjustable loan program within a matter of hours.

Unfortunately, mortgage brokers don't have control over the lenders they work with. Also, some brokers will attempt to sell borrowers loans they don't want since it's easier to get some types of loans approved than others. If you're set on a fifteen-year fixed loan and you know you can qualify for it, don't let a mortgage broker talk you into a thirty-year fixed or adjustable loan.

Mortgage brokers work on commission, just like real estate agents. The lender usually shares a portion of the points with the broker who originates the loan, but some of the larger lending institutions that accept loan applications directly from prospective borrowers will not pay an outside mortgage broker for bringing in a loan. If the lender won't compensate the broker, the broker will charge the borrower an extra fee. Let your mortgage broker know up front that you don't want to pay extra for a loan that is readily available to you for less.

Take the experience of Linda Cornell, who selected a mortgage broker based on his promise to obtain a loan requiring minimum documentation and only 20 percent down. One week before closing, the mortgage broker informed Linda that the loan program he promised her was no longer available, but he'd secured a loan commitment for her from a large savings and loan if she was willing to put 25 percent down and pay a two point loan origination fee. Linda was especially annoyed by the bait and switch routine, since she'd originally considered applying to the same savings and loan herself but didn't want to put 25 percent down if she didn't have to. If she'd gone directly to the lender, her loan fee would have been one and a half points, not two.

FIXED VERSUS ADJUSTABLE RATE MORTGAGES

A fixed rate home mortgage has a constant interest rate and equal monthly payments during the term of the loan, whereas the interest rate and monthly payments of an adjustable rate loan fluctuate. Lenders prefer adjustables because they shift the risk of future increases in interest rates to the borrower. However, it's a mistake to think that there is no risk involved in selecting a fixed rate loan. Although such a loan is good protection against rising interest rates, the borrower is stuck with the initial rate if interest rates drop. Statistics show that home buyers who have chosen adjustable rate mortgages since 1981 have saved thousands of dollars. The percentage of home buyers applying for adjustable rate mortgages has risen substantially over the years, and adjustables currently account for over 50 percent of new home loans. As rates in general drop, home buyers tend to revert to the fixed loans; when rates rise, the preferred choice is the adjustable loan.

There is usually a 2 to 2.5 percent difference in interest rates between an adjustable rate mortgage (ARM) and a thirty-year fixed rate loan. If you're planning on moving again within three or four years, an ARM makes sense even if rates do nothing but rise during that period of time. Calculate the difference between the initial cost of both loans (including the loan origination fees, which are almost always higher on a fixed rate loan). Figure out what the savings will be during the first year or so of ownership if you select an ARM. The bottom line figure should speak for itself.

Always look at the worst case scenario. Compute what you'll pay in two or three years if you take an adjustable and interest rates go up and stay there. Can you live with the monthly payments if they increase to the maximum amount the lender is permitted to charge under the terms of the note?

Individuals on fixed incomes should stick to a fixed rate loan. The security of knowing that the monthly payments and interest rate will never change will more than offset a possible disappointment if rates decline. Should rates drop and stay down for an extended period of time, there's always the option of refinancing. Be sure to find a lender who does not charge a penalty for early prepayment.

One benefit of adjustables that should not be overlooked is that they are usually assumable. This is a particularly attractive feature if you don't plan to stay in your new home for an extended period of time. Having an assumable loan on your home may enable you to sell when others can't because of high interest rates or a shortage of mortgage money.

THIRTY-YEAR VERSUS FIFTEEN-YEAR FIXED INTEREST RATE LOANS

The fifteen-year fixed rate home loan has recently been touted as the premium way to finance the purchase of a new home for those who have a large enough income to support sizeable monthly payments (approximately $200 per month higher for each $100,000 financed at a 10 percent interest rate than a thirty-year fixed rate loan). The amount of interest paid during the term of the loan, however, is much less on a fifteen-year than it is on a thirty-year; the longer the term of the loan, the larger the amount of the total finance charge paid by the borrower. In addition, fifteen-year home loans are offered at a lower interest rate than are thirty-year loans: customarily one half to one percent less.

It makes sense to finance your home purchase with a fifteen-year fixed rate loan if you're planning to retire within the next ten to twenty years and intend to stay in your present home. If you're starting out with a low cash down but earn a large income and anticipate trading up to a more expensive home in the future, you might prefer a fifteen-year loan because it ensures enforced savings. The equity build-up in a fifteen-year fixed loan increases at a much faster pace than it does in a thirty-year loan: it takes twenty-four and one-half years to pay down one-half of a fixed loan that's amortized over thirty years. If you do select a fifteen-year fixed loan in order to obtain maximum equity build-up in the shortest period of time, make certain that the lender will not charge a prepayment penalty, as this could diminish a good portion of your enforced savings.

To summarize the pros and cons of the two fixed rate loan programs, consider the following: The fifteen-year loan has a lower interest rate, is paid off in a shorter period of time, costs much less in total financing charges during the term of the loan, and provides the borrower with quick equity build-up. On the other side of the coin, the fifteen-year loan is harder to qualify for, the monthly payments are higher, the borrower has less flexibility to adjust financing parameters, and it could provide less of a tax shelter.

A thirty-year fixed rate home mortgage leaves borrowers more in control of how much interest they ultimately pay, how much interest write-off and tax shelter they receive, and how much their monthly payments will be. Keep in mind that, barring explicit restriction, a thirty-year fixed rate loan can be paid off in half the time if the borrower makes double payments each month. The attractive feature of this loan is that it gives the borrower the flexibility to make additional payments, an option that can be critical for some home buyers, particularly those who are self-employed and are unsure about their future income.

Thirty-year fixed rate loan borrowers who plan to make periodic supplemental loan payments should check with their lender when they make principal pay-downs to be sure that the payments are properly recorded. Make a notation on the additional payment check to indicate that the money is to be applied to principal reduction; many lenders provide a space on the payment coupon to enter any extra principal payments.

The benefit of making an early payoff on a thirty-year fixed loan will depend on how low the interest rate on the note is. The lower the interest rate, the less advantageous an early loan payoff will be. Also, the lower the amount of the remaining loan balance, the less the benefit of making an early prepayment. One factor to consider is how much the money you pay down on the loan could earn for you if it were invested elsewhere. Also, keep in mind that making extra principal payments on a thirty-year fixed rate loan does not relieve you of the responsibility for making regular monthly payments. You owe twelve monthly payments per year no matter how much extra you pay in any one month.

A thirty-year fixed rate mortgage with a bi-weekly payment plan provides a compromise between the fifteen- and thirty-year fixed rate loans. The bi-weekly payment plan is a relatively new mortgage product that requires the buyer to make a payment once every two weeks rather than once a month. Each payment is equal to one-half of the monthly payment on an ordinary thirty-year loan. The interest rate or fee may be slightly higher on a bi-weekly loan to cover the increase in processing fees. The benefit to the borrower is that a thirty-year loan on a bi-weekly schedule will be paid off in approximately twenty years, resulting in a large savings in total interest paid. If you have a thirty-year fixed rate loan that is not set up for bi-weekly payments, don't send one-half of your monthly payment to the lender on the fifteenth of the month expecting it to be credited toward reducing the remaining principal balance; it won't. The lender will either send your check back to you or hold it until the other half of the monthly payment is received. In other words, the borrower can't arbitrarily convert to the bi-weekly plan; the loan must be set up on this payment schedule initially.

Beware of fixed-rate loans amortized over thirty years but due in five or seven years. These loans often have a prepayment penalty, they may not be assumable, and there is a large loan amount to refinance within a relatively short period of time.

SELECTING AN ADJUSTABLE RATE MORTGAGE

The initial interest rate is important, but should not be the most important factor in deciding which adjustable rate mortgage is right for you. The interest rate on ARMs will fluctuate in response to a combination of factors. This brief discussion will explain in general how ARMs work. The list of questions at the end of this section will be helpful to you in evaluating various ARM programs.

Most ARMs are tied to an index which is a measure of a general cost of borrowing money. Usually, when the index rises so will the interest rate on the adjustable loan. When the interest rate change becomes effective and how it affects the monthly payment will depend on the specific ARM program.

The most common indexes used in California are an average of the cost of funds to the Eleventh Federal Home Loan Bank District institutions (referred to as the Eleventh District cost of funds index), and the rates on three-month, six-month, one-year, three-year, or five-year Treasury securities.

Historically, the Eleventh District cost of funds index has been more stable than Treasury rate indexes. This means that in periods of rising interest rates, ARMs tied to the Eleventh District index move up more slowly than do adjustables indexed to a T-bill rate; in periods of falling interest rates, however, an ARM with an Eleventh District index drops more slowly. Although the Eleventh District cost of funds index has been the more stable in the past, this should not be construed as a guarantee of how the index will behave in the future. When comparing one T-bill index with another, keep in mind that the longer the term of the index, the more the borrower is protected from short-term erratic interest rate fluctuations.

The effective interest rate on an ARM loan is calculated by adding a margin of a few percentage points to the index rate. The margin will vary from one loan program to the next but typically remains constant during the life of the loan. Avoid a loan that has a fluctuating margin or allows the lender to make modifications arbitrarily. To compare two ARMs tied to the same index, ask the loan officer for the current index rate and for the amount of the margin; then compare the resulting ARM interest rates. For instance, say you're considering two loans that are both tied to the six-month T-bill rate, which is currently at 7.5 percent. One loan has a 2 percent margin; the other 3 percent. In the first case the ARM interest rate would be 9.5 percent, as opposed to 10.5 percent in the second case. Often higher loan origination fees (points) are charged for the privilege of obtaining a loan with a lower margin, so be sure to compare the up-front fees charged before making a final determination.

Lenders will often offer an initial interest rate that is lower than the ARM rate (the note index rate plus the margin, also referred to as the fully indexed rate). This is called a discounted, or teaser, rate. For instance, rather than having a starting interest rate of 9.5 percent, a loan might be offered at 8.5 percent initially. Again, check the amount of the loan origination fees charged; these could offset any savings to be gained by virtue of the lower initial rate. Also, find out how long the discounted rate will be in effect. Some loans have adjustment periods as frequently as every six months. If the index rate on the loan were to rise 2 percent during the first six months, your payment could rise very sharply within a short period of time if the increase is added to the ARM rate rather than to the teaser rate (the method of computing the initial increase in interest rate varies from lender to lender). This rapid jump in payments is referred to as payment shock. Since the borrower is usually qualified based on the teaser rate and not the ARM rate, it's important to consider whether or not the loan will be affordable when the discounted rate expires.

Conservative adjustable rate mortgages are available that protect the borrower in the unlikely eventuality of perpetually escalating interest rates. These ARMs have interest rate caps written into the note that set limits on how high the lender can raise the interest rate per adjustment period (periodic cap) and over the life of the loan (life-time cap). These caps often also set a lower limit on interest rate adjustments, but this varies with the lender.

Adjustment periods differ: they range from once every six months to once a year, although there are ARMs fixed for longer periods. On an ARM that adjusts every six months, the cap per adjustment is usually .5 to 1 percent. ARMs that adjust once a year typically have an annual interest rate cap of 1–2 percent. Lifetime caps are typically in the 3.5–6 percent range. Often, the lower the initial interest rate, the higher the lifetime cap.

A lower cap offers more protection for borrowers during periods of escalating interest rates; however, if rates drop significantly within a short period, it will take time for this drop to be reflected in the borrower's monthly mortgage payment if there is a periodic cap on how low the interest rate can go. Be aware that the periodic adjustment cap may not apply to the first adjustment if the initial rate on the loan is a teaser rate.

Some ARMs have payment caps which limit the amount that the monthly payment can increase at the time of each periodic adjustment. A payment cap usually limits an increase to 7.5 percent of the previous payment amount. This protects the borrower from a large jump in a monthly payment. However, if the payment increase is not sufficient to cover the increased interest owed, the unpaid interest is added to the remaining loan balance. In this case, the loan balance increases rather than decreases; this is called negative amortization.

In periods of high appreciation, negative amortization is less risky than it is when prices are stable or are dropping, particularly for the borrower who made a small cash down payment to begin with. The combination of negative amortization and depreciation in home prices can result in a loan balance that is higher than the market value of the home.

ARMs with payment caps and negative amortization are usually reamortized so that the remaining loan balance can be fully paid off during the term of the loan. This could necessitate a substantial increase in the monthly payment. Some ARMs have a cap on negative amortization so the borrower never owes more than 125 percent of the original loan amount.

Negative amortization can be avoided by paying the additional interest owed monthly. ARMs that don't have payment caps usually do not have negative amortization.

A feature to beware of when shopping for an ARM is warehousing or shelving. This refers to the ability of the lender to save, hold over, or shelve any interest that couldn't be charged to the borrower at the time of an adjustment due to the periodic cap on the interest rate. If the loan permits the lender to warehouse uncharged interest, the borrower could be stuck with a higher interest rate when interest rates have dropped. For instance, if an ARM has a 2 percent annual interest rate cap and the index rate goes up 3 percent in a year, the lender can only increase the ARM interest rate by 2 percent at the next adjustment. But if rates drop 2 percent the following year, a lender who is permitted to shelve uncharged interest rate increases can charge the borrower the uncollected 1 percent the following year.

One of the benefits of the adjustable rate mortgage is its assumability. Make sure that the loan is assumable by another qualified buyer at the same rates and terms available to you; some ARMs have provisions that entitle the lender to raise the index rate or margin at the time the loan is assumed. Also, make certain that the loan has no penalty for early prepayment.

The convertible adjustable rate mortgage has been gaining in popularity since it offers the best of two worlds: the initial lower interest rate of an ARM plus the option of converting to a fixed-rate loan in the future. The points and interest rate on convertible adjustable loans will be a bit higher than on ARMs without conversion, and a fee is charged to convert. The conversion fee is usually less than it would cost to refinance, so this is a worthwhile loan to consider if you plan to stay in your new home and fixed rate loans are too high at the time of purchase.

Shop carefully for a convertible adjustable to be sure that you don't overpay for the conversion privilege. You may never convert the loan, so the adjustable rate and terms should be competitive with other ARMs. Also, compare the formulas used to compute the fixed rate at the time of conversion; if converting doesn't result in a fixed rate that's close to the current market rate, the convertible loan may not be a good deal. Buyers putting less than 20 percent cash down should be aware that some lenders are qualifying ARM borrowers on the maximum interest rate the lender can charge in the second year of the loan, not on the initial interest rate.

QUESTIONS TO ASK ABOUT ADJUSTABLE RATE MORTGAGES

1. What is the initial interest rate? Is this a discounted rate?
2. What is the ARM note interest rate?
3. What interest rate is used to qualify the borrower?
4. What is the index?
5. Is the index constant throughout the term of the loan?
6. What is the current index rate?
7. Will you provide a history of index rate changes?
8. What is the margin?
9. Is the margin constant throughout the term of the loan?
10. How often are interest rate adjustments made?
11. How much can the interest rate increase on the first adjustment?
12. What is the interest rate cap per adjustment?
13. What is the lifetime interest rate cap?
14. Do the caps set upper limits on the interest rate or upper and lower limits?
15. Are the caps based on the ARM interest rate or on a teaser rate?
16. Is there a monthly mortgage payment cap?
17. Is there a possibility of negative amortization?
18. Is there a cap on negative amortization? What is the cap? How will the cap affect future payments?
19. When is the loan reamortized?
20. Is the lender permitted to warehouse (or shelve) uncharged interest?
21. Is the loan assumable? On what terms and conditions?
22. Is there a prepayment penalty?
23. Is the loan convertible? On what terms and conditions?
24. Will you provide a full loan disclosure brochure?

These questions are to supplement the general list of questions provided in the section devoted to shopping for a lender. You will want to compare the points and other loan origination fees, lock-in policies, qualifying criteria, Property Mortgage Insurance, or impound account requirements.

DETERMINING WHAT SIZE CASH DOWN PAYMENT TO MAKE

Tax reform has altered many homeowners' opinions about how much mortgage debt they should carry on their homes. This particularly affects the trade-up buyer who has a large amount of equity in a home.

Many tax professionals are recommending that their clients trade up to a larger home and apply for the largest home loan possible to achieve the biggest income tax write-off obtainable. For individuals with a rising income, this could make good sense.

On the other hand, retiring homeowners often wonder which way to purchase the retirement home: pay all cash or secure a modest loan against the property? While there is peace of mind in owning a property, it's not always the best strategy for a senior citizen to pay all cash for a retirement home.

A better strategy for seniors might be to reserve liquid cash assets to cover unexpected emergencies and secure a small mortgage against the retirement home. The monthly interest payments could offset income tax payment obligations, and the cash assets ought to earn income if invested wisely.

FINANCING FOR THE MARGINALLY QUALIFIED BUYER

Alternatives are available for the prospective buyer who has less than two years on the job or an insufficient down payment. Enterprising buyers who can substantiate a job history and a good record of repayment of consumer debt should apply with a portfolio lender if they receive the cold shoulder from a conventional lender. Portfolio lenders do not have to comply with the Freddie Mac or Fannie Mae loan qualifying criteria and are packaging loans for their own investment portfolio rather than for outside investors. They have more flexibility in loan approval and are more willing to stretch their qualifying limits for borrowers they feel are a good risk. But keep in mind that a portfolio lender may not offer the best rate.

Graduated mortgage payment loans are available for the home buyer who anticipates an increase in income in the future. These loans commence at an interest rate lower than the note rate, but the rate will increase at predetermined intervals. If you're applying for an adjustable rate, graduated payment loan, be sure to review the questions at the end of the ARM loan section of this chapter.

Buy down rates are a possibility for the buyer and seller who agree to the specific terms. With an interest rate buy down program, the seller agrees to pay toward either reducing a portion of the loan origination fees (points) or the interest rate (for a stipulated period of time), or both, for the buyer. As with a teaser rate, the buyer should be aware that after the buy down ceases, the preferential rate will stop and the buyer will be stuck with paying the actual cost of the mortgage.

Quick qualifiers are an option for buyers who can't meet the qualifying criteria but have 25 percent cash down or more. Most of the quick, or easy, qualifiers are adjustable rate mortgages, but some lenders are providing fixed rate easy qualifiers. Your credit must be approved, but if you can substantiate that you have the required cash to close the escrow, it doesn't matter if your qualifying ratios deviate from the ordinary.

Federal Housing Administration and Veterans Administration financing are alternatives for borrowers with little cash down who meet the qualifying limits. FHA loans require 5 percent cash down, and VA loans can be obtained with no down payment. Both of these government-backed programs require the seller to pay part of the closing costs that are normally considered a buyer's expense. In a seller's market, VA or FHA loan programs may not be a workable alternative to conventional financing. Besides the additional fees, the seller could be required to complete repair work if it's called for in the appraisal of the property, and the time period necessary for processing the loan application is longer than it is for conventional loans.

Until recently, FHA and VA financing have accounted for less than 20 percent of the loans originated in California because the upper loan amount limits were low relative to the average price of homes in the state. Recently, the FHA loan amount limit increased to $101,250 in many high cost areas such as San Francisco, Los Angeles, Anaheim, and San Diego. The VA loan amount limit was raised to $144,000 in 1988. It's expected that these increases in FHA and VA financing will make housing affordable for an additional 20,000 California home buyers.

California veterans may qualify for a Cal Vet low-interest rate home loan program. However, the loan amount limitation of $75,000 makes this program of little use to most California home buyers.

Occasionally local government entities offer low-interest rate mortgages, usually backed by public bond money, to help make housing more affordable for low-income home buyers. At the state level, an experimental program is offered by the California Housing Finance Agency which is called the Match Down Payment Program. This program provides matching funds to buyers who have been able to save a specified amount of cash for a down payment. The state takes a second deed of trust against the property which is due when the home is sold. Income requirements for qualification and home price limits vary with the region.

The Urban Homestead Act Program offers federally-owned, one to four unit family residences for sale to first-time buyers (or buyers who are not current homeowners) for a nominal fee. Priority is given to applicants whose income is at or below average for the area. The properties must be owner-occupied, usually for five years, and the buyer must have a good credit history and proof of employment, as well as agree to repair and maintain the property. The Urban Homestead Act Program is not available in all communities. Write to a U.S. Department of Housing and Urban Development (HUD) Regional and Field Office for information. In California, direct your inquiry to the HUD Community Planning & Development Division (1615 W. Olympic Blvd., Los Angeles, CA 90015-3801).

Relocating couples find it difficult to qualify for a new home mortgage when one spouse is transferred but the other spouse has not yet lined up a job. Some lenders are making exceptions for double income transferring couples. These lenders recognize the likelihood that the unemployed spouse will be able to find work in the new location and will take the spouse's past income into account in qualifying the couple for the new loan. A condition of approval on such a loan might be that the buyers put an amount in escrow sufficient to cover six months' mortgage payments until they can provide proof that the unemployed spouse has a job.

SUBMITTING THE LOAN APPLICATION

Completing the residential loan application and submitting it to your lender as soon as possible after you enter into a purchase agreement is critical to speedy loan approval. A sample Fannie Mae loan application is included in this chapter; this is the standard form used by most residential lenders in California.

The front of the form asks for the loan terms you are applying for, the source of your cash down payment and settlement costs, your employer, gross monthly income, and the details of the purchase (which your Realtor can help you with). The bottom of the first page asks miscellaneous questions regarding your financial history. If you or your co-borrower will be answering "yes" to any of these questions, let your loan representative know before you submit the application. A "yes" answer to one of the questions could preclude loan approval; falsifying an application can have more serious consequences. The back of the form requires that you list all assets and liabilities (installment debts), details about any real estate you own, and previous credit references. The form must be signed and dated at the bottom.

The loan package from the lender will also include forms authorizing the lender to verify the source of the cash down payment and employment. The verification of the cash required for the down payment and closing costs must be one or more of the following: evidence of account balances from financing institutions, a certified copy of a final closing statement if the source is proceeds from the sale of another property, or a gift letter. A gift letter must state that the gift is to be used for the purchase of the specific property and that no repayment is required. Most lenders will accept a gift letter only if it's from an immediate relative and will require that the borrowers contribute to the cash down payment (usually at least 5 percent of the purchase price). Contact your loan officer if part of the cash down payment is a gift or if the cash is coming from another source. Some quick qualifier loans do not require the borrower to verify the source of funds.

Self-employed individuals and commissioned employees will need to provide the lender with copies of income tax returns for the last two years, as well as a current profit and loss statement. Borrowers who have partnership or corporation income will need to provide those additional tax returns as well. If you've been at your current job for less than two years, the lender will require that you verify your previous employment. Find out who should be contacted to verify employment and follow up to make sure that the form has been returned to the lender. Misdirected verification forms or forms that sit unopened on someone's desk are a common cause of delayed loan approval.

Income reported by the borrower that is coming from sources such as rental property, alimony, or monthly payments on a note carried back on a property will require additional verification. Be aware that lenders will count only 75 percent of verifiable rental income in qualifying a borrower for a home loan to allow for unanticipated tenant vacancies.

A copy of the purchase agreement, including counteroffers and addenda, should be included with your loan application and request for verification forms. Ask your real estate agent to provide you with an extra complete copy of the purchase contract. The lender will also need two copies of the preliminary title report on the property and will usually request a copy of the termite report. Your agent can instruct the title company to send the preliminary title reports to the lender when they are available, as well as provide the termite report if required.

Some home buyers submit loan applications to more than one lender. One lender, for instance, may offer a preferred program that the buyers are not sure they'll qualify for; submitting double applications will maximize the buyers' ability to close the escrow. Find out

Residential Loan Application

MORTGAGE APPLIED FOR	☐ Conventional ☐ VA ☐ FHA	Amount $	Interest Rate %	No. of Months	Monthly Payment Principal & Interest $	Escrow/Impounds (to be collected monthly) ☐ Taxes ☐ Hazard Ins. ☐ Mtg. Ins. ☐ ____

Prepayment Option

Subject Property

Property Street Address	City	County	State	Zip	No. Units

Legal Description (Attach description if necessary) Year Built

Purpose of Loan: ☐ Purchase ☐ Construction-Permanent ☐ Construction ☐ Refinance ☐ Other (Explain)

Complete this line if Construction-Permanent or Construction Loan ☞	Lot Value Data	Original Cost	Present Value (a)	Cost of Imps. (b)	Total (a + b)	ENTER TOTAL AS PURCHASE PRICE IN DETAILS OF PURCHASE.
	Year Acquired $	$	$	$		

Complete this line if a Refinance Loan		Purpose of Refinance		Describe Improvements [ ] made [ ] to be made
Year Acquired	Original Cost	Amt. Existing Liens		
	$	$		Cost: $

Title Will Be Held In What Name(s) Manner In Which Title Will Be Held

Source of Down Payment and Settlement Charges

This application is designed to be completed by the borrower(s) with the lender's assistance. The Co-Borrower Section and all other Co-Borrower questions must be completed and the appropriate box(es) checked if ☐ another person will be jointly obligated with the Borrower on the loan, or ☐ the Borrower is relying on income from alimony, child support or separate maintenance or on the income or assets of another person as a basis for repayment of the loan, or ☐ the Borrower is married and resides, or the property is located, in a community property state.

Borrower				**Co-Borrower**			
Name		Age	School Yrs ___	Name		Age	School Yrs ___
Present Address	No. Years ___	☐ Own	☐ Rent	Present Address	No. Years ___	☐ Own	☐ Rent
Street				Street			
City/State/Zip				City/State/Zip			
Former address if less than 2 years at present address				Former address if less than 2 years at present address			
Street				Street			
City/State/Zip				City/State/Zip			
Years at former address		☐ Own	☐ Rent	Years at former address		☐ Own	☐ Rent
Marital Status ☐ Married ☐ Separated ☐ Unmarried (incl. single, divorced, widowed)		DEPENDENTS OTHER THAN LISTED BY CO-BORROWER NO. AGES		Marital Status ☐ Married ☐ Separated ☐ Unmarried (incl. single, divorced, widowed)		DEPENDENTS OTHER THAN LISTED BY BORROWER NO. AGES	
Name and Address of Employer		Years employed in this line of work or profession? ___ years Years on this job ___ ☐ Self Employed*		Name and Address of Employer		Years employed in this line of work or profession? ___ years Years on this job ___ ☐ Self Employed*	
Position/Title	Type of Business			Position/Title	Type of Business		
Social Security Number ***	Home Phone	Business Phone		Social Security Number ***	Home Phone	Business Phone	

Gross Monthly Income				Monthly Housing Expense**	Details of Purchase	
Borrower	Co-Borrower	Total		Rent		Complete If Refinance

in advance if there are non-refundable fees involved if you don't take a loan that's offered to you.

Within several days after a loan application is submitted, the lender sends the prospective borrower a Good Faith Estimate of settlement, or closing, costs and a copy of a booklet entitled "Settlement Costs and You." Verification forms are sent out at this time, and a credit report and property appraisal are ordered. Be sure that your loan agent knows if you need a letter of lender prequalification within a certain number of days. Contact your lender at least once a week to verify that the approval process is on schedule. In all of these matters you should feel free to seek the assistance of your real estate agent.

Item					PRESENT PROPOSED			Do Not Comp	
Base Empl. Income	$	$	$	First Mortgage (P&I)		$	a. Purchase Price	$	
Overtime				Other Financing (P&I)			b. Total Closing Costs (Est.)		
Bonuses				Hazard Insurance			c. Prepaid Escrows (Est.)		
Commissions				Real Estate Taxes			d. Total (a + b + c)	$	
Dividends/Interest				Mortgage Insurance			e. Amount This Mortgage	(	)
Net Rental Income				Homeowner Assn. Dues			f. Other Financing	(	)
Other† (Before completing, see notice under Describe Other Income below.)				Other:			g. Other Equity	(	)
				Total Monthly Pmt.	$	$	h. Amount of Cash Deposit	(	)
				Utilities			i. Closing Costs Paid by Seller	(	)
Total	$	$	$	Total	$	$	j. Cash Reqd. For Closing (Est.)	$	

Describe Other Income

B–Borrower C–Co-Borrower	NOTICE: † Alimony, child support, or separate maintenance income need not be revealed if the Borrower or Co-Borrower does not choose to have it considered as a basis for repaying this loan.	Monthly Amount
		$

If Employed In Current Position For Less Than Two Years, Complete the Following

B/C	Previous Employer/School	City/State	Type of Business	Position/Title	Dates From/To	Monthly Income
						$

These Questions Apply To Both Borrower and Co-Borrower

If a "yes" answer is given to a question in this column, please explain on an attached sheet.

	Borrower Yes or No	Co-Borrower Yes or No
Are there any outstanding judgments against you?		
Have you been declared bankrupt within the past 7 years?		
Have you had property foreclosed upon or given title or deed in lieu thereof in the last 7 years?		
Are you a party to a law suit?		
Are you obligated to pay alimony, child support, or separate maintenance?		
Is any part of the down payment borrowed?		
Are you a co-maker or endorser on a note?		

	Borrower Yes or No	Co-Borrower Yes or No
Are you a U.S. citizen?		
If "no," are you a resident alien?		
If "no," are you a non-resident alien?		

Explain Other Financing or Other Equity (if any). _____

*FHLMC/FNMA require business credit report, signed Federal Income Tax returns for last two years; and, if available, audited Profit and Loss Statement plus balance sheet for same period.
**All Present Monthly Housing Expenses of Borrower and Co-Borrower should be listed on a combined basis.
***Optional for FHLMC
FHLMC 65 Rev. 10/86

Fannie Mae Form 1003 Rev. 10/86

THE PROPERTY APPRAISAL

An appraisal is a professional—although somewhat subjective—opinion of the most probable price a property should sell for in the current market. The appraiser is retained by the loan broker or lender, almost always at the buyer's expense, to provide an independent written evaluation of the market value of the specific property.

The appraiser customarily examines the property and then compares it with three similar properties located nearby that have sold during the past six months. A dollar value is assigned to features on the subject property which the comparable properties lacked. Likewise, value is deducted from the property in question if the comparable properties featured amenities that it doesn't have.

It's important for the buyer's real estate agent to meet the appraiser at the property in order to make access easy and to provide the appraiser with recent comparable sales information. This will save the appraiser time, which is critical in busy real estate markets when

This Statement and any applicable supporting schedules may be completed jointly by both married and unmarried co-borrowers if their assets and liabilities are sufficiently joined so that the Statement can be meaningfully and fairly presented on a combined basis; otherwise separate Statements and Schedules are required (FHLMC 65A/FNMA 1003A). If the co-borrower section was completed about a spouse, this statement and supporting schedules must be completed about that spouse also. ☐ Completed Jointly   ☐ Not Completed Jointly

Assets		Liabilities and Pledged Assets				
Indicate by (*) those liabilities or pledged assets which will be satisfied upon sale of real estate owned or upon refinancing of subject property						
Description	Cash or Market Value	Creditors' Name, Address and Account Number		Acct. Name if Not Borrower's	Mo. Pmt. and Mos. Left to Pay	Unpaid Balance
Cash Deposit Toward Purchase Held By	$	Installment Debts (Include "revolving" charge accounts)			$ Pmt Mos	$
		Co.	Acct. No			
Checking and Savings Accounts (Show Names of Institutions (Account Numbers) Bank, S & L or Credit Union		Addr			/	
		City				
		Co.	Acct. No			
Addr.		Addr.				
City		City				
Acct. No.		Co.	Acct. No.			
Bank, S & L or Credit Union		Addr				
		City			/	
Addr		Co.	Acct. No.			
City		Addr				
Acct. No		City			/	
Bank, S & L or Credit Union		Co.	Acct. No.			
		Addr.				
Addr.		City				
City		Other Debts including Stock Pledges				
Acct. No.						
Stocks and Bonds (No Description)						
		Real Estate Loans Co.	Acct. No			
		Addr				
		City				
Life Insurance Net Cash Value Face Amount $		Co.	Acct. No			
		Addr.				
Subtotal Liquid Assets		City				
Real Estate Owned (Enter Market Value from Schedule of Real Estate Owned)		Automobile Loans Co.	Acct. No.			
Vested Interest in Retirement Fund		Addr.				
Net worth of Business Owned (ATTACH FINANCIAL STATEMENT)		City			/	
Automobiles Owned (Make and Year)		Co.	Acct. No.			
		City			/	
Furniture and Personal Property		Alimony/Child Support/Separate Maintenance Payments Owed to			/	
Other Assets (Itemize)						
		Total Monthly Payments			$	
	A $	Net Worth (A minus B) $			Total Liabilities	B $

appraisals can run as much as four to six weeks behind.

Difficulties with appraisals may arise in real estate markets in which fast appreciation or depreciation is taking place. Escrows typically take approximately sixty days to close. If a house down the street sold two weeks ago for $25,000 more than anything else in the neighborhood, it will be difficult for the appraiser to ascertain the new market value until that escrow closes. On the other hand, if market values are dropping, a property could appraise for higher than current market value if very recent sales have not yet closed escrow. In slow markets or in areas with very low turnover, appraisals are tricky because of insufficient comparable home sales information.

Another problem that has complicated appraisals recently is that appraisers often require proof that building permits were taken out

Total Assets

SCHEDULE OF REAL ESTATE OWNED (If Additional Properties Owned Attach Separate Schedule)

Address of Property (Indicate S if Sold, PS if Pending Sale or R if Rental being held for income)		Type of Property	Present Market Value	Amount of Mortgages & Liens	Gross Rental Income	Mortgage Payments	Taxes, Ins. Maintenance and Misc.	Net Rental Income
			$	$	$	$	$	$
TOTALS →			$	$	$	$	$	$

List Previous Credit References

B—Borrower C—Co-Borrower	Creditor's Name and Address	Account Number	Purpose	Highest Balance	Date Paid
				$	

List any additional names under which credit has previously been received _____

AGREEMENT: The undersigned applies for the loan indicated in this application to be secured by a first mortgage or deed of trust on the property described herein, and represents that the property will not be used for any illegal or restricted purpose, and that all statements made in this application are true and are made for the purpose of obtaining the loan. Verification may be obtained from any source named in this application. The original or a copy of this application will be retained by the lender, even if the loan is not granted. The undersigned ☐ intend or ☐ do not intend to occupy the property as their primary residence.

I/we fully understand that it is a federal crime punishable by fine or imprisonment, or both, to knowingly make any false statements concerning any of the above facts as applicable under the provisions of Title 18, United States Code, Section 1014.

_____ Date _____   _____ Date _____
Borrower's Signature   Co-Borrower's Signature

Information for Government Monitoring Purposes

The following information is requested by the Federal Government for certain types of loans related to a dwelling, in order to monitor the lender's compliance with equal credit opportunity and fair housing laws. You are not required to furnish this information, but are encouraged to do so. The law provides that a lender may neither discriminate on the basis of this information, nor on whether you choose to furnish it. However, if you choose not to furnish it, under Federal regulations this lender is required to note race and sex on the basis of visual observation or surname. If you do not wish to furnish the above information, please check the box below. (Lender must review the above material to assure that the disclosures satisfy all requirements to which the Lender is subject under applicable state law for the particular type of loan applied for.)

Borrower: ☐ I do not wish to furnish this information
Race/National Origin:
☐ American Indian, Alaskan Native ☐ Asian, Pacific Islander
☐ Black ☐ Hispanic ☐ White
☐ Other (specify): _____
Sex: ☐ Female ☐ Male

Co-Borrower: ☐ I do not wish to furnish this information
Race/National Origin:
☐ American Indian, Alaskan Native ☐ Asian, Pacific Islander
☐ Black ☐ Hispanic ☐ White
☐ Other (specify): _____
Sex: ☐ Female ☐ Male

To Be Completed by Interviewer

This application was taken by:
☐ face to face interview
☐ by mail
☐ by telephone

Interviewer _____

Name of Interviewer's Employer _____

Interviewer's Phone Number _____

Address of Interviewer's Employer _____

FHLMC Form 65 Rev. 10 86   **REVERSE**   Fannie Mae Form 1003 Rev. 10 86

for large additions and remodels made to the property. If this proof cannot be provided, the appraiser may not count the additional square footage in the evaluation of property value. This could make a big difference if, for instance, the addition turned a small two bedroom, one bath home (with an approximate value of $175,000) into a three bedroom, two bath home (with a current market value of approximately $225,000). It is possible, in some instances, to obtain city building permits after the fact for a fee.

Lenders are less concerned when the loan amount the buyer is requesting is low in relation to the market value of the property than they are when the buyer is making a small cash down payment. If the appraisal comes in a little low, the lender will usually be more lenient in approving the loan if the borrower has a large cash down, since the equity position of the lender in this case is relatively secure.

Sometimes a property will appraise for lower than fair market value because the appraiser is not familiar with the local neighborhood, in which case an appraisal review should be requested and the buyer's agent should provide the appraiser and the lender with comparable sales information. If the appraisal comes in low and the lender cannot be convinced to revise it upwards, there are several alternatives. Buyers who are convinced they paid over fair market value for their home can terminate the contract and their deposit will be refunded. If, on the other hand, the buyers and sellers want to carry on with the transaction, either the buyers can make up the difference between the loan amount requested and the amount approved by the lender in cash or the sellers can agree to carry back a note for the buyers. Another alternative is to take the loan to another lender who might be more flexible.

WHAT TO DO ABOUT A BAD CREDIT REPORT

A minor blemish on a credit report may require nothing more than a simple letter of explanation from the prospective borrower to the lender. For example, if a payment due on your department store charge card was late one month because you were out of town on business and your spouse forgot to pay the bill, a letter to this effect will probably suffice to clear up the problem as far as your loan approval is concerned.

There are sometimes mistakes in credit reports. Or a late payment could show up as a result of the fact that your bank put a hold, or stop-payment, on a check in error. You are entitled to information about a negative entry in your credit file, and you have the right to challenge such an entry according to the National Foundation for Consumer Credit. Ask your loan agent who to contact if you suspect there's a mistake on your credit report.

Good credit is imperative. An easy qualifier lender may be willing to give you a loan, without verifying your income or cash down payment, if you have 25 percent cash to put down; but loan approval will be conditioned upon an acceptable credit report. A previous bankruptcy can remain in a credit file for up to ten years; foreclosures are normally reported by credit agencies for at least seven years. If your credit history was shaky in the past but has improved recently, ask previous creditors to remove disparaging comments from your credit record.

FINAL LOAN APPROVAL

Having your new home loan approved should mean that you have an unconditional commitment from the lender to loan you the amount of money you requested on the loan application at the interest rate and terms you stipulated. The commitment should be in writing and will state a date by which the escrow must be closed. In periods of rising interest rates, the loan commitment may expire before the close of escrow date stated in your purchase agreement. If this occurs, have your agent contact the seller's agent and request an early close of escrow in order to protect your loan commitment. The sellers may need to keep possession of the property after close if they are unable to push their move date forward to coincide with the earlier close of escrow.

Make certain that the loan approval is firm, not conditional, before removing the financing contingency from the purchase agreement. For example, a lender might approve a loan conditioned upon approving additional documents, such as a copy of the maintenance agreement on a shared driveway or private road; a copy of a certified closing statement on the home you just sold; verification that you've paid down a charge card debt; a copy of a note that the seller has agreed to carry for you; confirmation that the seller has completed a repair on the property that you requested as a part of the purchase agreement; a certified copy of your divorce decree; or even, as absurd as it may sound, a letter from you stating that you like your current job and don't anticipate making a job change in the near future.

Final approval may require an additional confirmation from an underwriter or a private mortgage insurance company. Again, make sure that the loan is *fully approved* before removing the loan contingency.

How to Finance a Home Purchase When Interest Rates Are High

When rates are high, the most attractive alternative to conventional financing, aside from seller financing (which will be discussed in the next section of the chapter), is a buyer takeover of an existing low interest rate assumable mortgage. Most adjustable rate mortgages are assumable. Sellers who agree to an assumption will want to be sure that they are relieved of future responsibility for loan repayment. Buyers will want to read and review the existing loan documents before committing to take on the responsibility of repayment. Check with the lender to determine the fees charged for an assumption as well as the terms and conditions of assumption.

Most assumable loans now require that the buyer be qualified to make the loan payments. Therefore, a qualification procedure, similar to that required for a new mortgage, will be necessary to secure approval. Be sure to allow at least thirty days for processing, since qualifying a buyer for an assumption is likely to rank low on the lender's priority list. Lenders are understandably less interested in facilitating assumptions of low interest rate loans than they are in originating new loans at higher rates.

When the amount of the remaining balance on the assumable

loan is low in relation to the purchase price, the seller may offer to carry back a second deed of trust in order to make up the difference between the remaining balance on the first loan and the amount of the buyer's cash down payment.

Buyers and sellers are cautioned against entering into any agreement conditioned upon the buyers taking over the existing loan if that loan is not expressly assumable. If the lender discovers that the non-assumable loan (which contains a "due on sale clause") has been taken over by the buyers without permission, the note is likely to be called immediately due and payable, which could put the buyers in a difficult position if affordable financing is not available.

The lease option is another possibility during periods of high interest rates and low real estate sales activity. With this method of home purchase, the seller retains title to the property, accepts an amount of money from the buyer (the option money), and leases the property to the buyer for a specified period of time. When the term of the loan is up, the buyer either pays the balance agreed upon in the option agreement and completes the purchase or forfeits the option money and the seller retains title to the property.

A lease option agreement works well for the buyer short on cash and the seller who is unable to sell. A seller should make any agreement to lease option a property conditioned upon approval of the potential buyer's financing statement and credit report within a specified number of days following acceptance of the lease option contract.

A contract of sale is a creative financing device similar to the lease option. Title to the property does not transfer to the buyer until certain terms and conditions are met. Usually the seller continues to make the existing mortgage payments, as is the case with the lease option arrangement. The buyer occupies the property and makes payments to the seller on a monthly basis until title to the property transfers to the buyer.

The buyer and seller both incur potential risks by entering into a lease option or a contract of sale arrangement. A buyer could end up with more debt than anticipated if the seller doesn't keep the existing mortgage payments current or if the seller further encumbers the property without the buyer's consent. The seller could find that the property is unsalable if the prospective buyer lets it fall into a state of disrepair and then doesn't follow through with the purchase.

SELLER FINANCING

Seller financing offers benefits to both buyers and sellers, but risks are involved that should be thoroughly understood. The benefits include tax relief for the seller, transaction completion at times when conventional financing is not readily available or is prohibitively expensive, and good investment opportunities for both the buyer and seller.

A buyer must ascertain that seller financing is not being offered as a concession for an inflated price. This is especially important if the seller-carry loan has a short term. If the note is not fully amortized and comes due and payable in two or three years, the buyer will need to pay the remaining principal balance (the balloon payment) by selling or refinancing the property. Problems for the buyer may also arise if interest rates are exorbitantly high or housing values are deflated when the note comes due. The house might not sell or be appraised for enough to provide the buyer with funds sufficient to pay off the remaining loan balance. Whenever possible, buyers should negotiate an extension provision allowing for an automatic extension of the term of the loan if refinancing cannot be obtained at the time the note is due.

California Civil Code 2966 requires that the seller send a special notice to the buyer within ninety to one hundred fifty days before a balloon payment is due. This applies to residential property containing one to four units. Buyers and sellers should also be aware that in cases when the seller is carrying a second mortgage for the buyer, most lenders will require that the due date of the loan be at least five, and often seven, years after the close of escrow. This is to help ensure that the buyer will not be caught short of funds when the balloon payment comes due.

Regardless of how creditworthy a buyer may appear to be, sellers are cautioned to avoid a "no-cash down deal." The California Association of Realtors has recently issued warnings to brokers and sellers against participating in seller-financed real estate transactions in which the buyers invest none of their own money. A "no-money down" transaction might work as follows. The buyers agree to purchase the seller's home at an inflated price, and then secure a new first loan against the property with the seller to carry back a large second. The total of the two loans exceeds the current market value of the property, and the buyers walk away from the escrow with cash in hand. They may occupy the property for a period of time and make the mortgage payments, but when they disappear, the seller's only recourse is to foreclose. It's unlikely, however, that the seller will be able to recover the full amount of the seller-carry loan since the market value of the property will not be enough to cover the amount of both loans.

California Civil Code Section 2956, which came into effect in 1983, requires detailed disclosure of the terms and conditions of seller financing when an arranger of credit is involved in the transaction. A real estate agent, acting either as an agent or as a principal in a transaction involving the sale of one to four residential units, is considered to be an arranger of credit under the provisions of this requirement. California Association of Realtors form SFD 11, a sample of which is included in this chapter, was developed to help real estate agents comply with this law. This form should be completed and signed by buyers, sellers, and their respective agents at the time the purchase agreement is negotiated.

Section A of the Seller Financing Disclosure Statement refers to the credit documents used to evidence the extension of credit. The note and deed of trust are the most commonly used credit documents. The note is an agreement that states the amount and terms of the loan. The deed of trust secures the note against the property. The installment land sale contract is the same as the contract of sale referred to in the previous section of this chapter.

An all-inclusive note and deed of trust, also called a wrap-around loan, is a second mortgage that the seller carries for an amount that includes both the existing first loan balance and the amount of the seller-carry second. The buyer makes one lump loan payment to the seller out of which the seller makes the payments on the underlying first loan. This method of seller financing should only be used in situations when the first loan is assumable; otherwise the underlying first loan is likely to be called due and payable when the first lender becomes aware that the property has transferred title.

The credit terms itemized in the SFD 11 form should duplicate those agreed to by the buyer and seller in the financing section of the purchase agreement. The interest rate is negotiable but will undoubtedly be determined by current interest rates charged on conventional home loans, as well as by the interest the seller could earn if the money were placed in another form of investment. Sellers should be aware that the IRS requires that a minimum interest rate be charged; otherwise interest is imputed at a specific rate and the sellers are taxed as if they had received the imputed rate.

A seller will usually want to make a late charge part of the note to encourage the buyer to make monthly loan payments on time. A customary late charge is 6 percent of the payment if it is not made within ten days of coming due.

A buyer will probably want to be able to stipulate that prepayment of the loan be without penalty. This should not cause a problem unless the loan payments are a source of retirement income, in which case early prepayment could have negative financial repercussions for the seller.

Most sellers prefer to have a due on sale provision included in the note, but this can be a negotiable item. Buyers who are concerned

SELLER FINANCING DISCLOSURE STATEMENT
(California Civil Code 2956-2967)
CALIFORNIA ASSOCIATION OF REALTORS® (CAR) STANDARD FORM

This three page disclosure statement from the purchaser (buyer) and vendor (seller) is prepared by an arranger of credit [defined in Civil Code 2957 (a)] and provided to **both** the purchaser (buyer) and vendor (seller) in a residential real estate transaction involving **four or fewer** units whenever the seller has agreed to extend credit to the buyer as part of the purchase price.

Buyer: _____

Seller: _____

Arranger of Credit: _____

Real Property: _____

A. Credit documents: This extension of credit by the seller is evidenced by note and deed of trust ☐, all-inclusive note and deed of trust ☐, installment land sale contract ☐, lease/option (when parties intend transfer of equitable title) ☐, other ☐, (specify)_____ .

B. Credit terms:
1. ☐ See attached copy of credit documents referred to in Section A above for description of credit terms; **or**
2. ☐ The terms of the credit documents referred to in Section A above are: Principal amount $_____ interest at _____ % per annum payable at $_____ per_____ (month/year/etc.) with the entire unpaid principal and accrued interest of approximately $_____ due_____ 19_____ (maturity date).

Late Charge: If any payment is not made within ____ days after it is due, a late chage of $_____ or _____ % of the installment due may be charged to the buyer.

Prepayment: If all or part of this loan is paid early, the buyer will ☐, will **not** ☐, have to pay a prepayment penalty as follows: _____
_____
_____ .

Due On Sale: If any interest in the property securing this obligation is sold or otherwise transferred, the seller has ☐, does **not** have ☐, the option to require immediate payment of the entire unpaid balance and accrued interest.

Other Terms: _____
_____
_____ .

C. Available information on loans/encumbrances * that will be **senior** to the seller's extension of credit:

	1st	2nd	3rd
1. Original Balance	$ _____	$ _____	$ _____
2. Current Balance	$ _____	$ _____	$ _____
3. Periodic Payment (e.g. $100/month)	$ _____ / _____	$ _____ / _____	$ _____ / _____
4. Amt. of Balloon Payment	$ _____	$ _____	$ _____
5. Date of Balloon Payment	_____	_____	_____
6. Maturity Date	_____	_____	_____
7. Due On Sale ('Yes' or 'No')	_____	_____	_____
8. Interest Rate (per annum)	_____ %	_____ %	_____ %
9. Fixed or Variable Rate: If Variable Rate:	☐ a copy of note attached ☐ variable provisions are explained on attached separate sheet	☐ a copy of note attached ☐ variable provisions are explained on attached separate sheet	☐ a copy of note attached ☐ variable provisions are explained on attached separate sheet
10. Is Payment Current?	_____		_____

☐ SEPARATE SHEET WITH INFORMATION REGARDING OTHER SENIOR LOANS/ENCUMBRANCES IS ATTACHED.

* IMPORTANT NOTE: Asterisk (∗) denotes an estimate.

D. Caution: If any of the obligations secured by the property calls for a balloon payment, then seller and buyer are aware that refinancing of the balloon payment at maturity may be difficult or impossible depending on the conditions in the mortgage marketplace at that time. There are no assurances that new financing or a loan extension will be available when the balloon payment is due.

OFFICE USE ONLY
Reviewed by Broker or Designee _____
Date _____

Copyright© 1983, CALIFORNIA ASSOCIATION OF REALTORS®
325 South Virgil Avenue, Los Angeles, California 90020   FORM SFD-11-1

SF-Jan-88

that they might be forced to sell during a period of high interest rates can request that the note be assumable by a future buyer, and sellers ought to find this provision agreeable as long as they have the right to approve the future buyer's credit report and financial statement.

Section C provides for disclosure of all loans or encumbrances secured against the property that will be senior to the seller financing. If the buyer is assuming an existing loan, the particulars of the loan need to be provided, and copies of any notes and variable interest rate disclosures should be attached and initialed by the buyer and seller. When the buyer is obtaining new financing as a part of the transaction, all particulars should be provided along with copies of any notes and adjustable rate mortgage disclosures.

Sellers should be wary of carrying back a second for a buyer who makes a small cash down payment and obtains a large adjustable rate first mortgage (ARM) that includes negative amortization. If interest rates rise dramatically, the remaining principal balance on the first loan could rise to a point where it jeopardizes the seller's equity.

Section G contains an important disclosure that sellers should note. California Civil Code section 580(b) protects buyers from personal liability in the event that they default on a seller financed arrangement, leaving foreclosure — even if the foreclosure sale proceeds are not sufficient to pay off the debt — as the seller's only remedy.

A seller should require the buyer to carry property insurance naming the seller as loss payee. A Request for Notice of Default should be recorded so that the seller is notified if the buyer goes into default on any senior loans. Most sellers and buyers will want title insurance to protect their respective interests and a tax service to monitor the payment of property taxes.

The security document should be recorded to ensure that the buyer's or seller's interest in the property is not jeopardized by intervening liens, judgements, or subsequent transfers of title. With a land contract of sale, for instance, title remains in the seller's name; this means that the seller could further encumber the property and jeopardize the buyer's interest.

A simple seller-carry note is often drawn up by the escrow company. However, if the note is complex or if the rate is adjustable, the escrow officer will usually require that the principals engage the services of a real estate attorney. A seller who plans to sell the note after the close of escrow should use Fannie Mae forms. Fannie Mae will buy private notes, at a discount, if they meet certain credit and appraisal standards, are on standard approved forms, and are serviced by an approved lender (who will charge a servicing fee).

Seller-carry loans are normally treated as installment sales for

SELLER FINANCING DISCLOSURE STATEMENT
(California Civil Code 2956-2967)
CALIFORNIA ASSOCIATION OF REALTORS® (CAR) STANDARD FORM

E. Deferred Interest:
"Deferred interest" results when the buyer's periodic payments are less than the amount of interest earned on the obligation, or when the obligation does not require periodic payments. This accrued interest will have to be paid by the buyer at a later time and may result in the buyer owing more on the obligation than at origination.
☐ The credit being extended to the buyer by the seller does **not** provide for "deferred interest", **or**
☐ The credit being extended to the buyer by the seller does provide for "deferred interest."
    The credit documents provide the following regarding deferred interest:
    ☐ All deferred interest shall be due and payable along with the principal at maturity (simple interest); **or**
    ☐ The deferred interest shall be added to the principal_____ (e.g., annually, monthly, etc.) and thereafter shall bear interest at the rate specified in the credit documents (compound interest); **or**
    ☐ Other (specify) _____

F. All-Inclusive Deed of Trust or Installment Land Sale Contract:
☐ This transaction does **not** involve the use of an all-inclusive (or wraparound) deed of trust or an installment land sale contract; **or**
☐ This transaction **does** involve the use of either an all-inclusive (or wraparound) deed of trust or an installment land sale contract which provides as follows:
    1) In the event of an acceleration of any senior encumbrance, the responsibility for payment or for legal defense is:
    ☐ **Not** specified in the credit or security documents; **or**
    ☐ Specified in the credit or security documents as follows:
    _____
    _____

    2) In the event of the prepayment of a senior encumbrance, the responsibilities and rights of seller and buyer regarding refinancing, prepayment penalties, and any prepayment discounts are:
    ☐ **Not** specified in the credit or security documents; **or**
    ☐ Specified in the credit or security documents as follows:
    _____
    _____

    3) The financing provided that the buyer will make periodic payments to _____
    [e.g., a collection agent (such as a bank or savings and loan); seller; etc.] and that_____
    will be responsible for disbursing payments to the payee(s) on the senior encumbrance(s) and to the seller.
CAUTION: The parties are advised to consider designating a neutral third party as the collection agent for receiving buyer's payments and disbursing them to the payee(s) on the senior encumbrance(s) and to the seller.

G. Buyer's creditworthiness: Section 580(b) of the California Code of Civil Procedure generally limits a seller's rights in the event of a default by the buyer in the financing extended by the seller, to a foreclosure of the property.
☐ No disclosure concerning the buyer's creditworthiness has been made to the seller; **or**
☐ The following representations concerning the buyer's creditworthiness have been made by the buyer(s) to the seller:

1. Occupation: _____	1. Occupation: _____
2. Employer: _____	2. Employer: _____
3. Length of Employment: _____	3. Length of Employment: _____
4. Monthly Gross Income: _____	4. Monthly Gross Income: _____
5. Buyer has ☐, has **not** ☐, provided seller a current credit report issued by: _____	5. Buyer has ☐, has **not** ☐, provided seller a current credit report issued by: _____
6. Buyer has ☐, has **not** ☐, provided seller a completed loan application.	6. Buyer has ☐, has **not** ☐, provided seller a completed loan application.
7. Other (specify): _____	7. Other (specify): _____

H. Insurance:
☐ The parties' escrow holder or insurance carrier has been or will be directed to add a loss payee clause to the property insurance protecting the seller; **or**
☐ No provision has been made for adding a loss payee clause to the property insurance protecting the seller. Seller is advised to secure such clauses or acquire a separate insurance policy.

FORM SFD-11-2

OFFICE USE ONLY
Reviewed by Broker or Designee _____
Date _____

EQUAL HOUSING OPPORTUNITY
SF-Jan-88

SELLER FINANCING DISCLOSURE STATEMENT
(California Civil Code 2956-2967)
CALIFORNIA ASSOCIATION OF REALTORS® (CAR) STANDARD FORM

I. Request for notice:
☐ A Request for Notice of Default under Section 2924(b) of the California Civil Code has been or will be recorded; **or**
☐ No provision for recording a Request for Notice of Default has been made. Seller is advised to consider recording a Request for Notice of Default.

J. Title Insurance:
☐ Title insurance coverage will be provided to **both** seller and buyer insuring their respective interests in the property; **or**
☐ No provision for title insurance coverage of **both** seller and buyer has been made. Seller and buyer are advised to consider securing such title insurance coverage.

K. Tax service:
☐ A tax service has been arranged to report to seller whether property taxes have been paid on the property. _____ [e.g., seller, buyer, etc.] will be responsible for the continued retention and payment of such tax service; **or**
☐ No provision has been made for a tax service. Seller should consider retaining a tax service or otherwise determine that the property taxes are paid.

L. Recording:
☐ The security documents (e.g., deed of trust, installment land contract, etc.) will be recorded with the county recorder where the property is located; **or**
☐ The security documents will **not** be recorded with the county recorder. Seller and buyer are advised that their respective interests in the property may be jeopardized by intervening liens, judgments or subsequent transfers which **are** recorded.

M. Proceeds to buyer:
☐ Buyer will **NOT** receive any cash proceeds at the close of the sale transaction; **or**
☐ Buyer will receive approximately $ _____ from _____ [indicate source from the sale transaction proceeds of such funds]. Buyer represents that the purpose of such disbursement is as follows: _____
_____

N. Notice of Delinquency:
☐ A Request for Notice of Delinquency under Section 2924(e) of the California Civil Code has been or will be made to the Senior lienholder(s); **or**
☐ No provision for making a Request for Notice of Delinquency has been made. Seller should consider making a Request for Notice of Delinquency.

The above information has been provided to: (a) the buyer, by the arranger of credit and the seller (with respect to information within the knowledge of the seller); (b) the seller, by the arranger of credit and the buyer (with respect to information within the knowledge of the buyer).

Arranger of Credit_____

Date_____ , 19_____ .   By_____

Buyer and seller acknowledge that the information each has provided to the arranger of credit for inclusion in this disclosure form is accurate to the best of their knowledge.

Buyer and seller hereby acknowledge receipt of a completed copy of this disclosure form.

Date_____ , 19_____ .   Date_____ , 19_____ .

Buyer _____   Seller _____

Buyer _____   Seller _____

A REAL ESTATE BROKER IS THE PERSON QUALIFIED TO ADVISE ON REAL ESTATE. IF YOU DESIRE LEGAL ADVISE, CONSULT YOUR ATTORNEY.

This form is available for use by the entire real estate industry. The use of this form is not intended to identify the user as a REALTOR®. REALTOR® is a registered collective membership mark which may be used only by real estate licensees who are members of the NATIONAL ASSOCIATION OF REALTORS® and who subscribe to its Code of Ethics.

OFFICE USE ONLY
Reviewed by Broker or Designee _____
Date _____

Copyright© 1983, CALIFORNIA ASSOCIATION OF REALTORS®
525 South Virgil Avenue, Los Angeles, California 90020   FORM SFD-11-3

SF-Jan-88

income tax purposes, which means that the seller's gain is taxed over the period that principal payments on the note are received. IRS rules regarding installment sales have changed several times in recent years, so be sure to consult with your tax advisor for more information about the tax ramifications of an installment sale before entering into a binding agreement with a buyer.

CHAPTER 11

THE ESCROW AND CLOSING

THE BLUEPRINT FOR A HASSLE-FREE ESCROW

Most buyers and sellers have a limited understanding of what escrow is and of the complexities involved in a satisfactory escrow closing.

An escrow holder is a neutral third party who acts as custodian for the funds and documents necessary to complete the real estate transaction. During the escrow period, the escrow officer handles such matters as payment of liens and encumbrances against the property and preparation of the final settlement papers. When all of the terms and conditions of the purchase contract have been satisfied, the escrow holder prepares and records the grant deed, which effectively transfers title to the property from the seller to the buyer.

The escrow officer acts as a limited dual agent for both parties in a transaction but cannot advise either party and acts only on instructions from the buyer and seller. The escrow instructions, which restate the terms of the real estate purchase agreement, delineate the escrow officer's responsibilities. In Southern California, escrow instructions are given to the escrow holder soon after the purchase agreement is accepted and they are signed by the buyer and seller at that time. In Northern California, a copy of the purchase agreement may or may not be sent to the escrow holder upon opening escrow, but the actual escrow instructions are not prepared and signed by the parties to the transaction until toward the end of the escrow period.

Many buyers and sellers operate under the misconception that the escrow holder is responsible for the closing. It's important to understand that nothing happens automatically in escrow, nor should it. The escrow officer acts on your instructions; without those instructions, the escrow officer has authority to do nothing.

The mutual efforts of a good escrow officer, conscientious real estate agents, and cooperative buyers and sellers make the difference between an escrow that proceeds smoothly and one that does not. Buyers and sellers should let their real estate agents and escrow officer know that they are available to help if necessary and that they want to be kept informed of the progress of the escrow, especially if a problem arises.

THE DEPOSIT MONEY

The buyer's deposit check is usually held by the escrow holder and is applied toward the total purchase price at closing. Some brokers have trust accounts set up for the purpose of holding the buyer's deposit money. The buyer should be aware that, once there's an accepted purchase contract, the deposit check will be cashed unless other provisions have been specified in the contract.

The escrow holder is not permitted to collect interest on the deposit money. Unless instructed otherwise, the buyer's deposit check will be placed into a non-interest bearing account, although it can usually be placed in an interest bearing account if the buyer requests this and the seller has no objection. Determining who is entitled to the interest on the buyer's deposit money can become a subject of some debate. In a probate sale, for instance, the buyer is required to make a cash deposit to the estate equal to 10 percent of the purchase price. Some attorneys who handle probate sales require that any interest earned on the buyer's deposit money during escrow go to the estate. To avoid confusion, an agreement should be made in writing between buyer and seller in advance. The party to benefit fills out a form giving the escrow holder relevant tax information.

Don't expect your money to earn any more than passbook account interest rates. Also, keep in mind that the escrow holder will need to withdraw your deposit money from the interest bearng account before close of escrow in order to have good funds available for closing. For a short escrow period, an interest bearing account may not merit the time and effort, but it's definitely worth pursuing if the deposit is large and the escrow period long.

When a purchase agreement calls for an increased deposit during the escrow period and the buyer and seller have initialed the liquidated damages clause, a Receipt for Increased Deposit and Supplement to Real Estate Purchase Contract must be filled out and signed by both parties. A sample of this form is included. Sellers should make certain that this form accompanies the buyer's deposit check if liquidated damages are part of the contract. This simple but critical bit of paperwork is often overlooked.

Also, make certain that your agent or escrow officer provides you with copies of receipts for your deposit checks. The seller should also receive copies of these receipts.

RECEIPT FOR INCREASED DEPOSIT AND SUPPLEMENT TO REAL ESTATE PURCHASE CONTRACT

CALIFORNIA ASSOCIATION OF REALTORS® STANDARD FORM

THIS IS INTENDED TO BE A LEGALLY BINDING CONTRACT. READ IT CAREFULLY.

Received from _____ herein

called BUYER, the sum of _____

Dollars ($_____) evidenced by cash ☐, personal check ☐, cashier's check ☐ as

additional deposit payable to_____

for the purchase of the property described in the Real Estate Purchase Contract and Receipt for Deposit dated

_____ , executed by _____

as BUYER and accepted by SELLER on _____ 19_____ .

Dated _____

Real Estate Broker_____   By _____

The following is hereby incorporated in and made a part of said Real Estate Purchase Contract and Receipt for

Deposit, which remains in full force and effect:

Buyer hereby increases the total deposit to $ _____ and Buyer and Seller Agree

that should Buyer fail to complete the purchase by reason of any default of Buyer, Seller shall

retain the total deposit as liquidated damages. If the described property is a dwelling with no more

than four units, one of which the Buyer intends to occupy as his residence, Seller shall retain as

liquidated damages the deposit actually paid, or an amount therefrom, not more than 3% of the

purchase price, and promptly return any excess to Buyer.

The undersigned agree to the above and acknowledge receipt of a copy hereof.

Dated _____   Dated _____

BUYER _____   SELLER _____

BUYER _____   SELLER _____

To order, contact California Association of Realtors®
525 S. Virgil Avenue, Los Angeles, CA 90020
Copyright² (1984), California Association of Realtors® Reviewed 1984   FORM RID-11

TT-L5-FG

Don't make the mistake made by Candice and Kevin Carpenter. The Carpenters sold their home to a buyer who removed contract contingencies in a timely fashion, but when their real estate agent instructed the escrow officer to prepare the final closing papers, the officer responded that the buyer's deposit check had never been received. The Carpenters' agent called the buyer's agent, who said that the buyer was planning to close the escrow and that the missing check was simply an oversight. The buyer ended up defaulting and the Carpenters had to hire an attorney to sue for damages. If the parties involved had made sure the buyer's check was received the day after acceptance, the buyer might have been less likely to default, knowing that the sellers could tie up the deposit money in escrow until they received satisfactory compensation for their damages.

How to Read a Preliminary Title Report

The buyer, seller, and their real estate agents should receive a copy of a preliminary title report (commonly known as the prelim) within five days after escrow is opened. The preliminary title report is a statement regarding the present condition of the title to the property. It shows who owns the property and details any liens and encumbrances affecting the title. The report also delineates the terms and conditions under which the title company will issue a policy of title insurance.

The title company's name and address, the title officer's name, and a reference number appear at the top of the report, followed by the address of the subject property and the buyer's name. A narrative statement from the title company outlining the scope and terms of the preliminary title report usually ensues. Next comes a statement regarding the estate or interest covered by the report, followed by the name of the vested owner and the manner in which title is currently held. A fee is the highest type of interest that a property owner can have; a fee interest or estate is freely transferable by the owner of record.

A list of exceptions and exclusions will follow. These will appear as exceptions to the policy of title insurance unless they are paid, released, or otherwise eliminated from the public record before the close of escrow. Exceptions include property taxes—the amounts due and current status, tax delinquencies, easements (rights of others to use a portion of the property), CC&Rs (Covenants, Conditions, and Restrictions), deeds of trust securing indebtedness against the property, tax liens, mechanics' liens, and judgements. The preliminary title report will also include a legal description of the property and a statement indicating whether there were any transfers of record during the six months preceding the date of the report.

The title company may require that a statement of identification (or identity) be provided by the sellers or buyers before a policy of title insurance will be issued. This requirement enables the title company to determine if there are any other liens or judgements that might affect title to the property and is almost always required when buyers or sellers have relatively common names.

A plat map is usually included with the preliminary title report for information only. The map is a reduced copy of the county assessor's map or the recorded subdivision map but is not a survey of the property boundary lines and is not a part of the report.

Paragraph five of the Real Estate Purchase Contract and Receipt for Deposit defines a time period for the buyer's review of the preliminary title report. This paragraph further states that the seller will deliver the property with title free of "liens, encumbrances, restrictions, rights and conditions of record known to Seller," except for current property taxes, CC&Rs, and public utility easements of record. The burden is on the buyer to reasonably disapprove, in writing, any title matter contained within the preliminary title report within the specified time period. If the seller is unwilling or unable to remedy the title matter disapproved by the buyer, the buyer may terminate the purchase agreement and the buyer's deposit will be returned.

A buyer should request that the title company provide complete copies of all easements (particularly those involving shared driveways and access easements) and CC&Rs. The prelim will list only the easements and CC&Rs, so the buyer should review the complete documents, which the title company will provide upon request, to make sure they don't contain an unacceptable restriction. Some CC&Rs that are listed in the prelim may contain expiration dates and may no longer be applicable.

Both the buyers and sellers need to verify that the vesting (ownership) indicated on the preliminary title report is accurate. Buyers should make sure that the owner of record shown on the prelim is the same person who signed, as the seller, on the purchase agreement. A problem could arise if only one seller signed the purchase agreement and there are multiple owners of record. When a vesting is in the name of a deceased owner, an heir may not have the legal capacity to transfer the property.

Sellers are advised to examine carefully the list of liens and encumbrances, particularly deeds of trust, securing indebtedness against the property. Sometimes an old debt, paid off long ago, will appear as a current lien on the property. This could indicate that the title company's search of the county records was incomplete, or it could mean that the deed of reconveyance (which is issued when the debt is paid in full) was never recorded. A seller can assist in clearing up this sort of title matter by providing the escrow officer with a copy of the recorded deed of reconveyance. When title matters are cleared up, make sure the title company issues an amended preliminary title report reflecting the corrections.

ENSURING GOOD TITLE

Title insurance is paid for one time only and protects the buyer from problems that might arise due to defects in the title. The title insurance policy remains in force during the buyer's period of ownership, but the policy is not transferable to a subsequent owner.

The coverage that most buyers obtain at the time of purchase (or refinance) is the California Land Title Association Standard Coverage Policy (commonly referred to as a CLTA Standard Coverage Policy), which protects against defects discoverable through an examination of the public records. A CLTA policy will not, however, protect the buyer from title risks discernible only from a physical inspection of the property. Boundary disputes and encroachments, unrecorded easements, and rights of persons in possession of the property are not covered under the CLTA Standard Coverage Policy.

More extensive title protection is provided under the American Land Title Association Loan Policy (commonly referred to as an ALTA Loan Policy), which does cover defects that can only be discovered from a physical inspection of the property. A lender will normally require that the buyer purchase an ALTA policy. In addition to protecting the lender from "off the record" title defects, the ALTA policy will ensure that the lender's deed of trust takes precedence over unrecorded claims against the property. A title company insuring the lender, but not the buyer, with an ALTA policy will usually issue a separate policy to the lender covering the deed of trust only.

A CLTA Standard Policy is less expensive since it does not involve an inspection of the property by the title company. Buyers who choose to purchase a CLTA policy will usually inspect the property on several separate occasions before making an offer to purchase or before removing the inspection contingencies from the purchase agreement.

Paragraph five of the CAR Real Estate Purchase Contract and Receipt for Deposit requires the seller to provide the buyer with a CLTA policy of title insurance. This should not be construed as a guarantee that CLTA is the title insurance of preference for your transaction. If you have any reservations about exceptions from the CLTA policy coverage, particularly where boundary lines or rights of parties in possession are concerned, pay the additional cost for ALTA owner (not lender) coverage. In addition, be aware that special endorsements are obtainable from the title company to cover specific problem situations. Consult a real estate attorney if you have any questions regarding which type of title insurance should be purchased to protect your interests.

Title insurance is commonly paid for by the buyer in Northern California and by the seller in Southern California. If the title record of a property has been searched within the past two years, either due to a transfer of ownership or a lender refinance, a discounted short term title insurance rate usually applies.

ADDENDA TO THE PURCHASE AGREEMENT

Rarely does a purchase agreement remain unchanged during the term of the escrow period. When modifications are made to the original purchase contract, it is important that they be agreed upon in writing by both buyer and seller. Let's say, for instance, that you would like to move the close date up, and the seller's oral response is that an early close date sounds acceptable. Based on this, you rearrange all your moving plans around what you assume will be the new close of escrow. Without having the modification in writing, however, the date is unenforceable and you may find yourself unhappily surprised to discover that you can't move in when you wanted to.

In periods of rising interest rates and short loan commitments, the buyer may be required by the lender to close escrow early. If the seller cannot vacate early, the buyer and seller can agree to an early close but retain the occupancy date they agreed to in the original purchase agreement. The seller in this situation may rent back the house from the buyer, after the closing, at a per diem rate that is mutually agreeable. This sort of a modification must be made in writing and should be accompanied with an Interim Occupancy Agreement that permits the seller to remain in possession for a specified period of time after the close of escrow.

TERMINATING AN UNSUCCESSFUL PURCHASE AGREEMENT SUCCESSFULLY

Once in a while, irreconcilable differences will occur during the escrow period. The inspection reports might reveal property defects that the seller is unable or unwilling to repair. If the buyer is unwilling to purchase the property unless the defects are remedied, a Release of Contract form, signed by buyer and seller, is usually sufficient to cancel the escrow and release both parties from their respective responsibilities. A less clear-cut situation exists if the buyer or seller has failed to remove a contingency within the requisite time period and a formal

RELEASE OF CONTRACT
THIS IS INTENDED TO BE A LEGALLY BINDING CONTRACT. READ IT CAREFULLY.
CALIFORNIA ASSOCIATION OF REALTORS® STANDARD FORM

The undersigned Buyer and Seller, the parties to that certain: ☐ Real Estate Purchase Contract and Receipt for Deposit,

☐ Mobile Home Purchase Contract and Receipt for Deposit, ☐ Business Purchase Contract and Receipt for Deposit, ☐ other

_____

dated _____, 19_____, covering the following described property:

_____

_____

_____

_____

_____

_____

_____

_____

hereby mutually release each other from any and all claims, actions or demands which each may have up to the date of this Agreement

against the other by reason of said Contract.

It is the intent of this Agreement that all rights and obligations arising out of said Contract are declared null and void.

_____holding
(Name of Broker or Escrow Holder)

the deposit under the terms of said Contract is hereby directed and instructed to disburse said deposit in the following manner:

$_____ TO _____

$_____ TO _____

$_____ TO _____

$_____ TO _____

Dated_____	Dated_____
Buyer_____	Seller_____
Buyer_____	Seller_____
Dated_____	Dated_____
Broker_____	Broker_____
By_____	By_____

NO REPRESENTATION IS MADE AS TO THE LEGAL VALIDITY OF ANY PROVISION OR THE ADEQUACY OF ANY PROVISION IN ANY SPECIFIC TRANSACTION. A REAL ESTATE BROKER IS THE PERSON QUALIFIED TO ADVISE ON REAL ESTATE OR BUSINESS TRANSACTIONS. IF YOU DESIRE LEGAL ADVICE CONSULT YOUR ATTORNEY.

written request for an extension of the contingency time period has not been made. A real estate purchase contract cannot be declared null and void by one party without the written consent and approval of the other party. This means that neither the escrow, nor the purchase contract, will be automatically cancelled if a contingency is not removed within the time frame specified in the purchase agreement.

What do you, as a buyer or seller, do if a contingency has not been removed, an extension has not been requested, and the time period for performance has passed? The first step is to ask your agent to put a request in writing that the other party perform within a reasonable time period: twenty-four to forty-eight hours should be sufficient. If the other party fails to respond to your inquiry or does not remove the contingency in question within that time period, consult with a real estate attorney to determine the next appropriate course of action.

In this situation, the seller should be careful not to elevate a backup offer into primary position without receiving a signed "Release of Contract" form from the first buyer. Make certain that you don't sell one property to two eager buyers. If both parties make a legal claim to your home, you could end up unable to convey free and clear title to either of them.

PAYOFF DEMANDS AND BENEFICIARY STATEMENTS

A payoff demand is a request sent by the escrow officer to the lender of record on a property in cases when the seller is to pay the loan off in full at the close of escrow. The demand asks the lender how much money is owed by the seller in order to pay the loan off in full. The cost of a payoff demand, or statement fee, varies from one lender to the next, but it is usually less than seventy-five dollars. The timing involved in ordering a payoff demand is important. If it's ordered too late in the escrow period and the precise figures are not available in time, closing could be delayed unless the seller is willing to leave excess funds in escrow to protect the escrow company in case the payoff demand includes unanticipated charges, such as late fees, delinquent payments, or prepayment penalties. A payoff demand that's ordered too early may necessitate an update during the escrow (usually done only for an additional fee) if the lender will not give revised figures to the escrow officer over the phone. Ideally the payoff demand should be ordered approximately thirty days prior to closing.

The seller should keep loan payments current during the escrow period in order to avoid having to pay late fees. Be aware, however, that a loan payment will usually not be credited to your account until the check you made the payment with has cleared. It might be worth your while to make a payment that's due just before the closing in person and with a cashier's check. Get a receipt from the lender so you can verify to the escrow officer that the payment was made. Any overpayments to the lender will be credited back to the seller after the close of escrow. A check covering the overpayment amount is usually sent to the seller in care of the escrow company.

A beneficiary statement is ordered when the buyer intends to take over the existing loan on the property. Like the payoff demand, it is a request for information on the condition of the loan. It asks, for instance, if the payments are current, whether there are any fees or delinquent payments owed by the seller, and the amount of the remaining principal balance due.

A seller should request to see a copy of the payoff demand or beneficiary statement as soon as it is received by the escrow officer. Call the lender directly if you think a billing error has been made, and don't be surprised if you're charged a corrected statement fee even though the lender made the mistake. Sellers who discover at the last minute, when closing documents are being signed, that an unanticipated prepayment penalty is due, may have no alternative but to pay it or risk a delayed closing. A prepayment penalty, by the way, can cost thousands of dollars, so it makes sense to confirm the lender's closing charges in advance. Buyers who are assuming an existing loan will want to review the beneficiary statement in advance of the closing and should request that any late charges or delinquent payments be brought current by the sellers at or before close of escrow.

DON'T WAIT UNTIL THE LAST MINUTE

Certain documents that are occasionally involved in residential property transfers require special approval from the legal department of the title company before the closing. Let's say, for instance, that your spouse is planning to be out of the country when the closing papers are signed and gives you a power of attorney to sign for both of you. The power of attorney must be in a legal form acceptable to both the title company and the new lender (if loan documents will be signed under its auspices), and it must be notarized and recorded in the county of the property.

A quitclaim deed is another document that needs title company approval before closing. This document relinquishes any interest that the grantor might have in the property. It's common, in a divorce situation, for one party to quitclaim interest in a property to the other party at the time a formal property settlement is made. The title company might request a copy of the divorce decree if the divorce is not final or if the decree has not been recorded.

The title company will want to approve a financing statement from the builder before transferring title to a new home if the lien period has not passed by the close of escrow. During the sixty-day lien period, which begins after the notice of completion is recorded, contractors who worked on the project can file mechanic's liens against the property. In addition to a satisfactory financial statement, the title company may require that the builder enter into an indemnity agreement stating that the title company will not be responsible for future liens recorded against the property.

Contact your escrow officer as soon as possible after the escrow is opened if you suspect that any aspect of the property transfer will require title company approval.

SHOP CAREFULLY FOR HOMEOWNER'S INSURANCE

Insurance rates vary by as much as 30 percent from one company to the next, so it pays to shop around before making a choice. Be sure, when making comparisons, that you receive quotes for equivalent coverage. In addition to cost, you will want to know whether the insurance carrier has a reputation for prompt and dependable service when claims are made.

Until recently, most lenders required that the borrower carry insurance at least in the amount of the loan. In most states this is still the case. California law now prohibits a lender from requiring the borrower to carry fire insurance in excess of the replacement value of the improvements on the property, even if this amount is less than the loan amount. The replacement value must, however, be established by the borrower's property insurer. Out-of-state readers should consult directly with their lenders if they feel the amount of insurance they are being required to carry is too high; some lenders will listen to reason, especially since legal precedent is being set in other states.

Over-insuring a property results in wasted dollars. Under-insuring can have more serious consequences. Guaranteed replacement cost coverage is available if the home is insured for 100 percent of the cost to repair or replace the structure. With guaranteed replacement cost coverage, the entire structure will be replaced at the insurance company's expense, even if this cost is more than the coverage amount. If you are not insured for 100 percent and your home burns to the ground, the insurance company will typically pay only 80 percent of the replacement cost, up to the coverage amount. Some insurance companies will not offer guaranteed replacement cost coverage on homes built before 1950.

Insurance in the amount of the purchase price is probably not necessary, because even when a house burns to the ground, a concrete foundation and the land usually remain. The foundation and land make up about 25 percent of the overall property value and will not need to be replaced in order to rebuild the structure.

Insuring for adequate protection, but not more than you need, is one way to save money. Another is to select a policy with a larger deductible amount. You can save approximately 10 percent on your insurance premium by accepting a $250 deductible rather than a $100 deductible. (The deductible is the amount paid by the homeowner on any given claim.)

Even if you are in the fortunate position of paying all cash, it's advisable to insure the property for its replacement value at the close of escrow. Buyers who take out a loan will be required to cover the house with a fire insurance policy that names the lender as loss payee. In addition to fire insurance, you will want to consider personal property coverage to protect against loss of your personal possessions and liability coverage to protect against claims for injury or damage. Earthquake insurance is available as an additional rider to a homeowner's insurance policy, but it usually has a very large deductible amount (as much as 5 percent of the replacement cost). If you live in an older home, the insurer may require that the home be secured to the foundation with anchor bolts, which can be installed by a contractor or structural pest control company. Flood insurance is customarily required by lenders in areas designated as "flood prone" under the National Flood Insurance Program. Purchasers of condominiums need insurance in addition to the general policy provided through membership in the homeowner's association which, in most cases, covers losses sustained to common areas but not damage to the inside of individual units or loss of personal possessions. Personal liability is also not covered by the general homeowner's association policy.

After you have selected insurance coverage for your new home, ask the insurance agent to contact your escrow officer to arrange for delivery of a policy or binder before closing. Most lenders will want the buyer to prepay the cost of the first year of coverage at the time of closing, although you may be able to arrange to pay semi-annually or quarterly, depending on the lender and the insurance carrier.

The insurance agent will want specific information about the property being covered before issuing the insurance policy. Since insurance premium discounts are available if the home is new or remodeled, has a smoke or security alarm, or is located close to a fire hydrant, make sure that your insurance agent has all the necessary information about the property before the policy is written.

How to Take Title to Your New Home

The manner in which you take title to property is an important consideration and should not be treated lightly. All too often, buyers give no consideration to this part of acquiring a home until they walk into the escrow office to sign the final closing papers.

Taking title as a single person is simple; there are no decisions to make since it's sole ownership. California is a community property state, so if you're married and are purchasing property that is to belong to you only, the title company will require a quitclaim deed in which your spouse relinquishes any interest in the property.

Two or more related or unrelated persons purchasing real property together have different options. How title is held between co-owners has legal, tax, and estate planning ramifications. Co-owners should consult with their legal or tax advisors before instructing the escrow officer how they want title to vest. The following is a brief summary of the three most common kinds of joint ownership used in California.

Unmarried co-owners can hold title with one another as joint tenants or as tenants in common. Joint tenancy provides for equal ownership interests and the right of survivorship, which means that at the death of one co-owner, that person's interest in the property passes to the remaining co-owner.

Tenants in common need not have equal interests in the property. Upon the death of one co-tenant, the decedent's interest in the property will pass to the heirs and not to the remaining co-tenants (unless they happen to be named as heirs under the will). In other words, the right of survivorship does not apply.

Married co-owners can hold title as tenants in common or as joint tenants. In California and in several other states, married individuals can also take title to real property as community property. Under community property ownership, the interests of the co-owners are equal, and each has the right to dispose of his or her one-half interest by will. In the absence of a will, the decedent's interest goes to the remaining spouse by right of succession.

The tax consequences of joint tenancy and community property ownership differ significantly when one spouse dies before the other. With community property, the entire tax basis of the property is stepped up to the fair market value at the date of the spouse's death. If the surviving spouse then sells the property for that fair market value, the taxable gain is zero. With joint tenancy, only one-half of the tax basis is stepped up to fair market value at the date of the spouse's death, which makes taxable gain at the time of sale a greater likelihood.

The estate of a deceased homeowner may need to be probated by the court, depending on how title was held during that person's life-time. Consult your legal and tax advisors regarding which method of holding title is best for you and your family.

ORDERING AND REVIEWING THE LOAN DOCUMENTS

Approximately two weeks before the close of escrow, the buyer's real estate agent or loan officer should instruct the escrow officer to order loan documents from the buyer's new lender. The timing is important, since loan papers usually contain an expiration date. Papers that are drawn too early may expire before closing; redrawing them usually involves an additional charge and can delay the closing. There is also a risk that the note could be redrawn at a higher rate if interest rates move upwards in the meantime.

It's not the escrow officer's responsibility to monitor the loan approval process: this should be taken care of by the real estate agent, the loan representative, and the buyers. But once the loan is approved, the escrow officer will need to be put in contact with the individual processing the loan for the lender (called a loan processor) in order to ensure a smooth closing.

Ask your escrow officer to provide you with a copy of the note to review in advance of signing the final closing papers. A fixed-rate note is fairly straightforward; you'll want to verify that the interest rate, monthly payment, and term of the loan are correct. An ARM note is much more complicated, and you won't be able to read and understand it in the half hour or so that you spend at the escrow company signing the final papers. Take time beforehand to study the way your ARM loan will work, making certain that the index, margin, periodic and life-of-loan caps, adjustment period, payment cap (if applicable), as well as the initial interest rate, monthly payment, and term of the loan are accurate on the note itself. Direct any questions you have to your loan agent, and if the lender has made an error on the note have it corrected at the lender's expense.

SETTLING UP: WHO PAYS FOR WHAT?

Before an escrow is closed, a final accounting of the charges owed by the buyers and sellers is prepared by the escrow officer. If time permits, ask for a copy of the settlement statement (see sample form included) so you can review the itemization of charges in advance. At the very least, have your agent review the settlement sheet with the escrow officer to make sure that no mistakes have been made.

The amount of your closing costs should not come as a surprise to you. Under the Real Estate Settlement Procedures Act, the lender is required to provide the buyers with an estimate of closing costs

A. Settlement Statement

U.S. Department of Housing
and Urban Development

OMB No. 2502-0265 (Exp. 12-31-86)

B. Type of Loan

1. ☐ FHA 2. ☐ FmHA 3. ☐ Conv. Unins.
4. ☐ VA 5. ☐ Conv. Ins.

6. File Number	7. Loan Number	8. Mortgage Insurance Case Number

C. Note: This form is furnished to give you a statement of actual settlement costs. Amounts paid to and by the settlement agent are shown. Items marked "(p.o.c.)" were paid outside the closing; they are shown here for informational purposes and are not included in the totals.

D. Name and Address of Borrower	E. Name and Address of Seller	F. Name and Address of Lender

G. Property Location	H. Settlement Agent
	Place of Settlement
	I. Settlement Date

J. Summary of Borrower's Transaction		K. Summary of Seller's Transaction	
100. Gross Amount Due From Borrower		**400. Gross Amount Due To Seller**	
101. Contract sales price		401. Contract sales price	
102. Personal property		402. Personal property	
103. Settlement charges to borrower (line 1400)		403.	
104.		404.	
105.		405.	
Adjustments for items paid by seller in advance		Adjustments for items paid by seller in advance	
106. City/town taxes to		406. City/town taxes to	
107. County taxes to		407. County taxes to	
108. Assessments to		408. Assessments to	
109.		409.	
110.		410.	
111.		411.	
112.		412.	
120. Gross Amount Due From Borrower		**420. Gross Amount Due To Seller**	
200. Amounts Paid By Or In Behalf Of Borrower		**500. Reductions In Amount Due To Seller**	
201. Deposit or earnest money		501. Excess deposit (see instructions)	
202. Principal amount of new loan(s)		502. Settlement charges to seller (line 1400)	
203. Existing loan(s) taken subject to		503. Existing loan(s) taken subject to	
204.		504. Payoff of first mortgage loan	
205.		505. Payoff of second mortgage loan	
206.		506.	
207.		507.	
208.		508.	
209.		509.	
Adjustments for items unpaid by seller		Adjustments for items unpaid by seller	
210. City/town taxes to		510. City/town taxes to	
211. County taxes to		511. County taxes to	
212. Assessments to		512. Assessments to	
213.		513.	
214.		514.	
215.		515.	
216.		516.	
217.		517.	
218.		518.	
219.		519.	
220. Total Paid By/For Borrower		**520. Total Reduction Amount Due Seller**	
300. Cash At Settlement From/To Borrower		**600. Cash At Settlement To/From Seller**	
301. Gross Amount due from borrower (line 120)		601. Gross amount due to seller (line 420)	
302. Less amounts paid by/for borrower (line 220)	( )	602. Less reductions in amt. due seller (line 520)	( )
303. Cash ☐ From ☐ To Borrower		603. Cash ☐ To ☐ From Seller	

Previous Edition Is Obsolete

HUD-1 (3-86)
RESPA, HB 4305.2

L. Settlement Charges

	Paid From Borrowers Funds at Settlement	Paid From Seller's Funds at Settlement
700. Total Sales/Broker's Commission based on price $ _____ @ _____ % = _____		
Division of Commission (line 700) as follows:		
701. $ _____ to _____		
702. $ _____ to _____		
703. Commission paid at Settlement		
704.		
800. Items Payable In Connection With Loan		
801. Loan Origination Fee _____ %		
802. Loan Discount _____ %		
803. Appraisal Fee _____ to		
804. Credit Report _____ to		
805. Lender's Inspection Fee		
806. Mortgage Insurance Application Fee to		
807. Assumption Fee		
808.		
809.		
810.		
811.		
900. Items Required By Lender To Be Paid In Advance		
901. Interest from _____ to _____ @$ _____ /day		
902. Mortgage Insurance Premium for _____ months to		
903. Hazard Insurance Premium for _____ years to		
904. _____ years to		
905.		
1000. Reserves Deposited With Lender		
1001. Hazard insurance _____ months@$ _____ per month		
1002. Mortgage insurance _____ months@$ _____ per month		
1003. City property taxes _____ months@$ _____ per month		
1004. County property taxes _____ months@$ _____ per month		
1005. Annual assessments _____ months@$ _____ per month		
1006. _____ months@$ _____ per month		
1007. _____ months@$ _____ per month		
1008. _____ months@$ _____ per month		
1100. Title Charges		
1101. Settlement or closing fee _____ to		
1102. Abstract or title search _____ to		
1103. Title examination _____ to		
1104. Title insurance binder _____ to		
1105. Document preparation _____ to		
1106. Notary fees _____ to		
1107. Attorney's fees _____ to		
(includes above items numbers: _____)		
1108. Title insurance _____ to		
(includes above items numbers: _____)		
1109. Lender's coverage $ _____		
1110. Owner's coverage $ _____		
1111.		
1112.		
1113.		
1200. Government Recording and Transfer Charges		
1201. Recording fees: Deed $ _____ ; Mortgage $ _____ ; Releases $ _____		
1202. City/county tax/stamps: Deed $ _____ ; Mortgage $ _____		
1203. State tax/stamps: Deed $ _____ ; Mortgage $ _____		
1204.		
1205.		
1300. Additional Settlement Charges		
1301. Survey _____ to		
1302. Pest Inspection to		
1303.		
1304.		
1305.		
1400. Total Settlement Charges (enter on lines 103, Section J and 502, Section K)		

within three days of receiving a residential loan application. In addition, your real estate agent should have prepared an approximate buyer's or seller's cost sheet at the time you negotiated the purchase agreement. Who pays what closing costs is not set by law and varies somewhat from one county to the next. Local custom usually prevails.

Buyer's closing costs usually include loan fees (points), appraisal and credit report fees, proration of interest on the new loan, all or part of a local transfer tax (where applicable), inspection fees, title insurance (in some counties), escrow fees (in some counties), document preparation fees, recording and notary fees, property tax proration, the fire insurance premium, and a tax service (if required by the lender). Buyers have the option of purchasing a home protection plan at the close of escrow if the seller does not offer one; sometimes this expense is shared between the buyers and sellers.

Proration of interest is a charge collected by the lender at closing if your first loan payment is not due exactly thirty days following the date of recordation. For instance, let's say escrow closes on May 15, and your first loan payment is due July 1; this payment will include interest owed for the month of June. The lender will collect a sum equal to the interest owed from May 15 to June 1 at closing, and this sum is referred to as prorated interest. Since interest paid on your home mortgage is tax deductible, make certain that the statement you receive from your lender indicating interest paid in your first year of ownership includes this prorated interest amount.

The IRS will generally consider the loan origination fee, or points, paid on your new home loan to be tax deductible in the year of purchase if payment is made directly from the borrower's own funds. If this fee is merely subtracted from the loan proceeds, however, the deduction might have to be taken over the loan term. If you plan to deduct the points in the year of purchase, make arrangements to pay them separately.

Prorations are based on a thirty-day month and on a 360-day year. Property taxes will be prorated at the day escrow closes. If the seller has prepaid property taxes, the buyer credits the seller for this amount in escrow; if taxes have been accruing but are not yet due, the amount owed by the seller is credited to the buyer, who then takes responsibility for the future tax bill when it becomes due. If escrow is to close several days before taxes are due, the escrow officer will often arrange to pay the bill through the escrow. Property taxes in California are paid in two installments. The first, which covers the period of ownership from July 1 through December 31, is due November 1 and becomes delinquent December 10; the second is due February 1, becomes delinquent April 10, and covers from January 1 through June 30.

Following close of escrow, the property is reassessed and a supplemental tax bill is issued which becomes a lien against the property. How soon the supplemental bill will arrive after the close varies from several weeks to six months or longer, depending on the county in which the property is located. If the sellers have recently acquired title to the property (through inheritance, for instance), their supplemental tax figures might not be available at the time of closing. In this case, the buyer should make sure that an agreement is drawn up stating that the sellers will pay for their supplemental tax bill when it becomes available.

A buyer is responsible for the payment of property taxes and monthly loan payments regardless of whether or not a tax bill or payment coupon is received. Mark the due dates of your first loan and property tax payments on your calendar as a reminder. If you haven't received the appropriate bills in time, call the escrow officer who can tell you where to make the loan payment and the account number that should appear on the check. The escrow officer can also find out the amount of property tax owed, the reference number to include on your check, and where you need to send the payment. Remember, lenders charge late fees that will probably be reflected on your credit record and there are penalties for delinquent property taxes.

Seller's costs customarily include payoffs of existing loans, prepayment penalties and late charges, accrued interest on existing loans, property tax proration, the documentary transfer tax ($1.10 per thousand), a portion of a local transfer tax (where applicable), a home protection plan (sometimes a shared expense), termite work, real estate commission, document preparation, title insurance (in some counties), escrow fees (in some counties), and recording and notary fees.

A seller is always one month behind on interest payments owed to the lender because interest is paid at the end, not the beginning, of each month. For example, the loan payment for May will include interest for the month of April. When a seller pays a loan off in full, the lender collects any remaining interest owed, which is usually at least one month's worth. This is referred to as accrued interest. In addition to this, the lender charges interest until the loan payoff check is received by the lending institution, which could be several days following the close date if the lender is not local. Ask the escrow officer to send the loan payoff check by express mail if your daily interest charge is more than the cost of express mail.

The above applies unless you have an FHA loan, in which case you will probably be charged an extra thirty-days' interest at loan payoff since a loan payment on an FHA loan can usually only be made once a month.

Rents are prorated to the close of escrow if the property is tenant-occupied and any deposits the seller is holding are transferred to the buyer at closing. If a seller is staying in possession after the close and is paying rent to the buyer, this will be reflected on the closing statement unless the rent money is held in the escrow account. In this case, prorated rent is released to the buyer at the time the seller vacates, and any unused portion is returned to the seller. Likewise, if the buyer moved into the property before transfer of title and agreed to pay rent to the seller, this will appear as a credit to the seller on the settlement sheet unless the buyer paid the rent money directly to the seller in advance.

SIGNING THE CLOSING DOCUMENTS
The closing papers are ideally signed at the escrow or title company, where a notary is available and last minute changes to documents can be made if necessary. In California, the buyer and seller usually do not sign papers at the same time, and papers must be signed several days before the actual close date.

A buyer can expect to sign the escrow instructions and settlement sheet, the note and deed of trust from the lender, miscellaneous additional paperwork from the lender, an affidavit of vendor and vendee (if required), copies of termite and other reports pertaining to the property (including the preliminary title report), and any special instructions to the escrow holder regarding such items as holdbacks for work to be completed after the close or seller rent-back agreements. The seller's papers are usually less cumbersome and include the settlement sheet and escrow instructions, the grant deed, an affidavit of vendor and vendee (if required), copies of relevant reports pertaining to the property, any special instructions to the escrow holder, and an IRS tax reporting form.

An affidavit of vendor and vendee is a form often required by the lender that specifies the purchase price and the amount of the new loan. The buyer and seller disclose any additional financing that the seller is providing for the buyer. Signatures on this form must be notarized; providing false information can result in serious consequences.

The IRS tax reporting form must be completed by sellers of one to four unit residential properties. There are penalties for not reporting a sale, and a sale must be reported to the IRS even if no capital gains tax is owed. The escrow holder is charged with the primary responsibility for ensuring that this form is completed at closing.

Buyers and sellers are cautioned that they should not sign reports pertaining to the property if they have not received and read copies of the reports beforehand. If you find yourself being asked to sign for receipt of documents you're unsure about, tell the escrow officer you'd like the opportunity to read them and return the reports to escrow later. If this is not possible, you can sign all documents and instruct the officer not to close the escrow until you give final authorization to do so.

Sellers need to tell the escrow holder what to do with the sale proceeds check when it becomes available. This will usually be sometime during the day that the grant deed is recorded and title transfers to the buyer. If the sale proceeds are not going immediately toward the purchase of a new home, the sellers can either pick up the proceeds check, have it delivered to their real estate agent, or have it wired into their bank account (this will require a deposit slip or bank branch, account number, and routing instructions). The seller is cautioned to keep homeowner's insurance in effect on the property until confirmation is received that the escrow has closed and title is transferred to the new owner's name.

COORDINATING TWO OR MORE ESCROWS

Most people who are buying are also selling. A seller who is transferring the proceeds from the sale of one property to an escrow set up for the purposes of acquiring another should communicate this intent to both escrow officers involved as soon as possible after the escrows are opened. If you are buying and selling properties located in different counties, it may be necessary to have both escrows handled by the same title company in order to close the escrows simultaneously. A safer strategy is to stagger the close dates so that the home you're selling will close a day or two before the home you're buying does. In any event, cooperation and timely communication are necessary to ensure that multiple escrow closings are coordinated satisfactorily.

FUNDING THE PURCHASE AND CLOSING THE ESCROW

Collected (negotiable) funds are required to close an escrow in California. This means that the funding check from the lender and the check covering the buyer's cash down payment and all closing costs must be deposited into the escrow trust account before escrow can close. Additionally, closing funds must be in the form of either cashier's checks, drawn on California banks, or wired funds, which are negotiable upon receipt. Out-of-state buyers who are purchasing homes in California commonly pay with wired funds.

A buyer who is providing a separate check to pay for loan points should make sure that this is a cashier's check unless a personal check was deposited to escrow far enough in advance to have cleared before the projected close date. Many buyers make the mistake of assuming that their money market account checks constitute collected funds. Most money market account funds are drawn on out-of-state banks, so make arrangements with your local account representative well in advance.

When wiring funds, get the appropriate information from the escrow holder regarding how and where funds are to be wired. There are usually special bank routing requirements, and you should follow up to make certain that the funds are received. Plan ahead to avoid an awkward or costly last minute foul-up.

After the closing papers are signed, the buyer's loan documents and settlement papers (referred to as the funding package) are returned to the lender for final approval. This is to verify that all the loan documents have been properly executed and that any additional documentation required by the lender is included with the signed documents. Funding packages are usually approved by the lending institution in the order they are received. A delay at your end will undoubtedly cause a delay for the lender.

When the funding package is finally approved, the buyer's lender issues a check for the loan amount (called the funding check). The escrow holder should volunteer to pick up the check to facilitate a speedy closing. According to California state law, the check for the loan amount, as well as the remainder of the buyer's funds required for closing, must be in the escrow holder's trust account the day before the close date. The escrow holder arranges for the grant deed to be recorded at the county recorder's office on the day of closing, thereby transferring title to the property from the seller to the buyer.

WHAT TO DO IF YOUR ESCROW DOESN'T CLOSE ON TIME
The following items typically cause a delayed close of escrow:

1. The homeowner's insurance policy is not ordered far enough in advance of closing, or it is not received by the escrow holder in time.
2. The buyer's funds don't arrive in time. This could happen if wired funds are accidentally misdirected or if the buyer provides the escrow holder with a personal check rather than a cashier's check drawn on a California bank.
3. The funding check from the buyer's lender is not issued on time.
4. A termite clearance is required by the lender before the escrow can close and the work is delayed.
5. The home being purchased is a new construction and the work required to finish the home isn't complete.
6. Two escrows are closing concurrently or sequentially and a delay in one ties up funds needed to close the other.

The first thing to do when you hear that your escrow is not going to close as scheduled is to stay calm. Be sure that your agent informs all other parties involved in the transaction that there is an unavoidable delay. Get a written extension of the close of escrow if the closing will be postponed for longer than twenty-four hours. The last thing you should do, no matter how frustrated you may feel, is to call the loan processor directly.

Normally, escrows handled by title and escrow companies are recorded at the county recorder's office once daily. In some counties, it's possible for the escrow holder to arrange for a "special" recording later in the day. Ask your escrow officer or real estate agent to set up a special recording if the cause of the delay is resolved quickly.

Ideally, buyers should not take possession of their new homes until the escrow has closed. Whenever possible, postpone the move until the last minute problem has been sorted out. In busy real estate markets, it may not be possible to reschedule professional movers late in the game. As a last resort, the buyer can ask the seller for permission to occupy the property before the closing and, if the seller is agreeable, an addendum should be drawn up indicating the terms and conditions under which the buyer can move in early. An interim occupancy agreement should also be signed by the buyer and seller, and the buyer's insurance must be in effect as of the date of occupancy.

CHAPTER 12

THE FINISHING TOUCHES

AFTER THE ESCROW CLOSES

Soon after closing you will receive various documents from the title company. Buyers should expect a copy of the final settlement sheet, the title insurance policy, a homeowner's insurance policy, and usually a refund check. Often the escrow holder will estimate closing costs (particularly interest and property tax prorations) on the high side to cover for the possibility that the closing will be delayed several days. The settlement sheet is adjusted as of the close date to reflect prorations, and the excess funds are returned to the buyer.

Sellers will receive a copy of the final settlement statement, which may or may not accompany the proceeds check. The escrow holder will usually prepare the checks first and copies of the final paperwork later. If the proceeds are not to be transferred immediately to another escrow, the seller should arrange to deposit the funds into an interest bearing account as soon as possible. Sellers who carry financing for the buyer will also receive the note, a recorded deed of trust in favor of the sellers, a copy of the title insurance policy, and a fire insurance policy to cover the seller as loss payee. Recorded documents, including recorded reconveyances of loans that were paid off at closing, will usually be sent to the sellers separately.

GETTING READY TO MOVE

Buyers and sellers should start planning the move no later than the date escrow is opened. A seller who is transferring across the country should begin even sooner.

Obtain bids from several movers in advance. One way to save money moving, if you have the time, is to do packing yourself. If you're undecided about whether you'll be doing the packing, ask each moving company representative to give you two estimates: one for moving and the other for both packing and moving. Many moving companies have free literature that can be helpful in planning and making your move. Be sure to ask each representative to provide you with whatever informational material they have available.

Select a mover and set the move date thirty to sixty days in advance. During periods of peak real estate activity, it may be necessary to schedule the move farther in advance. Find out what the moving company's maximum liability is for loss or damage to your possessions. Arrange for additional insurance coverage if necessary.

A surefire way to save on moving expenses is to throw out, sell, or donate surplus possessions before you move. Be sure to arrange to make donations in advance and obtain a receipt for the approximate value of your donated items. This amount can be deducted from your gross income at tax time if you itemize deductions. Once you've eliminated everything you're not moving, prepare an inventory of the possessions you're taking with you.

Start packing possessions you're not currently using and list the contents of each box on two sides. If labeling doesn't appeal to you, at least number each box and keep a list of the contents as this will simplify unloading and unpacking at the new home. Sturdy boxes suitable for packing are hard to find; moving boxes can be purchased directly from moving companies if necessary.

TRANSFERRING UTILITIES AND OTHER SERVICES

At least two weeks before the move, call the gas, electric, phone, water, garbage collection, and cable television companies in the new and old locations and arrange for the services to be transferred out of your name at the old house and into your name at the new house. It's preferable to have utilities transferred rather than shut off, as in this way you will avoid reconnect frees and the inconvenience of waiting for installers. Buyers who are not taking possession as soon as the seller vacates should make sure that utilities are transferred into their names so that lights can be left on and the yard watered.

Arrange to sell or transfer any club memberships if you're moving out of the area. Notify the post office of your change of address and send address change cards to magazine publishers, credit card companies, your present employer, banks, friends and relatives. Don't forget to notify important business contacts, the Department of Motor Vehicles, and your insurance carriers.

Stop services at the old location, such as the gardener, housekeeper, and newspaper. If the buyer is not immediately taking possession of the property, make arrangements for someone to water the yard.

Ask your dentist, doctor, lawyer, investment broker, and tax advisor for recommendations of professionals to work with in your new community. Transfer important documents, such as school and medical records. Open a bank checking account convenient to your new home and transfer funds in advance so that you have a source of cash when you arrive. If this isn't possible, at least purchase a good supply of traveler's checks to tide you over.

Have rugs and draperies you're taking with you professionally cleaned and packed for moving during the last week before the move. Have the car serviced if you'll be driving a long distance to your new location. Take care of overdue doctor or dentist appointments before you go. Moving companies usually will not move pets and sometimes won't move house plants. Make separate arrangements for both.

LEARNING THE IDIOSYNCRASIES OF YOUR NEW HOME IN ADVANCE
Ask your real estate agent to arrange for a meeting with the sellers to learn the intricacies of the home. It saves the buyer a lot of time, not to mention frustration, if the locations of outdoor lights, sprinkler system valves, and electrical panels are known in advance. Automatic sprinkler and security systems may require special instructions.

The buyer should inquire if there are any specific routine maintenance items required to keep the house in top condition. Do gutters need cleaning? How often? Are there any drains that need to be cleaned out periodically? Are there areas of the roof or around the foundation that require caulking? Ask the sellers to leave you the names and phone numbers of the tradespeople they have used to maintain the house in the past. Such recommendations are valuable, since these people have worked on the house and are familiar with it. If you're moving into a completely new community, ask the sellers to give you a rundown of the neighborhood and to introduce you to a few of your new neighbors.

Your agent should accompany you on this final meeting with the sellers. If you meet alone with the sellers and disclosure of a material defect is made which had not been made previously, you must get the information in writing. This information should have been included on the Real Estate Transfer Disclosure statement; if it wasn't, it needs to be in writing at this point.

A disclosure of a material fact affecting a residential property automatically institutes a three-day right of rescission period, during which time the buyer can terminate the contract and the deposit money will be returned. At this late date, the last thing the buyer will want is to rescind the contract. But full disclosure is required by California law, and the disclosure at least gives the buyer the opportunity to negotiate satisfactory compensation for a previously undisclosed problem. Failing to deal with the problem before the closing could result in more time-consuming and costly attempts at reconciliation after the close. When buyers and sellers don't have the opportunity to conduct a walk-through before taking possession of the home, the sellers should leave a note for the buyers detailing any relevant information, along with any operating manuals the sellers have in their possession.

ON MOVING DAY

Before the movers arrive, you should have packed a survival kit of clothes, toys for children, toilet articles, and food: everything you'll need until the remainder of your possessions arrive. You'll also want your driver's license, car registration, credit cards, checkbook and traveler's checks, pertinent addresses and phone numbers, and maps. Also take a phone book from your old house with you in case you need to reach someone in your former location.

You should be on hand to supervise the move and packing (if the movers are also packing your possessions).

> Ross Sutter had a pressing problem at work and was not home the day the movers came to pack his belongings and move them to his new home. The movers packed a number of items that were to remain in the house for the new buyers including the automatic garage door openers. This presented a considerable problem when the buyers attempted to move in, since the only way to move large pieces of furniture into the house was through the garage.

Leave the house keys with your real estate agent or a neighbor and make sure the buyers are informed about when and where the keys can be picked up. Extra keys should be left in the house along with automatic garage door openers. Make sure to leave your new mailing address at your old home, so the mail can be forwarded. If your house will be left vacant for some time before the buyers move in, notify the police and let your neighbors know.

Be available when the movers arrive to supervise the unloading. Make sure that your possessions are intact and that nothing is missing. Report any damage or suspected theft to the moving company immediately. The unloading will proceed quickly if you know in advance where you want your possessions placed.

INTEREST RATE %	15 YEAR TERM	30 YEAR TERM	INTEREST RATE %	15 YEAR TERM	30 YEAR TERM
7	8.99	6.65	11½	11.69	9.91
7¼	9.13	6.83	11¾	11.85	10.10
7½	9.28	6.99	12	12.01	10.29
7¾	9.41	7.17	12¼	12.17	10.48
8	9.56	7.34	12½	12.33	10.68
8¼	9.71	7.51	12¾	12.49	10.87
8½	9.85	7.69	13	12.66	11.07
8¾	10.00	7.87	13¼	12.81	11.26
9	10.15	8.05	13½	12.99	11.46
9¼	10.30	8.23	13¾	13.15	11.66
9½	10.45	8.41	14	13.32	11.85
9¾	10.60	8.60	14¼	13.49	12.05
10	10.75	8.78	14½	13.66	12.25
10¼	10.90	8.97	14¾	13.83	12.45
10½	11.06	9.15	15	14.00	12.65
10¾	11.21	9.34	15¼	14.17	12.85
11	11.37	9.53	15½	14.34	13.05
11¼	11.53	9.72	15¾	14.52	13.25

This chart indicates the dollar amount required monthly to amortize a loan of $1,000. Divide your Affordable Mortgage Payment (see Chapter One) by the appropriate factor and multiply by $1,000 to determine your Affordable Loan Amount. For example, if your Affordable Mortgage Payment is $1,020 and you want to know the size loan you can afford if you apply for an adjustable home loan with an 8 percent initial interest rate (thirty-year term), divide $1,020 by 7.34 and multiply by $1,000. Your Affordable Loan Amount is approximately $139,000.

To determine what the monthly payment (principal and interest only) will be on any loan amount, divide the loan amount by 1,000 and multiply by the appropriate factor. For instance, a $150,000 loan at 10 percent interest with a thirty-year term will have a monthly payment of $1,317. (Divide $150,000 by 1,000 and multiply by 8.78.)

To determine the cash required to purchase a home, once you know your Affordable Loan Amount, divide the loan amount by 80 percent (.80) or 90 percent (.90), depending on how much cash you have available. For example, if you can afford a $150,000 loan amount, your Approximate Affordable Purchase Price will be $187,500, if you obtain an 80 percent loan ($150,000 divided by .80). Buyers who are well qualified but short on cash may need to apply for 90 percent financing, in which case your Approximate Affordable Purchase

Price will be $166,667 ($150,000 divided by .90). Subtract the Affordable Loan Amount from the Approximate Affordable Purchase Price to determine your cash down payment. Don't forget to multiply the Affordable Loan Amount by 4 percent (.04) to determine your approximate closing costs and add this figure to your down payment to arrive at the approximate cash required to buy your new home.

The accuracy of the figures contained in the tables in this book is believed to be correct but cannot be guaranteed.

How to Use the Amortization Schedule

The amortization schedule can be used to determine the monthly principal and interest payment for any loan amount. Read down the far left column until you reach the loan amount in question, then read across the page to the appropriate interest rate and select a 15-year or 30-year amortization period. Monthly principal and interest payments for loan amounts not provided on the chart are computed by combining loan amounts and their corresponding monthly payment figures together. For example, to find the monthly principal and interest payment on a $92,000 30-year loan with an interest rate of 7¾%, add $644.77 (the monthly payment on a $90,000 loan with a 7¾% interest rate and a 30-year due date) to $14.33 (the monthly payment on a $2,000 loan with a 7¾% interest rate and a 30-year due date) for a total of $659.10. The monthly principal and interest payment on a $150,000 loan with a 9% interest rate and a 15-year due date is $1,521.40 and is calculated by adding $1,014.27 (the monthly payment on a $100,000 loan with a 9% interest rate and a 15-year due date) to $507.13 (the monthly payment on a $50,000 loan with a 9% interest rate and a 15-year due date).

DUE DATE YEARS	15	30	15	30	15	30	15	30
LOAN AMOUNT	7%		7¼%		7½%		7¾%	
1,000	8.99	6.65	9.13	6.82	9.27	6.99	9.41	7.16
2,000	17.98	13.31	18.26	13.64	18.54	13.98	18.83	14.33
3,000	26.96	19.96	27.39	20.47	27.81	20.98	28.24	21.49
4,000	35.95	26.61	36.51	27.29	37.08	27.97	37.65	28.66
5,000	44.94	33.27	45.64	34.11	46.35	34.96	47.06	35.82
6,000	53.93	39.92	54.77	40.93	55.62	41.95	56.48	42.98
7,000	62.92	46.57	63.90	47.75	64.89	48.95	65.89	50.15
8,000	71.91	53.22	73.03	54.57	74.16	55.94	75.30	57.31
9,000	80.89	59.88	82.16	61.40	83.43	62.93	84.71	64.48
10,000	89.88	66.53	91.29	68.22	92.70	69.92	94.13	71.64
20,000	179.77	133.06	182.57	136.44	185.40	139.84	188.26	143.28
30,000	269.65	199.59	273.86	204.65	278.10	209.76	282.38	214.92
40,000	359.53	266.12	365.15	272.87	370.80	279.69	376.51	286.56
50,000	449.41	332.65	456.43	341.09	463.51	349.61	470.64	358.21
60,000	539.30	399.18	547.72	409.31	556.21	419.53	564.77	429.85
70,000	629.18	465.71	639.00	477.52	648.91	489.45	658.89	501.49
80,000	719.06	532.24	730.29	545.74	741.61	559.37	753.02	573.13
90,000	808.95	598.77	821.58	613.96	834.31	629.29	847.15	644.77
100,000	898.83	665.30	912.86	682.18	927.01	699.21	941.28	716.41

DUE DATE YEARS	15	30	15	30	15	30	15	30
LOAN AMOUNT	8%		8¼%		8½%		8¾%	
1,000	9.56	7.34	9.70	7.51	9.85	7.69	9.99	7.87
2,000	19.11	14.68	19.40	15.03	19.69	15.38	19.99	15.73
3,000	28.67	22.01	29.10	22.54	29.54	23.07	29.98	23.60
4,000	38.23	29.35	38.81	30.05	39.39	30.76	39.98	31.47
5,000	47.78	36.69	48.51	37.56	49.24	38.45	49.97	39.34
6,000	57.34	44.03	58.21	45.08	59.08	46.13	59.97	47.20
7,000	66.90	51.36	67.91	52.59	68.93	53.82	69.96	55.07
8,000	76.45	58.70	77.61	60.10	78.78	61.51	79.96	62.94
9,000	86.01	66.04	87.31	67.61	88.63	69.20	89.95	70.80
10,000	95.57	73.38	97.01	75.13	98.47	76.89	99.94	78.67
20,000	191.13	146.75	194.03	150.25	196.95	153.78	199.89	157.34
30,000	286.70	220.13	291.04	225.38	295.42	230.67	299.83	236.01
40,000	382.26	293.51	388.06	300.51	393.90	307.57	399.78	314.68
50,000	477.83	366.88	485.07	375.63	492.37	384.46	499.72	393.35
60,000	573.39	440.26	582.08	450.76	590.84	461.35	599.67	472.02
70,000	668.96	513.64	679.10	525.89	689.32	538.24	699.61	550.69
80,000	764.52	587.01	776.11	601.01	787.79	615.13	799.56	629.36
90,000	860.09	660.39	873.13	676.14	886.27	692.02	899.50	708.03
100,000	955.65	733.76	970.14	751.27	984.74	768.91	999.45	786.70
LOAN AMOUNT	9%		9¼%		9½%		9¾%	
1,000	10.14	8.05	10.29	8.23	10.44	8.41	10.59	8.59
2,000	20.29	16.09	20.58	16.45	20.88	16.82	21.19	17.18
3,000	30.43	24.14	30.88	24.68	31.33	25.23	31.78	25.77
4,000	40.57	32.18	41.17	32.91	41.77	33.63	42.37	34.37
5,000	50.71	40.23	51.46	41.13	52.21	42.04	52.97	42.96
6,000	60.86	48.28	61.75	49.36	62.65	50.45	63.56	51.55
7,000	71.00	56.32	72.04	57.59	73.10	58.86	74.16	60.14
8,000	81.14	64.37	82.34	65.81	83.54	67.27	84.75	68.73
9,000	91.28	72.42	92.63	74.04	93.98	75.68	95.34	77.32
10,000	101.43	80.46	102.92	82.27	104.42	84.09	105.94	85.92
20,000	202.85	160.92	205.84	164.54	208.84	168.17	211.87	171.83
30,000	304.28	241.39	308.76	246.80	313.27	252.26	317.81	257.75
40,000	405.71	321.85	411.68	329.07	417.69	336.34	423.75	343.66
50,000	507.13	402.31	514.60	411.34	522.11	420.43	529.68	429.58
60,000	608.56	482.77	617.52	493.61	626.53	504.51	635.62	515.49
70,000	709.99	563.24	720.43	575.87	730.96	588.60	741.55	601.41
80,000	811.41	643.70	823.35	658.14	835.38	672.68	847.49	687.32
90,000	912.84	724.16	926.27	740.41	939.80	756.77	953.43	773.24
100,000	1,014.27	804.62	1,029.19	822.68	1,044.22	840.85	1,059.36	859.15

DUE DATE YEARS	15	30	15	30	15	30	15	30
LOAN AMOUNT	10%		10¼%		10½%		10¾%	
1,000	10.75	8.78	10.90	8.96	11.05	9.15	11.21	9.33
2,000	21.49	17.55	21.80	17.92	22.11	18.29	22.42	18.67
3,000	32.24	26.33	32.70	26.88	33.16	27.44	33.63	28.00
4,000	42.98	35.10	43.60	35.84	44.22	36.59	44.84	37.34
5,000	53.73	43.88	54.50	44.81	55.27	45.74	56.05	46.67
6,000	64.48	52.65	65.40	53.77	66.32	54.88	67.26	56.01
7,000	75.22	61.43	76.30	62.73	77.38	64.03	78.47	65.34
8,000	85.97	70.21	87.20	71.69	88.43	73.18	89.68	74.68
9,000	96.71	78.98	98.10	80.65	99.49	82.33	100.89	84.01
10,000	107.46	87.76	109.00	89.61	110.54	91.47	112.09	93.35
20,000	214.92	175.51	217.99	179.22	221.08	182.95	224.19	186.70
30,000	322.38	263.27	326.99	268.83	331.62	274.42	336.28	280.04
40,000	429.84	351.03	435.98	358.44	442.16	365.90	448.38	373.39
50,000	537.30	438.79	544.98	448.05	552.70	457.37	560.47	466.74
60,000	644.76	526.54	653.97	537.66	663.24	548.84	672.57	560.09
70,000	752.22	614.30	762.97	627.27	773.78	640.32	784.66	653.44
80,000	859.68	702.06	871.96	716.88	884.32	731.79	896.76	746.79
90,000	967.14	789.81	980.96	806.49	994.86	823.27	1,008.85	840.13
100,000	1,074.61	877.57	1,089.95	896.10	1,105.40	914.74	1,120.95	933.48
LOAN AMOUNT	11%		11¼%		11½%		11¾%	
1,000	11.37	9.52	11.52	9.71	11.68	9.90	11.84	10.09
2,000	22.73	19.05	23.05	19.43	23.36	19.81	23.68	20.19
3,000	34.10	28.57	34.57	29.14	35.05	29.71	35.52	30.28
4,000	45.46	38.09	46.09	38.85	46.73	39.61	47.37	40.38
5,000	56.83	47.62	57.62	48.56	58.41	49.51	59.21	50.47
6,000	68.20	57.14	69.14	58.28	70.09	59.42	71.05	60.56
7,000	79.56	66.66	80.66	67.99	81.77	69.32	82.89	70.66
8,000	90.93	76.19	92.19	77.70	93.46	79.22	94.73	80.75
9,000	102.29	85.71	103.71	87.41	105.14	89.13	106.57	90.85
10,000	113.66	95.23	115.23	97.13	116.82	99.03	118.41	100.94
20,000	227.32	190.46	230.47	194.25	233.64	198.06	236.83	201.88
30,000	340.98	285.70	345.70	291.38	350.46	297.09	355.24	302.82
40,000	454.64	380.93	460.94	388.50	467.28	396.12	473.65	403.76
50,000	568.30	476.16	576.17	485.63	584.09	495.15	592.07	504.70
60,000	681.96	571.39	691.41	582.76	700.91	594.17	710.48	605.65
70,000	795.62	666.63	806.64	679.88	817.73	693.20	828.89	706.59
80,000	909.28	761.86	921.88	777.01	934.55	792.23	947.31	807.53
90,000	1,022.94	857.09	1,037.11	874.14	1,051.37	891.26	1,065.72	908.47
100,000	1,136.60	952.32	1,152.34	971.26	1,168.19	990.29	1,184.13	1,009.41

DUE DATE YEARS	15	30	15	30	15	30	15	30
LOAN AMOUNT	12%		12¼%		12½%		12¾%	
1,000	12.00	10.29	12.16	10.48	12.33	10.67	12.49	10.87
2,000	24.00	20.57	24.33	20.96	24.65	21.35	24.98	21.73
3,000	36.01	30.86	36.49	31.44	36.98	32.02	37.47	32.60
4,000	48.01	41.14	48.65	41.92	49.30	42.69	49.95	43.47
5,000	60.01	51.43	60.81	52.39	61.63	53.36	62.44	54.33
6,000	72.01	61.72	72.98	62.87	73.95	64.04	74.93	65.20
7,000	84.01	72.00	85.14	73.35	86.28	74.71	87.42	76.07
8,000	96.01	82.29	97.30	83.83	98.60	85.38	99.91	86.94
9,000	108.02	92.58	109.47	94.31	110.93	96.05	112.40	97.80
10,000	120.02	102.86	121.63	104.79	123.25	106.73	124.88	108.67
20,000	240.03	205.72	243.26	209.58	246.50	213.45	249.77	217.34
30,000	360.05	308.58	364.89	314.37	369.76	320.18	374.65	326.01
40,000	480.07	411.45	486.52	419.16	493.01	426.90	499.53	434.68
50,000	600.08	514.31	608.15	523.95	616.26	533.63	624.42	543.35
60,000	720.10	617.17	729.78	628.74	739.51	640.35	749.30	652.02
70,000	840.12	720.03	851.41	733.53	862.77	747.08	874.19	760.69
80,000	960.13	822.89	973.04	838.32	986.02	853.81	999.07	869.35
90,000	1,080.15	925.75	1,094.67	943.11	1,109.27	960.53	1,123.95	978.02
100,000	1,200.17	1,028.61	1,216.30	1,047.90	1,232.52	1,067.26	1,248.84	1,086.69
LOAN AMOUNT	13%		13¼%		13½%		13¾%	
1,000	12.65	11.06	12.82	11.26	12.98	11.45	13.15	11.65
2,000	25.30	22.12	25.63	22.52	25.97	22.91	26.30	23.30
3,000	37.96	33.19	38.45	33.77	38.95	34.36	39.45	34.95
4,000	50.61	44.25	51.27	45.03	51.93	45.82	52.60	46.60
5,000	63.26	55.31	64.09	56.29	64.92	57.27	65.75	58.26
6,000	75.91	66.37	76.90	67.55	77.90	68.72	78.90	69.91
7,000	88.57	77.43	89.72	78.80	90.88	80.18	92.05	81.56
8,000	101.22	88.50	102.54	90.06	103.87	91.63	105.20	93.21
9,000	113.87	99.56	115.36	101.32	116.85	103.09	118.35	104.86
10,000	126.52	110.62	128.17	112.58	129.83	114.54	131.50	116.51
20,000	253.05	221.24	256.35	225.15	259.66	229.08	263.00	233.02
30,000	379.57	331.86	384.52	337.73	389.50	343.62	394.50	349.53
40,000	506.10	442.48	512.69	450.31	519.33	458.16	525.99	466.05
50,000	632.62	553.10	640.87	562.89	649.16	572.71	657.49	582.56
60,000	759.15	663.72	769.04	675.46	778.99	687.25	788.99	699.07
70,000	885.67	774.34	897.22	788.04	908.82	801.79	920.49	815.58
80,000	1,012.19	884.96	1,025.39	900.62	1,038.65	916.33	1,051.99	932.09
90,000	1,138.72	995.58	1,153.56	1,013.20	1,168.49	1,030.87	1,183.49	1,048.60
100,000	1,265.24	1,106.20	1,281.74	1,125.77	1,298.32	1,145.41	1,314.99	1,165.11

DUE DATE YEARS	15	30	15	30	15	30	15	30
LOAN AMOUNT	**14%**		**14¼%**		**14½%**		**14¾%**	
1,000	13.32	11.85	13.49	12.05	13.66	12.25	13.83	12.44
2,000	26.63	23.70	26.97	24.09	27.31	24.49	27.65	24.89
3,000	39.95	35.55	40.46	36.14	40.97	36.74	41.48	37.33
4,000	53.27	47.39	53.94	48.19	54.62	48.98	55.30	49.78
5,000	66.59	59.24	67.43	60.23	68.28	61.23	69.13	62.22
6,000	79.90	71.09	80.91	72.28	81.93	73.47	82.95	74.67
7,000	93.22	82.94	94.40	84.33	95.59	85.72	96.78	87.11
8,000	106.54	94.79	107.89	96.37	109.24	97.96	110.60	99.56
9,000	119.86	106.64	121.37	108.42	122.90	110.21	124.43	112.00
10,000	133.17	118.49	134.86	120.47	136.55	122.46	138.25	124.45
20,000	266.35	236.97	269.72	240.94	273.10	244.91	276.50	248.90
30,000	399.52	355.46	404.57	361.41	409.65	367.37	414.75	373.34
40,000	532.70	473.95	539.43	481.87	546.20	489.82	553.00	497.79
50,000	665.87	592.44	674.29	602.34	682.75	612.28	691.25	622.24
60,000	799.04	710.92	809.15	722.81	819.30	734.73	829.50	746.69
70,000	932.22	829.41	944.01	843.28	955.85	857.19	967.75	871.13
80,000	1,065.39	947.90	1,078.86	963.75	1,092.40	979.64	1,106.00	995.58
90,000	1,198.57	1,066.38	1,213.72	1,084.22	1,228.95	1,102.10	1,244.25	1,120.03
100,000	1,331.74	1,184.87	1,348.58	1,204.69	1,365.50	1,224.56	1,382.50	1,244.48

LOAN AMOUNT	**15%**		**15¼%**		**15½%**		**15¾%**	
1,000	14.00	12.64	14.17	12.84	14.34	13.05	14.51	13.25
2,000	27.99	25.29	28.33	25.69	28.68	26.09	29.03	26.49
3,000	41.99	37.93	42.50	38.53	43.02	39.14	43.54	39.74
4,000	55.98	50.58	56.67	51.38	57.36	52.18	58.05	52.98
5,000	69.98	63.22	70.84	64.22	71.70	65.23	72.57	66.23
6,000	83.98	75.87	85.00	77.07	86.04	78.27	87.08	79.48
7,000	97.97	88.51	99.17	89.91	100.38	91.32	101.59	92.72
8,000	111.97	101.16	113.34	102.76	114.72	104.36	116.10	105.97
9,000	125.96	113.80	127.51	115.60	129.06	117.41	130.62	119.22
10,000	139.96	126.44	141.67	128.45	143.40	130.45	145.13	132.46
20,000	279.92	252.89	283.35	256.89	286.80	260.90	290.26	264.92
30,000	419.88	379.33	425.02	385.34	430.20	391.36	435.39	397.39
40,000	559.83	505.78	566.70	513.78	573.60	521.81	580.52	529.85
50,000	699.79	632.22	708.37	642.23	717.00	652.26	725.65	662.31
60,000	839.75	758.67	850.05	770.68	860.39	782.71	870.78	794.77
70,000	979.71	885.11	991.72	899.12	1003.79	913.16	1015.92	927.23
80,000	1,119.67	1,011.56	1,133.40	1,027.57	1,147.19	1,043.61	1,161.05	1,059.69
90,000	1,259.63	1,138.00	1,275.07	1,156.01	1,290.59	1,174.07	1,306.18	1,192.16
100,000	1,399.59	1,264.44	1,416.75	1,284.46	1,433.99	1,304.52	1,451.31	1,324.62

ACCELERATION CLAUSE: Gives the lender the right to call all sums owed to the lender immediately due and payable upon the occurrence of a specific event, such as sale of the property or delinquent repayment.

ACQUISITION INDEBTEDNESS: Used by the IRS to indicate the initial debt incurred to purchase a primary residence or second home.

ADDENDUM: A list of items to be added to a purchase contract or escrow instructions.

ALL-INCLUSIVE DEED OF TRUST: A second deed of trust with a face value equal to the amount of the first loan plus that of the second loan. The borrower pays the second lender one payment from which the second lender makes the payment to the first lender. Also called a wrap-around mortgage.

AMORTIZED LOAN: A loan that is paid off in full with equal periodic payments of principal and interest over a fixed period of time.

APPRAISAL: An opinion about the value of a property based on a factual analysis.

ASSUMPTION: An agreement whereby the buyer takes on the liability for repayment of an existing loan on a property. Usually requires the lender's approval. The seller is not automatically relieved of liability.

ATTORNEY-IN-FACT: Someone who is authorized to act as an agent for another person under a power of attorney.

BACK-UP OFFER: An offer to buy a property that's accepted in secondary position, subject to the collapse of the primary offer.

BALLOON PAYMENT: A payment on an installment debt that is significantly larger than the other payments, usually the final payment. Loans with interest-only payments, rather than amortized payments, will have a balloon payment due at maturity.

BENEFICIARY STATEMENT: A statement issued by the lender stipulating pertinent information about the loan such as the remaining loan balance, interest rate, and monthly payment. Requested from the lender when a buyer is assuming the loan.

BUYDOWN: A payment made to the buyer's lender, usually by the seller, in order to reduce the buyer's interest rate on a new loan for a specified period of time.

CAPITAL GAIN: Generally the difference between the original cost and the selling price of a capital asset, such as real property, adjusted to allow for deductible expenses. Capital gain is currently taxed as ordinary income.

CC&Rs: Abbreviation for "Covenants, Conditions, and Restrictions," which describe restrictive limitations that apply to a property. Usually found in planned community developments.

CLOSING: The successful completion of a real estate transaction or refinance, including the transfer of documents and disbursement of funds.

CLOSING COSTS: Miscellaneous fees and expenses that buyers and sellers incur in a real estate sale.

CONTINGENCY: A condition that must be met before a contract becomes binding, i.e., an inspection of the property.

CONTINGENT SALE: An offer to purchase a property that is dependent upon the sale of another property.

CONTRACT OF SALE: A real property sales contract that provides for title to remain in the seller's name until a prescribed portion of the purchase price is paid by the buyer.

CO-SIGNER: A second person who signs a note with the primary borrower and is thereby equally responsible for repaying the loan.

COUNTEROFFER: An offer in response to an offer (as opposed to an acceptance).

DEED OF TRUST: A legal document, used in California instead of a mortgage, by which the borrower pledges a piece of real property as a guarantee for repayment of a loan.

DEFAULT: Failure to fulfill a promise or perform a legal duty.

DUAL AGENCY: One broker represents both the buyer and seller in a real estate transaction. Dual agency exists if two agents working for the same broker represent the buyer and seller in a transaction.

DUE ON SALE CLAUSE: A clause in a real estate loan stating that the amount owed to the lender is all due and payable when title to the property is transferred to a new owner.

EASEMENT: A right, privilege, or interest which one party has in land that belongs to another party.

ENCROACHMENT: Building improvements that are wholly or partly on another's adjacent property.

ENCUMBRANCE: Anything that limits the title to real property, including liens, easements, or restrictions of any kind.

EQUITY: The current value of a property, less any liens secured against it.

ESCAPE CLAUSE: A clause in a purchase contract that allows one party to withdraw from the contract under certain terms and conditions. Also called a Release Clause.

ESCROW: The deposit of the funds, documents, and instructions required to complete a real estate purchase with a neutral third party until all the terms of the purchase contract have been mutually fulfilled, at which time title to the property is transferred and the escrow is said to be closed.

EXCLUSION: An item of real property that is not included in the sale (such as a dining room light fixture). Or an individual who is an exception from the listing agreement. If the owners sell to the exclusion, a real estate commission is not owed to the real estate broker.

FANNIE MAE: (FNMA) Federal National Mortgage Association. A private corporation that buys and sells mortgages at a discount.

FIDUCIARY: A person acting in a relationship of trust and confidence, as between principal and broker.

FIRST DEED OF TRUST: A deed of trust that has priority over all other voluntary liens secured against a property.

FIXTURE: Personal property that is attached to real property and is therefore treated as real property, such as plumbing and light fixtures. Fixtures transfer with real property, unless specifically excluded from the sale.

FORECLOSURE: A procedure whereby a property that is pledged as collateral for a debt is sold to pay that debt in the event the borrower defaults on payments or terms.

FREDDIE MAC: (FHLMC) Federal Home Loan Mortgage Corporation. An organization that purchases loans from banks and savings and loans.

FSBO: (pronounced Fisbo) For Sale by Owner. A property offered for sale without the assistance of a real estate broker.

GRANT DEED: A type of deed used to transfer real property which contains an implied warranty that the property has not already been conveyed to another person and that the property is free from encumbrances placed by the person granting the deed.

HOMEOWNER'S POLICY: An insurance policy available to homeowners for a premium which provides coverage for the home and its contents in the case of damage or loss due to fire. Lenders almost always require that a homeowner policy be kept in effect.

HOME PROTECTION PLAN: An insurance policy to insure buyers and sellers against defects in a home they're buying or selling (usually in heating, electrical, and plumbing systems).

IMPOUNDS: An account set up by a lender for the collection of funds to pay for future property taxes, mortgage insurance, and homeowner's insurance premiums. These funds are usually collected with the note payment. Often required when the buyer is putting less than 20 percent cash down.

IN-HOUSE SALE: A sale of a property in which the buyer's and seller's agents both work for the same broker.

INSTALLMENT SALE: A tax term used to refer to a sale in which the seller carries financing for the buyer to spread capital gain liability over a number of years.

INTERIM LOAN: Also called a Swing or Bridge Loan. A temporary, short-term loan that enables a homeowner to liquidate the equity in one home, before it's sold, in order to make a cash down payment on another home. Also refers to a construction loan.

JUNIOR LOAN (OR LIEN): Any mortgage, deed of trust, or other lien against a property that is of lesser priority than the first mortgage or deed of trust. For instance, a second deed of trust.

KEYBOX: Also called lockbox. A metal box containing the house key that is hung on, or close to, the front door and that is opened by special keys issued only to member agents of the Multiple Listing Service.

LEASE OPTION: A lease giving the lessee the option to purchase the property at the specific price and terms set forth in the option agreement.

LESSEE: One who contracts to rent a property; a tenant.

LESSOR: An owner who enters into an agreement to rent to a tenant; a landlord.

LEVERAGE: The use of borrowed money and a small amount of cash to purchase a property or investment in order to maximize the return per dollar of equity invested.

LIEN: A type of encumbrance which makes a property the security for a debt or obligation.

LIQUIDATED DAMAGES: A predetermined sum, agreed to by the parties to a contract, to be considered full damages if a certain event occurs, i.e., a breach.

LISTING AGREEMENT: An employment contract between a property owner and an agent authorizing the agent to perform certain services involving the property.

LOAN TO VALUE RATIO: The percentage of a property's appraised value that a lender may be willing to loan to a borrower. Usually the higher the ratio, the higher the interest rate charged on the loan.

LOCKBOX: See keybox.

LOCK-IN: A guarantee from a lender to a borrower who's submitting an application that a specified interest rate will be held for a specified period of time.

LOSS PAYEE: A clause in a homeowner's policy stating the priority of claims in the event the property is destroyed. Lenders and sellers carrying financing for the buyer will usually be named as loss payees and will be paid the amounts owing to them before the buyer is paid.

MARKET VALUE: The highest price a willing buyer would pay and a willing seller would accept for a property that is exposed to the open market for a reasonable period of time, and with both buyer and seller being well informed and neither party acting under undue pressure.

MATERIAL FACT: A fact materially affecting the value or desirability of a property which is not known to or readily observable by the buyer.

MECHANIC'S LIEN: A lien created by statute which exists against real property in favor of persons who have performed work or provided materials for the purpose of improving that property.

MORTGAGE: Technically, a legal document by which property is hypothecated to secure payment of a debt or obligation. The term is commonly used to refer to a home loan, and it is often used interchangeably with "deed of trust" (although a mortgage and a deed of trust are different legal instruments).

MULTIPLE LISTING: A listing, usually an exclusive right to sell, taken by a member of an organization of real estate brokers with a provision that all members will have an opportunity to find a buyer for the property, thus ensuring wider market exposure for the seller.

NEGATIVE AMORTIZATION: A condition that occurs when the monthly payments on a loan are insufficient to pay the interest accruing on the principal balance. The unpaid interest is added to the remaining principal due.

NOTARY PUBLIC: One who has the authority to take the acknowledgements of persons signing documents and to affix an official seal.

NOTE: A signed written document acknowledging a debt and promising repayment on specific terms and conditions. When concerning real property, the note is secured by a deed of trust or mortgage.

NOTICE OF DEFAULT: A notice filed to show that a borrower is behind in payments due.

NOTICE OF DELINQUENCY: A notice filed to show that a borrower's payment is past due.

PAYOFF DEMAND: A written request for a lender to provide exact figures of the amount owed by the borrower in order to pay the loan off in full.

PITI: Abbreviation for Principal, Interest, Taxes, and Insurance, prorated on a monthly basis; the monthly housing expense.

POINTS: The origination fee charged by the lender. One point is equal to 1 percent of the loan amount.

PORTFOLIO LENDER: A lender that originates loans for its own portfolio, as opposed to a lender that packages loans to be sold on the secondary money market (to Freddie Mac or Fannie Mae).

POWER OF ATTORNEY: A legal document authorizing a person to act as an agent for the person granting it. A power of attorney can be general or specific.

PRELIMINARY TITLE REPORT: Also called a prelim. A report issued before the completion of a real estate sale or loan transaction indicating the condition of the title.

PREPAYMENT PENALTY: A charge paid by a borrower to a lender if the loan is paid off before its maturity and the loan agreement contains a provision stating that such a charge applies.

PRIVATE MORTGAGE INSURANCE: (PMI) Insurance that a borrower pays to protect the lender in case of default. Usually required with high risk home loans.

PRORATION: To divide property taxes, insurance premiums, interest, rental amounts, etc., between buyer and seller according to proportionate use as of the closing or an agreed upon date.

PURCHASE CONTRACT: An agreement between the buyer and seller that sets forth the terms and conditions of the sale.

QUITCLAIM DEED: A deed that relinquishes, without warranty, any interest in a property that the grantor may have.

RECONVEYANCE: A legal document commonly used when a debt is satisfied or paid in full under the terms of a deed of trust. Also called a deed of reconveyance or release.

RECORDING: Placing a document on file with a designated public official (usually the County Recorder) for everyone to see. Recording is governed by statute, and signatures on legal documents usually must be notarized before the documents can be recorded.

RED FLAG: Anything a real estate agent sees while completing a diligent visual inspection of a property that might indicate that a problem exists.

REFINANCE: To pay off an existing loan on a property and replace it with another loan.

SELLER FINANCING: Refers to a loan on real property, secured either by a first or second or third or fourth deed of trust that a seller carries for a buyer. The seller is the lender rather than a bank or savings and loan.

SINGLE AGENCY: One real estate broker represents one principal: buyer or seller, but not both.

SPECIFIC PERFORMANCE: A legal action to compel the performance of a contract requirement.

STATEMENT OF IDENTITY: Also called Statement of Identification. A confidential form that a title company requires the buyer and seller to complete as a condition of issuing title insurance to ensure that liens and judgments of record do not apply to the individuals in question.

STATUTE OF LIMITATION: A legal limit on the time period within which a court action must be initiated.

SUBJECT TO: Taking over an existing loan on a property without going through a formal assumption process. The original borrower is not released from responsibility for repayment of a loan.

TAX LIEN: A lien that attaches to real property if the property owner fails to pay property or income taxes when they are due.

TERMITE REPORT: A Structural Pest Control Inspection Report which covers active infection and infestation by wood destroying organisms, damage from such organisms, conditions that resulted in current structural pest control problems, and conditions that are deemed likely to lead to such problems in the future.

TITLE: Evidence of ownership and right to real property.

TITLE INSURANCE: Insurance issued by a title company to protect a property owner from loss due to imperfect title.

UNDERWRITING: The technical analysis completed by a lender to ensure that a contemplated loan is a sound investment.

VESTING: The manner in which title of ownership to a particular property is held, including the names and status of the owners.

WAIVER: To abandon or release a right to enforce or require something.

ZONING: The act of a governing authority specifying how property in specific areas can be used.

INDEX